Faith and Humility

Jonathan L. Kvanvig is Professor of Philosophy at Washington University in St. Louis. He was previously Distinguished Professor of Philosophy at Baylor University, and has held faculty positions at the University of Notre Dame, Texas A&M University, and the University of Missouri. His scholarly activities focus in metaphysics & epistemology, philosophy of language and logic, and philosophy of religion, with more than 15 books and over 100 articles published.

Faith and Humility

Jonathan L. Kvanvig

OXFORD
UNIVERSITY PRESS

OXFORD
UNIVERSITY PRESS

Great Clarendon Street, Oxford, OX2 6DP,
United Kingdom

Oxford University Press is a department of the University of Oxford.
It furthers the University's objective of excellence in research, scholarship,
and education by publishing worldwide. Oxford is a registered trade mark of
Oxford University Press in the UK and in certain other countries

First Edition published in 2018
First published in paperback 2021

Published in the United States of America by Oxford University Press
198 Madison Avenue, New York, NY 10016, United States of America

British Library Cataloguing in Publication Data
Data available

Library of Congress Cataloging in Publication Data
Data available

ISBN 978-0-19-880948-7 (Hbk.)
ISBN 978-0-19-289458-8 (Pbk.)

Contents

Introduction

Today is a good day to die. So said Low Dog before the Battle of the Little Bighorn in 1876, though often attributed to Crazy Horse. Low Dog's remark is not best understood as a threat against the 7th Cavalry nor as a suicidal remark, but rather as a statement of commitment to a cause that is important enough to die for if necessary. In his description of the battle and his motivation for participating, he ties his efforts to a rejection of the idea of living nothing but a humble life: "Why should I be kept as a humble man, when I am a brave warrior and on my own lands? The game is mine, and the hills, and the valleys, and the white man has no right to say where I shall go, or what I shall do." And when asked what role Sitting Bull played in battle, he is reported to have said, "If someone would lend him a heart he would fight."[1]

This story is a model of the relationship between faith and humility that I articulate here. My goal in recounting the story is not to endorse the idea of armed conflict or to take sides in the matter of dispute in question, though I note the transformative experience I had upon reading Brown (1970) and upon learning that the homestead land settled by my ancestors was taken by the US government when in 1868 it unilaterally re-wrote the 1851 Treaty with the Sioux. My goal, instead, is to see in Low Dog's remarks the danger of a humble life not balanced by commitment to goals and ideals worth pursuing and honoring. What I see in his stance is a way of living that aims to balance two important virtues: humility and faith worth having.

In the story of Low Dog, we can see these two virtues free from a disconcerting distortion when we attend only to the language of faith within religious contexts. That language, I will argue, suffers from something close to original sin. Christianity is a paradigm example. There was a dream, a hope, a promise, and all of these came to be seen by an original band of followers as being embodied in a first-century Jewish man. Commitment to the cause of Christ is the source of the religion that followed, and the lives of faith displayed by the original band have the same core elements as that displayed by Low Dog in refusing a humble life of subservience to whatever the United States government demanded of him. The religion in question, however, soon came to portray faith in terms of doctrinal belief, condemning to eternal judgment those who refused to sign on to the official orthodoxy. Moreover, the orthodoxy grows over time, so that cognitive assent is demanded not only concerning the life, death, and resurrection of Jesus, but also regarding doctrines that are arguably more peripheral (such as Virgin Birth and Immaculate Conception). My claim here is not that these doctrines are false, but rather that it is a distortion of the fundamental faith of the

---

[1] Low Dog's account of the battle was published in the Leavenworth, Kansas *Weekly Times* of 18 August 1881.

original followers to replace their commitment to a cause with a doctrinal faith that focuses on factual claims, just as it would be a remarkably mind-boggling suggestion to think of the faith displayed by Low Dog in resisting demands of subservience primarily in terms of which claims he took to be true and which false.

It is in these vignettes that I see the true nature of faith worth having and also the intimate relationship between faith and humility. This work is devoted to articulating this connection and exploring the nature, value, and virtues of faith and humility. The goal is to understand both in a way that does not discriminate between religious and mundane contexts, between sacred and secular. It arises from a conviction that these two character traits are important to a flourishing life, and intimately related to each other in such a way that the presence of one demands the presence of the other.

The result of such an inquiry, if that inquiry is successful, will require a re-orienting of discussions surrounding faith, including the interminable and, to my mind, stagnant debates about the relationship between faith and reason. Those debates involve something identified as faith, and though it may be such, it is a kind of faith that has never been central to my own experience of a life of faith and one that I don't find present in the examples of faith that grip me most. This work is my attempt to change the conversation, and even though the chances of success are perhaps somewhere near the chances of success for Low Dog to avoid the life demanded by the US government, it is a cause worth fighting for.

The plan for this book is as follows. I begin with the topic of faith worth having, and develop an account of this kind of faith along with the methodological underpinnings for approaching philosophical questions from such an axiological standpoint. The slogan for the view is that faith is a disposition in service of an ideal, and the source of the view is in John Dewey's *A Common Faith*, an under-appreciated work by this important American philosopher. The first five chapters focus exclusively on faith, first in ordinary, mundane contexts and then in religious contexts, specifically the context of Christian faith. Chapter 6 is the transitional chapter where I argue for the central thesis of this work, that faith and humility are balancing virtues, and in the remaining chapters, I develop an account of humility that can be used to sustain this thesis. The conclusion is especially important in the context of Christianity, where faith in Christ is crucially connected with the humility of Christ as an expression of Divine love, but its importance is not limited to that context. The generality of the results is part of the cumulative case argument presented for the importance of faith and humility and the relationship between the two.[2]

[2] This work was supported by a grant from Templeton Religion Trust. The opinions expressed in this publication are those of the author and should not be attributed to the Templeton Religion Trust.

1

Faith Worth Having

1.1 Introduction

We talk about faith and use the language of faith in a multitude of ways: faith in humanity, being a person of faith, having faith that the economy won't collapse, the catholic faith, etc. Faith is sometimes used as a synonym of trust, sometimes of belief. Such diversity prompts methodological reflection: is systematic treatment even possible here, except in taxonomic terms? Pessimism isn't much of a methodology, though, and the more optimistic will want to follow recognizable paths. Those familiar with the linguistic turn in philosophy may seek semantic or conceptual systematization,[1] and those of a different methodological persuasion may prefer conceptual genealogy, attempting a historical or perhaps mythical account of where our current concept comes from or might have come from (hoping to elucidate the phenomenon in question in the process).[2] One might also proceed more metaphysically, looking for something metaphysically fundamental, arguing that one can have equally true but different descriptions of the world, one of which "cuts nature at its joints" and one which does not.[3]

Here I articulate and defend a different strategy, one focused on faith worth having. One might think of such an approach as one that mixes metaphysics and value theory,

[1] The best defense of the need for such is Jackson (1998) and Jackson (2005).
[2] Examples of such include Craig (1990) on knowledge and Williams (2002) on truth. We will have opportunity to look more closely in a later chapter at such an approach to trust developed in Simpson (2012).
[3] A standard example is the white-black/whack-blite figure, due to Sider (2011). The figure is a rectangle composed of two squares, one black and one white. A diagonal line is then drawn from the upper left corner to lower right, with everything above the line counting as whack and everything below blite:

Regarding this figure, it is both truth that it is half white and half black as well as half whack and half blite. But the first purportedly "carves nature at its joints," while the second does not. (It probably goes without saying, but I will anyway: this issue of fundamentality is a metaphysical twist on a long-standing problem in confirmation theory, the new riddle of induction from Nelson Goodman (1955), replacing grue and bleen with whack and blite.)

thinking of the idea of fundamentality here in terms of axiological fundamentality.[4] For a basic tenet regarding faith is that it is not like being snub-nosed, which is true of some and not of others but nothing of deep interest turns on the difference, but rather something which is supposed to be a virtue and somehow central to a well-lived life. While one might prefer to bracket axiological questions in the interest of first giving a systematic treatment of the ways we use the language of faith (or of the variety of conceptualizations of this phenomenon), my approach will be to put axiology first, leaving open the possibility that a substantial portion of the logical space of the language of faith and the conceptualizations involved can be written off as uninteresting or unimportant. For example, perhaps there is an appropriate usage or conceptualization of faith on which Mark Twain was right: faith is believing what you know ain't so. Others who want to give an account of faith on which this claim comes out true are welcome to it. I have no interest in such a thing, any more than I care to make a big issue about who is snub-nosed and who isn't. Others want to find faith to be ubiquitous, perhaps as a way of shielding religious faith from criticism, identifying faith with any activity that involves risk. So, for example, smoking a cigar involves faith as does sitting down on a chair. If there is such a kind of faith, it is important to a well-lived life, but only to the "life" part and not to the "well-lived" part, since there is no possibility of risk-free activity (or inactivity). My interest is in a quite general human phenomenon, one that is purportedly central to human flourishing (rather than, like air, central to human existence), and seeing to what extent we can regiment the language of faith and conceptualizations of it in terms of this axiologically fundamental sort. Perhaps what we will learn in the process is to change the way we talk in light of what we learn is important about faith, rather than changing our account to accommodate the way we talk.

In order to deflect certain kinds of objections to this approach, it will be helpful to contrast the present approach with other approaches that have dominated philosophical inquiry for nearly a century and a half and to explain my dissatisfaction with them. Nowhere are these flaws more present than in the epistemology of the last fifty years or so, and we can make progress in seeing the case for approaching our topic from the standpoint of what is axiologically fundamental by looking at this history.

1.2 Fundamentality and Axiological Fundamentality

Standard philosophical practice in seeking what is fundamental about a given phenomenon is illustrated well in the history of epistemology. A central aspect of philosophy has always been the question of the varieties and scope of human

---

[4] My use of the term 'axiology' is not meant to restrict the focus to moral goodness alone. Instead, I use the term for value-theoretic inquiry more generally, and in the present context, for any value-theoretic inquiry into what the good life involves. Presumably, such inquiry will include moral goodness but not be limited to it.

knowledge. In order to address this question, epistemologists have an interest in understanding the nature of knowledge in hopes that such understanding will aid reflection on its scope. When we turn to the question of the nature of knowledge, we find various proposed necessary conditions for it: some maintain that you can't know what isn't true, others that knowledge requires belief or some other similar cognitive commitment to the claim in question, and still others that you can't know anything without satisfying some normative constraint, voiced as a requirement for, for example, justification or warrant or rationality.

This multiplicity of necessary conditions leads directly to a concern about what is fundamental to knowledge, and whether any of the proposed necessary conditions can take the lead in answering the question of fundamentality. The typical approach in western philosophy has been to contrast knowledge with belief (or opinion) and with true belief, with the former being much more difficult to attain than the latter two. Though this starting point might be simply a matter of convenience, it might also involve a philosophical commitment. The thought might be (and often is) that the legitimacy of the contrast arises because knowledge is an enhancement of belief and true belief, that what is fundamental about knowledge is that it is a specific form of true belief (or opinion).

There are two issues one might raise with such an assumption. The first is that the contrastive source of the view (that knowledge can be rightly contrasted with, and is harder to achieve, than true opinion) isn't sufficient for the conclusion drawn (that knowledge is a form of true opinion), as is shown by the source of the contrast in Plato's dialogues. The approach taken there contrasts knowledge with true opinion, taking them to be different things with different objects involved in each, thereby denying that knowledge is a form of true belief. The best source for this claim is found in the discussion of the divided line in *The Republic* 509d–510a and the cave analogy that follows it. The four parts of the line are the shadows and reflections of visible things, the visible things themselves which are the objects of natural science, the intelligible realm investigated via mathematical reasoning, and the intelligible world examined by philosophical dialectic, with the cognitive attitudes for each of the four parts being, respectively, *eikasia*, *pistis*, *dianoia*, and *noesis*. The realm of opinion is thus contrasted with the realm of knowledge, where the first two areas involve imagination and conjecture (*eikasia*) and the second involves belief about ordinary objects (*pistis*), while the realm of knowledge involves different objects and is investigated via proof and mathematical reasoning yielding understanding (*dianoia*) or philosophical reasoning yielding insight or theoretical wisdom (*noesis*). We might classify the first two as falling within the realm of the phenomenal (*doxa*) and the latter two as falling with the domain of the epistemic (*episteme*). This theme is carried through to the latest dialogue, the *Timaeus*, where at 37b, Plato contrasts the insight and knowledge or understanding (*nous*, *episteme*) with respect to the intelligible realm (*logistikon*) to the lesser, non-epistemic achievements of belief (*doxa*) and opinion (*pistis*) of the perceptual realm (*aistheton*). At the very least, then, one needs more than a contrast between knowledge and true belief to draw the conclusion that knowledge is a form of true belief, on pain of accusing Plato of a blunder akin to claiming that stallions are all bachelors.

This point meshes nicely with a second concern, one concerning the pervasiveness of necessary conditions. It maybe be necessary to believe in order to know, but knowledge is also impossible unless everything is identical to itself. Yet, no one is tempted to think that what is fundamental to knowledge is self-identity. In general, trying to determine what is fundamental to X by focusing on something the instances of X all have in common is not a sound practice. The result might say more about the psychology of the theorist than about the thing itself. Moreover, even where the necessary conditions identified are not trivial in the way self-identity is trivially necessary for knowledge, the fact that something has non-trivial necessary conditions should not be taken to show that what is fundamental to the thing should be located among these necessary conditions. For, as the example of Timothy Williamson (2000) reveals, one theoretical option to consider is that knowledge itself is fundamental and unanalyzable although it nonetheless requires true belief.

Even if we agree with the current assumption that Plato is mistaken to think that knowledge and opinion never coincide, there is a tendency to false consciousness in epistemological theorizing about knowledge, for it is well-known that the language of 'knows' is wider than always implying true belief. Witness the attributions of knowledge to students who hesitantly voice a correct answer ("See, you did know!"), where the behavior indicates more of a guess than a sincere avowal.[5] Notice as well the non-factive uses: "I just knew Kerry was going to win!", distraughtly uttered the morning after the election by someone who retired early, content that Kerry would win. Such non-factive uses are widespread and involve no misuse of language at all.

Some will say that such uses involve non-literal uses of the term in question, and thus should play no role in the theory of knowledge.[6] But it is a vexed question how to distinguish literal from non-literal meaning,[7] though there are clear examples of figurative uses of language where a non-literal reading is obvious (e.g. "Juliet is the sun"), and it is also a vexed question which uses of a term, if any, count as literal.[8] One finds several strands in the literature when attempting to characterize the distinction

---

[5] David Lewis (1996, p. 556) takes these examples to be decisive. Knowledge doesn't require belief, he concludes.

[6] I ignore in the text the complicating factor that one has to regiment the use of 'literal' to make this move. Witness the following passage from Frances Brooke's 1769 novel *The History of Emily Montague*: "He is a fortunate man to be introduced to such a party of fine women at his arrival; it is literally *to feed among the lilies.*" If we prefer to think of such uses as non-literal uses of 'literal', we should say that such non-literal uses are not new. We should also note that such uses introduce an important circularity worry in trying to articulate the thesis that certain uses are literal while others are non-literal.

[7] See e.g. Lakoff (1993).

[8] See, for example, the explosion of interdisciplinary work on metaphor that resists the traditional view that metaphor is a special rhetorical tool that allows language users to rise, at least momentarily, out of the mundane world of literal meaning, represented well in Gibbs (2008).

in question. Sometimes accounts advert to the concept of what is conventional: literal meaning is conventional, non-literal non-conventional. It is worth noting on this score that non-factive uses of 'knows' are clearly conventional.[9] Others focus on context-independence for literal meaning, but such a criterion for literalness would make all uses of 'knows' non-literal if contextualism is true![10] Moreover, it gives no ground for thinking that non-factive uses are to be classified differently from factive uses in terms of literality. Still others focus on the semantics/pragmatics distinction: semantics is the domain of the literal and pragmatics the non-literal. That viewpoint has the undesirable consequence of ruling out *a priori* the Lakoff thesis that many terms in natural language have a semantic value that involves metaphor (see Lakoff (1993)). Perhaps some would relish that conclusion, but that result strikes me as too cheap an argument against the thesis.

Careful attention to these issues should lead one to look for a better explanation of why epistemologists ignore, and why it is appropriate to ignore, certain quite common uses of the language of knowledge. I think there is one, and its existence provides support for the charge of false consciousness above.

That explanation supplements or replaces standard analytic assumptions (whether couched in terms of linguistic meaning or conceptual content) with axiological considerations. Instead of looking for what is fundamental by attending to certain pieces of language or intentional correlates of such, an axiological approach to fundamentality focuses from the outset on issues concerning what is worth theorizing about. In the context of epistemology, the driving concern is the question of whether there are connections between mind and world that count as successful connections, in a purely theoretical (as opposed to practical) sense. This issue becomes embodied in the challenges of the skeptics, who insist that we are fooling ourselves into thinking that any of our intellectual efforts count as successful in the intended sense. We thus have an axiological source, and an embodied one at that, for focusing on factive uses of the language of knowledge, for no skepticism worth its salt cares one whit whether attributions of non-factive knowledge turn out to be true: if they do, that still won't count as a successful connection of the intended sort between mind and world.

My suggestion, then, is that the attempt to rule out non-factive uses of 'knows' from epistemology by appeal to a distinction between literal and non-literal uses of language arises from a false assumption. That assumption is that what we are doing when we do philosophy, and especially when we are giving a theory of knowledge, involves nothing more than conceptual or linguistic analysis. Some are attempting to do such analysis, and even those who are actually being guided by axiological considerations tend to conceptualize their theorizing in terms of the dominant social milieu of

---

[9] If evidence be needed, note that one lexical entry in the *Oxford English Dictionary* is: "Be absolutely certain or sure about something."

[10] The kind of contextualism—attributor contextualism—is found in Cohen (1987), DeRose (1992, 1995), Cohen (1998, 1999) and DeRose (2008). It is also in Lewis (1996), though masked to some extent by a failure to respect the distinction between using a term and mentioning it.

philosophy in the English-speaking world since the late nineteenth century, in terms of linguistic or conceptual analysis. As a result, they suffer false consciousness, actually doing one thing and telling themselves and others that they are doing something else. Regardless of the merits of this charge of false consciousness, however, a better understanding is achieved by characterizing what epistemologists are doing in terms of looking for important connections between mind and world. In a context in which one encounters living, breathing skeptics, it is natural to adopt as a working hypothesis the idea that knowledge has pre-eminent position here.[11] The focus on knowledge here, however, is a focus driven by the axiological concerns arising in the disputes between skeptics and non-skeptics, not a linguistic or conceptual investigation of ordinary meaning or its associated cognitive content. We rule out non-factive uses of the language of knowledge because we are inquiring about connections between mind and world that *matter* from a purely theoretical point of view, and knowledge fits that bill. In the process, we search for something fundamental to theorizing about what matters here, and thus arrive at a standard view, according to which what is axiologically fundamental here is true belief is a special sort.

Furthermore, one doesn't need to look very far or hard to find the source of the false assumption. Philosophy, since the rise of Logical Positivism and perhaps earlier in British Empiricism, has been plagued by anxiety that it has nothing to offer when it comes to intellectual pursuits and inquiry. The voice of Hume echoes in our minds,

If we take in our hand any volume; of divinity or school metaphysics, for instance; let us ask, *Does it contain any abstract reasoning concerning quantity or number?* No. *Does it contain any experimental reasoning concerning matter of fact and existence?* No. Commit it then to the flames: for it can contain nothing but sophistry and illusion. (Hume 1777 [1748], p. 166)

To the Logical Positivists, managing to lift philosophical inquiry to the level of sophistry and illusion would be a *major accomplishment*, for you can't get to that level unless you first manage to *say something*. Feeding their notoriety, the Logical Positivists denied that philosophers managed to say something except when they were engaged in linguistic analysis, not quite appreciating the embarrassment of trying to say all this using sounds that were obviously not instances of linguistic analysis, nor of mathematics or science.

Thus arises the vexed soul-searching of much of philosophy in the twentieth century, finding unavoidable the question of what we are doing and why it is worth doing. For a variety of historical reasons, such soul-searching isn't as common any more,[12] but the turning of hearts and minds toward linguistic analysis engendered by the soul-searching remains. Old habits, apparently, die hard.

---

[11] A working hypothesis that is, in my opinion, false, as I argue in Kvanvig (2003).

[12] A central figure in this history is Saul Kripke, whose trenchant criticisms of the empiricist underpinnings of such anti-philosophy made the world safe for metaphysics in particular and philosophy more generally. See Kripke (1980), first given as lectures at Princeton in 1970.

There remains the possibility of a metaphilosophical defense of the idea that philosophers must engage in linguistic or conceptual analysis, but without the underlying empiricist assumptions that trapped the discipline in this box canyon, the case in favor of analysis and the case against everything else is much more difficult to make. The reason the case is so difficult is simple: philosophers are interested in the stuff of reality, not primarily the words we use to talk about it nor the mental entities that might exist which tie together language, mind, and world. There are parts of philosophy where the linguistic and the mental are the focus of inquiry: philosophy of mind and philosophy of language, for example. But it would be a remarkable coincidence, signaling an amazing human achievement, if the structure of the world matched precisely the structure of our language and the mental concepts involved in thinking about the world. Instead of relying on such a myth, it is better to say that philosophers should aim to theorize about reality, not 'reality'; about normativity, not 'normativity'; about knowledge, not 'knowledge'; about justice, goodness, and obligation, not 'justice', 'goodness', and 'obligation'. Look at reality itself and attempt to understand it, we should say, refusing to deflect one's gaze toward the words or concepts we use in the process—refusing even if there is no possibility of understanding reality without relying on words or concepts.

Once freed of the disastrous anxiety engendered by an exaggerated empiricism, we can embrace the ancient perspective on philosophy in which it is part of the pursuit of the great intellectual goods of knowledge, understanding, and theoretical wisdom. The motivation for such inquiry is, of course, not purely theoretical, but rather arises from the practical, existential, and moral search for the good life, and the hope that better understanding and wisdom will assist us in achieving such a life. Once we think of what we are doing in this way, it is easy to see why one can engage in, for example epistemological reflection in the way described above. We focus on knowledge that is factive, not because 'knows' is a factive verb, but because factive knowledge is a significant intellectual good, even if acquiring knowledge is not near as important as coming to understanding or possessing theoretical wisdom. It remains a theoretical possibility that engaging in such philosophical inquiry is an exercise in futility or, even worse, an activity that undermines any chance of finding the good life, but there is also the hope that the activity will not return void and that the process and products of such inquiry are integral aspects of the good life, or at least some good lives.

What goes for epistemology goes as well for pisteology, the study of the nature and value of faith. There are the usual linguistic and conceptual analysis approaches to the subject, and they always leave me wondering, "Why bother?" Why not, instead, look at the phenomenon in question and ask what, in the neighborhood of things pointed to by the language in question, is worth having and thinking about? If we start from this axiological point of view, we should notice, first, that if faith is to be a virtue, it should be the stuff of which virtue is made—namely, a disposition of a certain sort. Once we think about the topic of investigation in this way, we should also expect that the disposition in question will have, not only behavioral manifestations, but also affective and cognitive aspects as well. The complexity involved thus calls for reflection and clarification, for if faith worth having has behavioral, affective, and cognitive features to it, we can ask which of these features is fundamental. Is faith fundamentally a disposition, so that the faith can remain the same even if different combinations of factors involving the will, the emotions, and the intellect, are involved? Is it fundamentally a non-cognitive state (such as a certain kind of preference or hope or desire), or is it fundamentally a cognitive state (such as a belief)? Notice, however, how this investigation is imbued with axiology, so we will focus on proposals regarding fundamentality only to the extent that they offer some hope of providing a positive answer to the question of whether the kind of faith in question is good for anything, either theoretically or practically, just as we begin epistemology, appropriately done, by considering only those kinds of knowledge that are factive.

Starting in this way leaves open the possibility that standard assumptions about faith are correct, that faith is a type of belief or other cognitive state. The humor of the Twain remark, that faith is "believin' what you know ain't so," relies on this common assumption. In slogan form, a common assumption is that faith is fundamentally doctrinal: its primary form is in terms of faith that something is the case, and such faith-that is a form of belief-that. We turn, then, in the next chapter to consider the possibility that the disposition in question is one that is fundamentally cognitive.

2

Cognitive Versus Functional Accounts

2.1 Introduction

Our beginning assumption is that faith is a virtue, an important element of a well-lived life. This assumption, of course, may turn out to be false—there may be nothing in the vicinity of that part of logical space indicated by our language of faith. We begin, however, from this assumption in hopes of identifying something worth possessing.

If we begin from this point, we are beginning from an assumption that faith involves dispositions of some sort or other, for virtues are characteristics that fall within the broader category of dispositions. Moreover, on the standard view of faith—that it is a kind of belief—this starting point is embraced, for beliefs are one important kind of disposition toward behavior. To believe a claim may not be identical with any particular behavioral disposition, as behaviorism dictates, but beliefs are nonetheless the kind of thing that disposes a person to behave in some ways and not in others. So if we begin from the idea that faith is a disposition of a certain sort, which it must be if it is to be a virtue, one way to preserve this starting point is to hold that the fundamental character of faith is belief of a certain sort.

Such a view is certainly part of ordinary language about faith. Witness C. S. Lewis: "Roughly speaking, the word Faith seems to be used by Christians in two senses or on two levels, and I will take them in turn. In the first sense it means simply Belief—accepting or regarding as true the doctrines of Christianity" (Lewis 1952, p. 138). What Lewis says about Christian faith could be generalized to all faith, so that faith of any sort involves some set of beliefs that certain claims are true.

It would be an indefensible view, however, to say that faith is identical to belief, for that would require faith that $1 + 1 = 2$, which I believe but don't have as an object of faith. Here we find a common second step: not only is faith a form of belief, it is a form to be contrasted with reasonable belief. And not only Mark Twain here ("Faith is believin' what you know ain't so"): see, for example, Leiter (2012), "religious belief in the post-Enlightenment era involves culpable failures of epistemic warrant" (p. 82) and "Religious beliefs, in virtue of being based on "faith," are insulated from ordinary standards of evidence and rational justification, the ones we employ in both common sense and in science" (pp. 33–4). Such characterizations are far from exceptional, enjoying widespread endorsement. One can find endorsements of such by Stephen Pinker, Alexander Rosenberg, and Richard Dawkins, as documented in Howard-Snyder (2013). It is worth pointing out, in defense of such secular critics of religious faith, that they are agreeing with a long line of religious thinkers who endorse a similar position, contrasting faith with doubt and insisting that true faith often involves ignoring or rejecting grounds for doubt. (See Howard-Snyder (2013) for discussion of this position, which he labels "the Common View.")

We can think of the criticisms in question, and the characterization of faith on which they rely, as inherently cognitive. Such a picture arises quite naturally from our use of the term 'faith' to stand for the particular truth claims made by a given religion. We talk of the Christian faith and of the Baptist Faith and Message, for example.

From this use of the language of faith, it is easy to adopt a cognitive picture of what faith involves: to be, for example, a Christian is to endorse the Christian faith, it is to believe some vague but important subset of the truths that constitute the Christian faith. And the same can be said for faith of any sort, where the particular kind of faith involved is delimited by the kinds of claims that are the objects of belief.

2.2 Discomfort with Cognitivism

Even though cognitive approaches to faith have a long and distinguished history,[1] recently some have resisted. In place of cognitive approaches, others have claimed that faith is a feeling, that it is an attitude or affective state of a certain sort (Clegg 1979), that it is a special kind of trust (Audi 2011, Schellenberg 2009), that it can be a special kind of hope (Pojman 1986, Sessions 1994), that it is a preference of a certain sort (Buchak 2012), or that it is a kind of practical commitment or disposition toward certain patterns of action (Tennant 1943, Kvanvig 2013a).

Are there good reasons to abandon the standard cognitive approach? It is worth noting C. S. Lewis's first remark after noting that in the first sense faith means, simply, belief. He immediately points out a difficulty:

I must talk in this Chapter about what the Christians call Faith. Roughly speaking, the word Faith seems to be used by Christians in two senses or on two levels, and I will take them in turn. In the first sense it means simply Belief—accepting or regarding as true the doctrines of Christianity. That is fairly simple. But what does puzzle people—at least it used to puzzle me—is the fact that Christians regard faith in this sense as a virtue. I used to ask how on earth it can be a virtue—what is there moral or immoral about believing or not believing a set of statements? Obviously, I used to say, a sane man accepts or rejects any statement, not because he wants to or does not want to, but because the evidence seems to him good or bad. If he were mistaken about the goodness or badness of the evidence that would not mean he was a bad man, but

---

[1] For additional evidence, note such examples of what philosophers have claimed: that faith is a type of belief (Locke 1698), that it is a cognitive state such as acceptance (Alston 1996, Audi 1982), or that it is a kind of belief generated through the *sensus divinitatis* so as to result in knowledge (Plantinga 2000).

only that he was not very clever. And if he thought the evidence bad but tried to force himself to believe in spite of it, that would be merely stupid.

Well, I think I still take that view. But what I did not see then—and a good many people do not see still—was this. I was assuming that if the human mind once accepts a thing as true it will automatically go on regarding it as true, until some real reason for reconsidering it turns up. In fact, I was assuming that the human mind is completely ruled by reason. But that is not so. For example, my reason is perfectly convinced by good evidence that anaesthetics do not smother me and that properly trained surgeons do not start operating until I am unconscious. But that does not alter the fact that when they have me down on the table and clap their horrible mask over my face, a mere childish panic begins inside me. I start thinking I am going to choke, and I am afraid they will start cutting me up before I am properly under. In other words, I lose my faith in anaesthetics. It is not reason that is taking away my faith: on the contrary, my faith is based on reason. It is my imagination and emotions. The battle is between faith and reason on one side and emotion and imagination on the other.   (Lewis 1952, p. 138)

This is a rich quote, both for its insights and foibles, and I will focus here on two major things of note. The first is that Lewis shows a concern with the idea that a doxastic account of faith will have trouble explaining why faith is a virtue. There will be trouble, Lewis thinks, not because a doxastic account will not classify faith as a disposition, which it needs to be if it is to be a virtue, but that it is the wrong kind of disposition. Lewis is befuddled by the idea that there can be moral credit for thinking something to be true, and that is a puzzlement we should all share. The problem here is easiest to see in the context of religious faith where such faith is required for eternal bliss, and it is the problem of arbitrariness. If we are told that God will decide one's eternal destiny on the basis of one's ability to recite the Gettysburg Address backwards in under 30 seconds, we'd all be in trouble if the report were true. But the arbitrariness of the standard should give us reason to conclude that the report isn't true. It simply makes no sense, and though perhaps things don't make sense, the fact that a report doesn't make sense is good reason to walk away from it. On this score, doxastic accounts of religious faith suffer a similar fate.

Lewis's way of making this point is to claim that sane belief tracks evidence, so if faith were just a kind of belief, we should expect that the doctrinal requirements for religious faith would be nothing but what the evidence shows to be true. But, if that claim is true (and widespread disagreement about doctrinal claims, both intrareligious and interreligious, makes such a claim difficult to accept), the idea that such faith is an important moral, or all-things-considered, virtue gets lost in the shuffle. Believing the truth is an intellectual good, as is believing in accord with the evidence; but the importance of faith is disproportionate to the intellectual value and virtue of believing truths supported by evidence.

These two complaints are both important and complementary, but we must distance ourselves a bit from some questionable elements in Lewis's claims to appreciate these points. First, he relies on the dubious claim that sane belief tracks evidence. In addition, the second paragraph of the quote is mysterious, for it begins by endorsing the problem but then seems to angle toward rescuing the doxastic account of faith by pitting it against the emotions. He doesn't say so directly, but instead talks of the possibility of reason conflicting with emotion. Once this possibility is noted, however, he says, "In other words, I lose my faith . . .", a remark that requires the identification of faith with belief. Yet, if that viewpoint is subject to objection, then what we have here is a kind of faith that isn't up to the task set for it.

Whatever we wish to make of the details, however, Lewis's general point is still telling. The importance of faith, at least in religious contexts, vastly outreaches any importance that could be explained in terms of belief and possible evidence. And when we think of faith in democratic ideals, faith in humanity, faith in our friends and family, the same point is true: the importance of such faith vastly outstrips an importance that could be achieved by having true or justified beliefs regarding democratic ideals, humanity, friends, and family. So when we think of faith being a disposition that makes it possible for faith to count as a virtue, it is a mark against doxastic accounts of faith that, though they have a story to tell about why faith is a disposition, strain to explain how faith could be anything close to an important virtue.

Lewis's voice is not the only one expressing dissatisfaction with doxastic accounts of faith. Because such doxastic accounts are so deeply entrenched in ordinary language and thought, it is worth taking note of some quotes of disaffection signaling an attraction for an alternative picture of faith:

"Unbelief," like "theology" is a product of the Greek mind. . . . Where the word "belief" is used to translate the biblical Hebrew and Greek it means not the "belief that" of Plato, but "belief in," a matter not of cognitive assent but of faith, trust, and obedience. . . . Plato's "theology" is not in fact an accurate apprehension of traditional religion. It is the self-conscious intellectual's translation of that religion into terms that he can understand. (Bellah 1991, p. 216)

Those inclined toward cognitive construals of faith won't be moved much by the argument in this passage. The quote claims that faith is a matter of belief-in, not belief-that, adding that belief-in is a matter of faith, among other things. It is easy to see where a defender of a cognitive approach will resist. Yet, if we listen to understand rather than to resist, the central idea is clear and worth thinking about: the idea that belief-in is more a matter of trust and obedience, and it is belief-in that is playing surrogate here for the idea of faith. In that light, consider another passage:

While belief now refers to a state of mind, a disposition to assent to a set of propositions, even within the early Christian intellectual tradition historically it had as much or more to do with love, loyalty, and commitments akin to pledging one's allegiance to a person as Lord or to a cause or to entering into a covenant such as marriage. The Latin word credo (apparently a compound of cor, cordis 'heart' and -do, -dere, 'to put' derived from the proto Indo-European root for placing one's heart upon something, *kred-dhē) means 'I set my heart' upon the entity or doctrines in question. Even for scholastics such as Aquinas . . . credo meant to pledge allegiance to, to give one's self and one's loyalty. The Latin terms most closely expressing today's meaning of belief and opinion, *opinio* ('opinion, belief, supposition') and *opinor* (*opinari*, to be of the opinion, to believe) played an almost negligible role in Christian thought.

(McKaughan 2013, pp. 107–8)

The idea that is at least hinted at in these quotes is that when we ask about the nature of faith, we are not asking about necessary and sufficient conditions for it, though of course that is a topic that will arise in the inquiry. We are asking more about its essence (if it has one), about species and genera, that of which it is a particular instance and what makes it be the particular instance it is. When we want to know what it is to be a person or a human being, we will find it frustrating to be told that it's a featherless biped or a thing inclined to don attire. Even if these claims are true, they don't give us what we want. Just so with accounts of faith. We want to know what faith is, not what it co-varies with, even if necessarily. Thus, the standard cognitivist approach tells us that faith is an instance of belief, and then goes on to describe which particular instance it is.

Both quotes signal dissatisfaction with such an approach. Whatever faith is, to these authors, it is not primarily or fundamentally a cognitive mental state. That leaves open the possibility that various mental states, including cognitive ones, are involved in having faith, but the project is one of understanding the nature of faith, and for that we must look first at what is fundamental and primary: what is it that faith is an instance of, and what makes it the particular instance of that phenomenon?

Attention to the history of Christian doctrine reinforces such discontent with cognitive approaches. Very early in this history, doctrinal disputes arose, and the language of anathema was quickly adopted for those with non-standard views. See, for example, the seemingly hyperbolic language of the Athanasian Creed: "Whosoever will be saved, before all things it is necessary that he hold the catholic faith. Which faith except every one do keep whole and undefiled; without doubt he shall perish everlastingly. . . . This is the catholic faith; which except a man believe truly and firmly, he cannot be saved." The lesson is clear here. The faith is defined in terms of propositional content, and salvation requires believing truly and firmly the members of the set of propositions in question.

Disaffection toward such doxastic requirements for faith and salvation should result immediately when we consider heroes of faith: Abraham, Moses, Job, and even the Apostles. It is mind-boggling to think of them as satisfying the cognitive standard embraced. Imagine any of these at the beginning of their lives of faith endorsing any of the language of the Athanasian Creed: " . . . we worship one God in Trinity, and Trinity in Unity; Neither confounding the Persons; nor dividing the Essence. . . . our Lord Jesus Christ, the Son of God, is God and Man; God, of the Essence of the Father; begotten before the worlds; and Man, of the Essence of his Mother, born in the world. Perfect God; and perfect Man, of a reasonable soul and human flesh subsisting. Equal to the Father, as touching his Godhead; and inferior to the Father as touching his Manhood." Whatever status we want to give to such orthodoxy, it is essential to distinguish the life of faith and the central, salvific role faith plays in such a life from the alethic concerns about what is true and what is not that dominate the creeds. In short, no reasonable approach to our topic can fail to distinguish salvific adequacy from alethic adequacy when it comes to purely cognitive issues, for failure to do so triggers Lewis's concern that any attempt to explain why faith is a virtue, under such an assumption, will be in vain. So, once this distinction is made, it becomes clear that what is central to faith, the kind of faith intimately connected with salvific adequacy, must be somewhere else or something else than something purely cognitive. Thus arises the idea of searching for a less cognitive, or non-cognitive, account of faith, one more attuned to what exemplars of faith display, both in religious and other contexts. We can think of Christian and religious concerns about salvation as specific instances of the more general and not necessarily religious concern for a well-lived life, and once generalized in this way, it is fairly easy to see how easy it is to be attracted to an alternative to the cognitive view of faith when considering the question of finding a kind of faith that is a virtue and thus worth having.

2.3 A Dispositional Alternative

If we resist the standard approach, there is a natural alternative, one that is theoretically minimal. First, if we consider faith that matters, our attention will turn first to thoughts of the virtue of faith, since that is the primary way in which the significance of faith is discussed. Once our focus is on faith as a virtue, we should notice that we are thinking about a dispositional character trait, and thus we would seem to be considering something that is fundamentally a disposition to behavior or responses of a certain sort rather than a cognitive state of some kind. I am not suggesting that faith can't be both, since many if not all cognitive states are or involve dispositions toward behavior. I am only pointing out that if we are looking for a virtue, we will look first look for the disposition and only locate it within cognition when given an argument that the disposition in question cannot help but be located within a cognitive state of a certain sort. Second, a proper understanding of the language of faith in the Biblical languages of Hebrew and Greek shows a predominant usage elsewhere than in any language of faith that takes a proposition as object, so the usual approach according to which faith is fundamentally doctrinal suffers a failure of fit with at least the typical Biblical language concerning faith. Third, a proper understanding of the development of Judaism places loyalty and commitment to Yahweh as the central feature to note concerning the use of the term *emunah* and its variants, translated as "faith" when in noun form and "believe" when in verb form. An excellent example of this centrality appears in Deuteronomy 9:23, where Moses berates the Israelites: "And when the Lord sent you from Kadesh-Barnea, saying, 'Go up and possess the land which I have given you'; then ye rebelled against the commandment of the Lord your God, and ye believed Him [he'emantem] not, nor hearkened to His voice." Using a standard Hebrew device of repetition for emphasis, the believing not and the hearkening not are to be understood in terms of failure to follow through on the command given, not simply or primarily in terms of some underlying cognitive commitment to the truth or falsity of certain propositions. It would be incoherent, after all, to try to characterize what it is to "believe" a command in terms of believing that a certain claim is true. Just consider an example: what is it to believe or hearken with respect to the command to bring me my glasses? The obvious answer is to bring me my glasses, whether or not one also believes something like, "it is right and good that I bring you your glasses." The dispositional response is central, and is adequate in itself to explain the case, so any detour through cognitive commitments to some truth or other is strained at best. Moreover, it is this same feature that is present in the first description of Abraham as the father of faith, for it is his *emunah* that is credited to him as righteousness in Genesis 15:6, a credit that makes perfect sense when understood in terms of loyalty, commitment, and reliance (and would be perplexing if understood only or primarily in terms of cognitive commitment to certain propositional truths). This understanding of *emunah* fits well with the underlying narrative concerning the rise of Judaism, which emerges in a struggle with the temptations of idolatry generated by surrounding cultures, with the accompanying demand of loyalty, commitment, and obedience to the one true God. If in this development there are cognitive commitments to propositional claims, they are ancillary to the central character of faith.

My suggestion, then, is that when we inquire about the phenomenon of faith, we should begin by asking what kind of thing faith is that could be something truly worth having, and for such an inquiry, we need to think first about the function of faith in human life. What is faith for, not only in religious contexts, but elsewhere as well? And in particular, what is it for, that could possibly sustain a theology built around it, or uphold the idea that it is a major virtue of a well-lived life? In short, we look at the variety of ways in which we talk about faith and variety of things that get labeled using that word, and we sort through the jumble, looking for something of value. We should look for, not what is analytically, conceptually, or metaphysically fundamental to faith, but rather what is axiologically fundamental.

The first step in such a process has already been noted: if we are looking for something of value here, it will be a trait that some people have and others don't, and in order to be a trait that is capable of being considered to be a virtue, it will have to be a trait of character. Traits of character can be characterized functionally, in terms of their input and output conditions. So, when we look at faith in this way, we may begin by asking how it functions, what dispositional difference it makes in the lives of those who have it, and whether this function is one that counts as a good thing for a person who has it.

When approached in this way, the first thing one might notice is that faith has a kind of directedness to it. Some faith is directed at humanity itself, some at the future, some at God and his kingdom, some at one's prospects or the prospects for one's children. This list is not meant to be exhaustive, but only illustrative. The lesson it teaches, however, is that faith is a special kind of character trait, one involving an attachment or commitment to something as an ideal, a *telos*, something worth achieving or pursuing. So, we can begin by describing faith worth having in terms of a disposition to behave or respond to the circumstances of life in service of an ideal. It is the kind of disposition that provides structural unity or integrity to a personality over a wide variety of circumstances, with the depth or degree of faith a measure of how wide the variety.

Looked at in this way, it becomes clear why we should not be tempted toward accounts of faith that lack this feature of directedness. One such approach focuses on the risk-taking element involved in faith, wanting to find faith at work when one, for example, sits down in a chair, risking it not able to hold the weight. One concern about such an account is that it will find faith present in every circumstance of life. Even if the language of faith supports the idea that you display faith in a chair by taking a seat, such faith won't be the right kind of faith to consider when attempting to locate the virtue of faith. All of life is a risk, but central to whatever risk-taking is essential to faith is some story or explanation of why the particular risk-taking in question is something worth pursuing, and an answer to that question will invoke just the kinds of elements of directedness I've been arguing for. Even if risk-taking ends up being part of the story, it is too ubiquitous to be the right kind of starting point to endorse at this point in our inquiry. Instead, we should begin from the idea that faith is a disposition that involves a direction or focus or intention toward something of significance, toward an ideal of a certain sort, not simply some bodily movement that subjects one to the risk of harm.

2.4 Lives of Faith

Thought of in this way, a natural starting point begins by noting that there can be both unified approaches to life and approaches that involve disunity or disconnectedness. In the latter category are lives that instance the Humean view of causation: just one damn thing after another, with no attempt on the part of the individual in question to do anything beyond coping with whatever comes one's way. Such patterns of life are difficult to sustain (note that merely planting a garden takes one beyond such a Humean existence, since planting a garden is tied to the idea of harvest at some later time), but it is not uncommon to see lives that display it in significant temporal chunks. In contrast to such patterns of behavior are approaches that pursue unity, that aim at connecting the multiplicities in experience into some sort of plan or purpose, and the boundary of such a search involves plans, purposes, and goals that are all-encompassing. The development of such typically arises out of conative or affective aspects of human life, such as negative or positive emotional experiences. Among the negative emotional experiences are fear, horror, regret, guilt, worry, sorrow, shame, anger, misery, meaninglessness, and despair; among positive affective states are joy, compassion, awe, wonder, and experiences of beauty and the sublime.[2] Such aspects of human life can provoke an interest in finding meaning or in developing a plan or purpose or goal that reaches beyond merely coping with each particular episode in life as it comes. In some cases, the call of the goal is merely attractive, in other cases it takes on the guise of the mandatory. In either case, these features of human life need not prompt the kind of unification that interests me, but the possibility exists, and is often realized, of responding to such by adopting a pattern of life that involves longer-term projects, goals, and plans. It is, I am claiming, in such unification that the notion of an ideal arises, that notion that will play a central role in understanding faith worth having. Ideals involved in the disposition in question are, first and foremost, forces for unification and integration in the life of a person displaying faith worth having.

It is on these affective origins of the pursuit of ideals of one sort or another that I want to focus initially, for these unifying responses, I want to suggest, are responses that involve faith of one sort or another. To adopt a longer-term project or goal or plan involves a kind of hope that success may be possible, or at least a decision not to give in to feelings of hopelessness, and a kind of self-trust and trust or reliance on the structure of the universe and the society in which one hopes to flourish, regarding the accomplishment of some plan. None of these underlying attitudes or dispositions need to be ones brought to consciousness in deliberate reflection on the experiences that prompt them, nor need they be part of any fully deliberate approach taken to the motivations for them. Responses to such motivations range from the spontaneous to the fully deliberate. What is important about the responses in question is not how reflective they are but that they involve a setting of a direction for the individual, one which a person may faithfully pursue.

I should caution that the teleological point here should not be taken to imply that faith can be present for any goal one might care to select. Just as it would be unwise to think that faith is present in every case of risk-taking, it would also be a mistake to think that the kind of faith worth having, in the way that can explain why it is a virtue, is present whenever goal-directed activity occurs. One takes a shower in order to avoid offense, but the goal-directedness no more involves the kind of faith in focus here than does the risk-taking involved in sitting down.

Faith, in this sense, is an orientation of a person toward a longer-term and more all-encompassing goal, an orientation or disposition toward the retaining of the goal or plan or project in the face of difficulties in achieving it, one prompted by affections of various sorts and involving complex mental states that are fundamentally affective even if they involve cognitive dimensions as well. A plan, purpose, or goal

---

[2] Some might think that the experiences of beauty and the sublime should be classified with the cognitive rather than the affective. Since nothing I say here turns on the issue, I'll bypass extended discussion of the issue here by simply noting the attraction of views that treat normative and evaluative experiences and judgments as essentially involving a pro-attitude or con-attitude. So by classifying these experiences as conative and affective, my intention is to signal the way these attitudes can function in the story of faith in much the same way as the emotions cited.

is developed, and the culmination of this process involves a commitment by the individual to such a plan, and in following through on such a commitment the person can display the kind of faith that I am describing. People can be faithful to their commitments, or not, and when faithful, they follow through in a way that displays an orientation or disposition toward retaining the goal or plan or project in the face of difficulties encountered.

I have avoided describing such faith in terms of the language of mental states or attitudes, since even though such faith may involve specific attitudes, it would be unwise to begin from that assumption. It is, to be sure, an orientation of the person, a disposition of the self, toward a certain ideal.[3] The metaphysics of such is interesting in its own right, but I will not pursue that topic at this preliminary stage of our investigation except to caution against any assumption that all such personal features must fall into the the the category of intentionality, displaying a characteristic "aboutness" whether of the *de re* or *de dicto* sort. The caution I'm voicing is that we shouldn't begin by insisting that the discussion be herded into the arena of intentionality. Perhaps some attitudes are not intentional in the required sense: perhaps a person can be angry without being angry about anything (and certainly not angry about everything),[4] just as a person can have undirected anxiety, or moments of pure joy without there being any good answer to the question "Concerning what?". More generally, however, it is clearly possible to have dispositions or orientations that don't involve intentional aboutness at all: dispositions such as being loving or caring or miserly or mean. So too we should assume about the kind of faith I speak of: perhaps one can display it without it being about anything. It is an orientation of a person, a stance taken, that displays itself in a faithful pursuit of a goal or ideal. I do not rule out the possibility of some fancy story that reduces such to the level of the intentional, but we should not start there.

To return to the issue of the nature of this orientation of a person, the first lesson to note is that such faith is thoroughly mundane, and the reason for focusing on the affective features of it is that they are worn on its face, whereas whatever cognitive dimensions there might be are more variable and harder to discern. We can see these points more clearly by considering a specific example. Suppose a young Little League pitcher gives up a game-winning home run and experiences the typical despondency

---

[3] I use the language of an ideal, even though the reality will be much more specific, in terms of the realization of some goal or the following of some pattern of life. What all of these have in common is an appearing under the guise of the good or a felt attraction for the object in question, and it is for this reason that I choose to use the language of ideals to describe the varieties of objects toward which a life of faith might be directed.

[4] Thanks to Kris McDaniel for reminding me that defenders of Brentano's thesis that intentionality is the mark of the mental, displaying a characteristic "aboutness", have rebuttal resources here. For example, undifferentiated anger can be treated in terms of being angry at the world. I won't pursue this issue here, since there are plenty of other grounds for resisting a treatment of faith in terms of intentional attitudes of a *de re* or *de dicto* sort, but will merely note that I don't find this story plausible. Being angry at the world (earth? universe?) is one thing, and simply being angry is another.

for having done so. One reaction is to adopt a goal of becoming a better pitcher and never having to feel that way again. Such a reaction can generate an orientation or disposition toward various efforts at becoming better, in hopes of doing so (or at least some aversion to the idea that any efforts of any sort are hopeless), and display a kind of self-trust or self-reliance and perhaps some trust of others who may be recruited to help in the project. Our youngster makes a commitment to a certain kind of future. It might be intense commitment or more casual in its firmness, but when he carries through on this commitment, he will be properly characterized as being faithful to the ideal in question, or pursuing it faithfully.

Our question about such a mundane example is what kind of mental states, cognitive or affective, must all of this involve? We have already seen the affective source and sustenance of the faith; we might even characterize it as a kind of affective faith, involving an attraction toward a certain ideal and an aversion toward its alternative. These affective states not only cause the disposition or orientation toward the ideal of becoming a better pitcher, they are inherent in it. And what of cognition? What role can we find for it? Doesn't he have to have certain types of belief here, and aren't there beliefs that inhere in the faith in the same way that the affections inhere in the faith?

I doubt it. Let's consider what particular beliefs might be involved in being faithful to the ideal of becoming a better pitcher. Certainly our youngster needn't believe that he will succeed, nor that it is likely that he will succeed, or even that there is some chance that he will succeed—his commitment to the ideal and the way in which he follows through with his plan reveals some hope of success, and that is enough to make sense of the process in question. Nor need our young athlete believe that the ideal is worthy of pursuit or that achieving the ideal is a good thing.[5] Such beliefs might be present, but it is equally possible that our young athlete either hasn't formed any beliefs with such lofty axiological components and possible that the conceptual elements required of such beliefs are simply not present yet. Beliefs of the sort described may be present, but they are not constitutive of the faith in question nor necessary for it. Might we insist on a role for other beliefs, such as believing that there is such a thing as the game of baseball, that there are coaches, and teammates, and (obnoxious) parents involved in Little League?

I expect he does believe these things, though I'm not sure he has to believe them. Perhaps cases of this sort could occur in which the affective faith remains, but only dispositions to believe are present rather than occurrent or dispositional beliefs.[6] A further possibility is to be in cognitive states that differ from belief, a possibility we will investigate at some length later on. Perhaps, for example, our young pitcher only presupposes these claims, or assumes them in such a way that his belief box remains empty of the sought items. There is, of course, the reductive project of showing that presuppositions and assumptions are kinds of belief, but reductive projects do not

---

[5] Cf. Howard-Snyder (2013) for a contrary view on this point.   [6] See Audi (1982, 1994).

have an impressive track record in philosophy. Among cognitive features of human persons are not only beliefs, but expectations, assumptions, and presuppositions, as well as mental assents to certain claims without actually believing them, and a committing of the self to a viewpoint or cause, whether or not such commitment involves something like a mental state having a certain proposition as its content. One can, as it were, nail one's theses to the wall, taking one's stand on them, all the while knowing that one falls short of believing them. My point is that there is a lot of philosophical work required before we can say that belief is present, even if our Little Leaguer is properly characterized in some way or other in terms of the claims just cited.

In any case, the relevant point at this stage of our inquiry is elsewhere. Even if there are beliefs or other cognitive elements present, they are merely background conditions for the faith in question and not constitutive of it nor doing the work that the affective elements are doing in sustaining it. The cognitive elements were already in place prior to the emergence of the affective faith in question, and form no part of the attraction of the ideal in question or the aversion to its central contrast. They are, at most, background conditions already in place that make possible the story, no more a part of the affective faith in question than his background beliefs that he exists and has hands.

On the idea here that there is a difference between explainers and background conditions, it is worth noting that the distinction between the two is hard to characterize. This difficulty leads some to claim that there is no such distinction: there is merely what we treat as background and then what appears in the foreground as a result. Vary what we hold fixed, vary what we treat as background, and any of the features involved in the story will turn out to be an explainer.

Such skepticism overreaches. In a theory of rationality, we distinguish between conferrers of rationality and enablers: the absence of defeaters of the confirming power that some piece of information provides for a given action or belief is an enabler but not a conferrer; a belief that entails that another belief is true or that an action must be done, is a conferrer of rationality and not an enabler. A full account of rationality, however, has to include both the presence of conferrers and enablers, on pain of violating the defeasible nature of rationality. Since adequate explanations are subject to the same defeasibility feature (X can explain Y, whereas X&Z doesn't), we need both the feature that is doing the explanatory work and the features that are enabling the explanatory work to be done. In the case of the faith in question, the story is told to make this clear: what is doing the work is the affective state in question. For it to do its work, various other conditions, some cognitive in nature, may be needed. None of the particular items mentioned is itself needed, perhaps—but at least one of a broad variety of enabling possibilities must be realized. But these enabling conditions are not doing the work here and do not enter into the nature of the faith in question. Only the features present that are doing the work partially define or partially constitute the nature of that faith.

Moreover, the disposition or orientation of our young pitcher has a kind of deictic element to it, pointing to the affective element central to the example. The disposition in question is not merely one of becoming a better pitcher. It is, rather, a disposition to work to become a pitcher who doesn't let *that* happen again. Of course, it is possible over time for all this to change, but that is not the kind of case we are presently considering. Our case is, instead, one where the source of the goal is embedded in, and active in sustaining, the motivation that leads to the faithful pursuit of that goal.

2.5 Conclusion

One might make one last try to force a cognitive dimension here, based on the plausible idea that even affective faith involves a dimension we might characterize in terms of closure of inquiry regarding various claims surrounding the plan or goal in question. For example, consider the issue of the possibility of success. If one raises the question of what our Little Leaguer thinks about the possibility of success, and he retains the plan and his faith in it in the presence of the question, the question will get shrugged off or met with an affirmation. The question is a closed one, and will remain so as long as the plan, and the faith that undergirds it, remains in place.[7] His being closed to inquiry on the issue is a personal feature of the boy, an attitude or disposition toward the possibility of success. But we need not suppose that our young possessor of mundane faith is in some particular mental state with this possibility as its content in order to be closed to inquiry on the issue. We should thus abandon the search for a defensible cognitive approach to faith worth having, drawing the more defensible conclusion that such faith is better thought of as dispositional and affective, and consider more directly what we can learn about such faith from this and other examples of faith worth having. We turn, in the next chapter, to look at non-cognitive accounts, especially those that still contrast with a purely functional account.

---

[7] For further exploration of this dimension of faith, see Buchak (2012).

3

Non-Cognitive Accounts

3.1 Varieties of Non-Cognitivism

If we are unsatisfied with cognitive accounts of faith worth having (and the point of the last chapter was to begin the case for why we should be, a case that will be pursued in the remainder of this book), we will want to see what the options are for a non-cognitive account of the matter. To that end, we can begin with an account of the contours of the logical space of non-cognitivism that are relevant here.

The historical literature on non-cognitivism is primarily in the domain of ethics, and the early non-cognitivists, from the positivist era, thought of moral judgments in terms of expressions of emotions. Later non-cognitivists adopt a point of view on which moral claims involve expressions of attitudes, not just emotions. Other varieties are on offer as well, and we can distinguish two central common claims among non-cognitivists. The first is a semantic thesis, to the effect that moral judgments (or, more generally, normative judgments) are not suited for alethic evaluation in the way factual judgments are: they are not the sort of thing that can be true or false, or have truth conditions; or at least, they don't have these features in the robust way that factual judgments do, even if in some minimal and purely formal sense the predicates 'is true' and 'is false' can be correctly attached to such judgments. The second is a psychological thesis, to the effect that what is expressed by a moral or normative claim is not solely a belief or other mental state that falls within the cognitive aspect of a person.

These remarks can be made more specific by thinking of the meaning of normative sentences instead of talking about such sentences in use in the form of judgments. When talking of the meaning of a normative sentence, the non-cognitivist insists that part of the meaning of such sentences is that they are used to express non-cognitive attitudes. Perhaps part of the meaning is something else as well, and perhaps that additional part involves ordinary propositional content of the sort that characterizes non-normative language.

The connection between this use of the cognitive/non-cognitive distinction and the use to which I will put it is indirect. First, the above use of the distinction lands all such discussions squarely at the meta-level: it is a topic in metaethics whether cognitivism is true, not a topic in normative ethical theory. The distinction regarding various approaches to faith is, however, not one about the meaning of sentences involving a notion of faith, nor about the judgments people make about faith or that count as expressions of faith. The topic here is faith itself, and thus the discussion is in the material mode rather than the formal mode.

Even so, there is some connection, for the sense in which some approaches to faith are non-cognitivist is a sense much like the second sense above, which is a psychological thesis concerning whether a given state of a person is one that can be understood in cognitive or non-cognitive terms. So, in what follows, we look for specific varieties of non-cognitivism in terms of the psychological condition alone.

Examples of non-cognitivist approaches to faith start with the cognitivist contrast. The standard cognitivist view is that faith is a type of belief (Locke 1698), but there are other possibilities. It may also be taken to involve a degree of belief, perhaps a maximal one,[1] or that it involves a non-doxastic cognitive state such as acceptance (Alston 1996), or that it is a kind of belief generated by the *sensus divinitatis* in such a way that the belief rises to the level of knowledge (Plantinga 2000). In the last few decades, however, new approaches have been championed, claiming that faith is an attitude or affective state of a certain sort (Clegg 1979), that it is a special kind of trust (Audi 2011, Schellenberg 2009), that it involves hope (Pojman 1986, Sessions 1994), that it is a preference of a certain sort (Buchak 2012), or that it is a kind of practical commitment or disposition toward certain patterns of action (Tennant 1943).

Our starting point regarding faith is that it is a disposition of a certain sort, since our goal is to find a kind of faith worth having, a kind of faith for which there is some promise of claiming it to be a virtue. In line with this minimal beginning is the possibility that the best account of the matter will be a purely functional one, so that a proper characterization of faith doesn't move toward any specific substrate for the disposition, but rather allows considerable variability for how the functional state in question is realized in any particular instance. Contrasting with functional accounts are ones that focus on particular mental states or attitudes, claiming that the generic functional account is too generic. One way to make such a claim is to insist that faith is fundamentally a cognitive attitude, and the last chapter was devoted to showing the weakness of such an approach. Another way to resist a functional approach is to focus on non-cognitive attitudes or states that are more specific than a purely functional account endorses. Such non-cognitive accounts are the focus of this chapter, and we can begin to see how to assess such non-cognitive approaches to

---

[1] Some may want to express this idea by saying that faith is a feeling of confidence, and since feelings are clearly non-cognitive, one might be inclined to think that such an account is non-cognitive. I resist that move, thinking that talk of feelings of confidence is a misnomer, one arising from the common sloppiness in ordinary speech of confusing thoughts and feelings. We hear things like "I feel that we know a lot less than we think we know," "I felt that Obama was going to have trouble getting legislation passed." At some point, we'll have to say that the meaning of 'feeling' has become ambiguous between referring to an emotional state or a cognitive one, but I think we aren't there yet, and that such uses involve either a nice metaphor or the mistake of confusing a thought with a feeling.

faith by examining two quite promising versions of the view, one according to which faith is a kind of trust and the other according to which it is an affective state involving preferences.

3.2 Faith as Trust

I begin with the idea that faith is trust for primarily historical reasons. It is, perhaps, the most common explanation of faith to come to mind when looking for a replacement for cognitive accounts. Moreover, it lays claim to being the conception of faith at the heart of the Reformation; as William Cunningham writes,

With respect to the nature of saving faith, the principal ground of controversy was this, that the Romanists held that it had its seat in the intellect, and was properly and fundamentally assent (*assensus*), while the Reformers in general maintained that it had its seat in the will, and was properly and essentially trust (*fiducia*). The great majority of eminent Protestant divines have adhered to the views of the Reformers upon this point, though some have taken the opposite side, and have held faith, properly so called, to be the mere assent of the understanding to truth propounded by God in His word; while they represent trust and other graces as the fruits or consequences, and not as constituent parts and elements, of faith. (Cunningham 1862, p. 122)

We thus begin with faith as trust, but in doing so, we face difficulty immediately. For if we wish to identify faith with trust, it would be nice if we were clarifying the more obscure by the less obscure, but when we ask what trust itself is, we get a stupefying variety of opinion. Russell Hardin identifies trust with belief: "The declarations "I believe you are trustworthy" and "I trust you" are equivalent" (Hardin 2002, p. 10). Annette Baier (1986) thinks of trust as involving dependence on the goodwill of another, while Karen Jones (1996) claims that trust is constituted by an attitude of optimism about the goodwill of another. James Coleman (1990) characterizes trust as a kind of action that one places or not, depending on decision-theoretic calculations of the ordinary variety, and Richard Holton (1994) thinks it is crucial that an account of trust include normative, reactive attitudes involving dispositions to feel betrayed or grateful, depending on whether one's trust is violated.

How could such disparate approaches occur if people are actually looking at the same phenomenon? One answer to that question is given by Thomas W. Simpson (2012):

The ways that the word is used are simply too various to be regimented into one definition. Sometimes 'trust' is naturally understood as referring to a sort of affective attitude ('I will trust my husband, I will not be jealous'); at other times to a conative one ('Come what may, I will trust you to the end'); and at yet others to cognitive ones ('I know you are an honourable woman, so I trust you'). Sometimes it is not a mental state but action which is described as trust ('The patrol followed the scout, trusting him to spot any ambush'). Similarly, it is used in situations where the motivation to trustworthiness is dramatically varied: love, or mutual gain, or moral considerations may all count as reasons not to betray someone's trust. These all support the inductive argument against the plausibility of analysing of trust. Counter-examples can be given so easily because there are so many ways the word may permissibly be used, and so it would be foolish to seek a single definition.   (Simpson 2012, pp. 553–4)

And what is Simpson's solution? He recommends abandoning the project of analysis and substituting the methodology of genealogy in its place:

An alternative way of thinking takes the value of trust as of first importance. A genealogical approach addresses the concept obliquely, by asking why we might have the concept that we have, given some broad facts about how we live and the projects we pursue.

The claim is that if we can give a 'role description' for an important concept that looks and feels very similar to a notion that we actually operate, explaining what is needed of a concept in order to do a particular job, then that sheds light on the content of our actual one. Rather than trial by thought-experiment, it instead accommodates the vagueness and conflicting intuitions that surround difficult and abstract notions. No doubt all the advocates of the 'trust is this' claims I critiqued above have replies to my counter-examples. But the sorts of replies on offer will tend to consist in argument over the cases, and ultimately a discovery that we use the word 'trust' to describe different things on different occasions. . . . What would be genuinely revealing is an explanation of why the term permits this variability. As well as yielding a clearer grasp on the content of the concept, such an approach also makes it entirely perspicuous where its value comes from. Two results for the price of one enquiry is no bad thing in these straitened times.

(Simpson 2012, p. 555)

Simpson is well aware that his case for an alternative methodology is not compelling. Even without such an argument, however, we should recognize that he is onto something important here. We can engage philosophically in an analysis of anything in the dictionary, but we don't, and the reason we don't, when it is justifying of our practice, is because we presuppose the value or importance or significance of what we focus on in our philosophical explorations. It is also true that much of what passes for linguistic analysis is simply bad faith: we aren't attempting lexicographical improvement over what the dictionary says, but are instead attending to the phenomenon that our language indicates, however much or little it happens to cloud our view. We then say things like, "I don't care what the ordinary concept of knowledge is, I don't care what 'knows' means; I'm interested in knowledge, not 'knowledge',"[2] in much the

---

[2] Compare here Keith Lehrer (2000, p. 5):

> . . . [L]et us consider the distinction between analysing the meaning of the term 'know' and analysing the kind of knowledge denoted. Many philosophers have been interested in the task of analysing the meaning of the word 'know'. . . . Indeed, many would argue that there is no need for philosophical analysis once we have a satisfactory analysis of the meaning of the term 'know'. This restrictive conception of philosophical analysis is sustained by a dilemma: either a theory of knowledge is a theory about the meaning of the word 'know' and semantically related epistemic terms, or it is a theory about how people come to know what they do. The latter is not part of philosophy at all, but rather that part of psychology called learning theory. It follows that if a theory of knowledge is part of philosophy, then it is a theory of knowledge about the meaning of the word 'know'. . . .
> It is not difficult to slip between the horns of the dilemma. A theory of knowledge need not be a theory about the meaning of epistemic words any more than it need be a theory about how people come to know what they do. Instead, it may be one explaining what conditions must be satisfied and how they may be satisfied in order for a person to know something.

same way as we have come to expect scientists to disavow any interest in the ordinary meaning of terms like 'mass' and 'motion' when they attempt to give theories about the physical world. In each such case, the process of inquiry presupposes the importance of the topic in question, and one way to get past the remaining vestiges of the disease of ordinary language philosophy is to argue explicitly concerning what is valuable and worth theorizing about prior to offering a theory of it. In the process, we may find ordinary language to have a distorting effect and we may be in a position to do what philosophy has always claimed some promise or hope of doing: to improve our lives by improving our understanding of ourselves and the world we inhabit.

Even if Simpson is onto something important, the intrusion of geneaology into the story is nonetheless unfortunate. Genealogical accounts, by the use of the term, ought to be relying on some history or supposed history, and this is their flaw. Looking again at Simpson's description above, there are two things to note here—one good, one bad. The good is the value-driven heart of the approach, and the bad is the bad metaphysics. The bad part is a direct result of including the historical part of what is claimed for the genealogical approach, hoping perhaps for something like what Bernard Williams is looking for in his discussion of truth when he claims that the genealogical method is broadly naturalistic in that it "helps to explain a concept or value or institution by showing ways in which it could have come about in a simplified environment containing certain kinds of human interests or capacities." (Williams 2002, p. 21)

That is, the historical aspect of the genealogical account is supposed to point us to the fundamental reality the importance of which motivates our theorizing, and do so in a way (perhaps) that lets us see how to defend our favorite metaphysical picture in the process. But no historical or historically-tinged mythology will accomplish either of these tasks, at least when considered purely abstractly. The only thing one could hope for is preventing the metaphysical picture from refutation by the item in question, but even for that, the genealogical project can't be a substitute for identifying the nature of the thing that poses a threat to the metaphysics. For the threat is a threat from the thing itself, not some close relative of it. This characterization fits nicely with Williams' project, a project in which one attempts a perhaps mythical explanation of how the item in question—in his case truth—might have arisen in a broadly naturalistic way. Such a result is important, not for telling us what the nature of truth is, but for helping to block refutation of a naturalistic metaphysics because of the existence of truth. So, perhaps in particular cases, genealogy might be useful to add to our value-driven approach, but the general idea that the value-driven approach is itself part and parcel of genealogy is unmotivated. It is wrongheaded in a way that favors value-driven approaches over genealogical ones, since the latter requires more

---

We might add: there are many ways to slip between the horns of this dilemma, one of them occurring when we offer a theory of knowledge, focusing on its constituents or lack of them, and ending in discoveries which may or may not be reflected in semantic facts about the meanings of epistemic terms.

backfilling in order to justify the relevance of the historical dimension, mythical or otherwise, it touts.

3.3 Value-Driven Inquiry and Affective Faith

So, to repeat, the methodology I favor here focuses on what is important in a given domain. In this domain, I thus address what I take to be an important, and perhaps fundamental, kind of faith—one that is common ground between religious and mundane examples of this phenomenon that is central to a flourishing life.

This kind of faith emerges when we examine different possible approaches to life. We begin as noted earlier, with a distinction between lives that are unified or integrated and those that involve disunity or disconnectedness. In the latter category are lives that instance the Humean view of causation, denying that there is anything that ties one thing to another except temporal succession. Avoiding Humean disconnectedness involves generating an ideal, something taken to be worth pursuing and dedicating a significant portion of one's life to, and a disposition to pursue the ideal, a disposition that is not itself easily undermined by difficulties and trials along the way. Because the ideal in question is one that becomes an ideal for a person in virtue of an affective source and identity, we can think of the faith in question as an affective faith, and the mundane example I used in the last chapter involves the response of a young Little League pitcher who gives up a game-winning home run and experiences the typical despondency for having done so. One reaction is to adopt a goal of becoming a better pitcher and never having to feel that way again. Such a reaction can generate an orientation or disposition toward various efforts at becoming better, in hopes of doing so (or at least some aversion to the idea that any efforts of any sort are hopeless), and display a kind of self-trust or self-reliance and perhaps some trust of others who may be recruited to help in the project. Our youngster makes a commitment to a certain kind of future, and when he carries through on this commitment, he will be properly characterized as being faithful to it, or pursuing his goal faithfully. In a short motto, we grasp the noun form of what (this kind of) faith is from the adjectival and adverbial form involving being full of faith: faith is what faithful people have and faith is that which underlies and explains patterns of behavior and activity that are engaged in faithfully.

Such a kinship between affective faith with faithfulness is also well-suited to explaining important and central examples of religious faith, such as the faith displayed by Abraham in leaving Mesopotamia for Canaan.[3] The narrative in Genesis 12 is sparse—we are told only that the Lord said, "Go," and "So Abraham went." Later

---

[3] There is some uncertainty about the details here as to when the first call came to Abraham. Genesis 12 has the initial response involving leaving Haran, not Ur, whereas Stephen, in Acts 7, has the call coming to Abraham to leave Mesopotamia before he was in Charran (Haran). These uncertainties are irrelevant to our discussion, so I will bypass further discussion of them here.

accounts of the matter attribute his behavior to faith: "By faith Abraham, when he was called to go out into a place which he should after receive for an inheritance, obeyed; and he went out, not knowing whither he went." (Heb. 11:8) The explanation here is quite natural: Abraham is faithful to the divine command to leave for Canaan; his doing so is "by faith." We do not know the details, but several natural non-cognitive explanations of his behavior come to mind easily: perhaps he experiences a felt obligation to a divine command, or perhaps a deep attraction to a life guided by a divine being and being the recipient of divine favor and blessings; perhaps these were mixed with fear of divine displeasure with disobedience. What we can be confident of, however, is that the source of his behavior and the attitude that underlies it are just as fundamentally affective as they are in the case of the Little League pitcher. In both cases, affective faith is expressed by faithfulness to an ideal.

What we should resist are interpretations of Abraham's faith that are overtly cognitive. As Abraham's life with God progresses, he receives specific promises about what his future will be like, and (we are told) believes God regarding these promises. But his initial acts of faith are not described in terms of belief but instead in terms of following the command of God. It is the following that is essential here, not the believing, since we can easily make sense of his behavior as a display of faith even without any belief in the promise of God (for example, it might have been only a deep hope). How things develop is one thing, where things start is quite another.

One might resist this conclusion that the initial faith of Abraham is typical of saving faith, maintaining that it would not have been adequate faith without the more full expression of Abraham's faith involved in the Akedah. The idea here is that the real substance which is faith is expressed in the binding of Isaac and the willingness to sacrifice him, and prior events come to be classified correctly as examples of faith only in light of this later event, as something like honorific attributions appropriate only because they foreshadow the real thing to come later. Moreover, if seen in this way, we might then prefer more cognitive accounts of faith if more cognitive accounts fit better with this crowning achievement of faith on Abraham's part. On this matter, Eleonore Stump writes,

And so this is indeed a test of Abraham, as the narrative says. God's command to sacrifice Isaac tries the measure of Abraham's commitment to the goodness of God. The way in which Abraham dealt with Ishmael makes the form of this test the right one for him, too. For Abraham to treat Isaac in the same way as he treated Ishmael is for Abraham to commit himself whole-heartedly to the belief that God is good.

. . . [I]t is precisely Abraham's willingness to believe in God's goodness, even against strong temptations to the contrary, that makes him the father of faith. When Abraham passes the test, he passes it just because he believes that God is good and will not betray his promises. . . .

(Stump 2010, pp. 298–300)

There is much to say here about how different a perspective I have on the life and times of Abraham, but the following will suffice for present needs. First, even if the story of offering to sacrifice Isaac is the central jewel in the crown that is Abraham's faith, it is not the substance of it. Whatever is central to Abraham's faith was already present in his leaving Mesopotamia at the command of God, and so if faith requires believing that God is good and keeps his promises, we'd have to find some sign of that in the early relationship between God and Abraham. As pointed out already, there is none, and any attempt to treat the initial ascriptions of faith as honorific—correct only insofar as they are a poor shadow of the real thing yet to come—takes liberties with the text that are unjustified.

A reservation we should have about Stump's account is that it makes the divine command ancillary to the point of the story. God's command generates a test for Abraham, but the central factors at work in her account relegate the significance of the command to secondary status. The accomplishment of displayed faith, on her account, could have been present even without the command. As far as I can tell, her account of Abraham's faith leaves open the possibility that such faith could have been expressed even if Abraham had decided on his own to sacrifice Isaac, perhaps vowing to sacrifice Isaac on the model of Jephthah,[4] and then displaying the same degree of belief in God's goodness as she attributes to Abraham in the actual story.

Stump makes much of the contrast between Jephthah and Abraham, arguing that the usual reasons for taking Abraham to be the father of faith (having to do with his willingness to kill his only son) are reasons for giving the title to Jephthah instead, since (according to one traditional interpretation) he carried through on his vow to sacrifice his child. But her account isn't better in terms of explaining why Jephthah shouldn't have a higher status, if we add that he did what he did in full confidence of the goodness of God.

Most important here is that neither an approach emphasizing doxastic states or even the conative condition of being willing to kill explain the central difference between Abraham and Jephthah, which is the instigation by God of the decision Abraham has to make. To my mind, that isn't terribly surprising, since I doubt there can be a good explanation within the story itself of why God issued the command or what sense can be made of that aspect. Stump compares God's command with Abraham's treatment of Ishmael, claiming that because of the way in which he had

---

[4] From Judges 11:30–9 (NIV): "And Jephthah made a vow to the Lord: "If you give the Ammonites into my hands, whatever comes out of the door of my house to meet me when I return in triumph from the Ammonites will be the Lord's, and I will sacrifice it as a burnt offering." Then Jephthah went over to fight the Ammonites, and the Lord gave them into his hands. He devastated twenty towns from Aroer to the vicinity of Minnith, as far as Abel Keramim. Thus Israel subdued Ammon. When Jephthah returned to his home in Mizpah, who should come out to meet him but his daughter, dancing to the sound of timbrels! She was an only child. Except for her he had neither son nor daughter. When he saw her, he tore his clothes and cried, "Oh no, my daughter! You have brought me down and I am devastated. I have made a vow to the Lord that I cannot break." "My father," she replied, "you have given your word to the Lord. Do to me just as you promised, now that the Lord has avenged you of your enemies, the Ammonites. But grant me this one request," she said. "Give me two months to roam the hills and weep with my friends, because I will never marry." "You may go," he said. And he let her go for two months. She and her friends went into the hills and wept because she would never marry. After the two months, she returned to her father, and he did to her as he had vowed. And she was a virgin."

treated Ishmael, the test was "the right one for him, too." There is a sense in which this may be correct—if you play cavalier with the life of a less-favored son, perhaps you deserve to face the possibility of losing your most-favored one. But the propriety here is hard to see as all-things-considered justifying of the instruction, and so difficult to see as making sense of the central role of God's command in the story. What is clear, however, is that it is the command of God that makes the story as gripping as it is and makes Abraham's response one that warrants calling him the father of faith.

Even if there is no good explanation within the story itself of why such a command was given, there is a good explanation available within the context of the recording of the story itself. As I see it,[5] the story is a central component in the development of the ethical monotheism distinctive of the Abrahamic traditions, culminating in the explicit denunciation of child sacrifice in the prophetic literature. Such an emphasis on authorial intent doesn't help us understand the experience of Abraham in responding to God's command, but when the question is one of who deserves the title "father of faith," it is the perspective of the author or final redactors that is central, not the experience of the characters in the stories themselves. So there is an account available that explains the central role of God's command in the story, and it is an account that makes Abraham's response a test of faith precisely because it tests the reach of his disposition to follow God's instructions. In this most trying of situations, the disposition in question is not masked by other interests or concerns, and in this way, it reveals itself to be enormously strong. Such an explanation is explanation enough, showing no inadequacy for not including precisely what Abraham might have been thinking or feeling at the time.

I should also point out what I regard as excessive optimism in Stump's account of the sacrifice event, since a more realistic assessment of Abraham will be central to my reservations about identifying faith with trust. Stump notes the duplicity and double-mindedness that has characterized Abraham's relationship with God and his promises prior to the command to sacrifice Isaac, and she emphasizes as well his continued double-mindedness towards God's promise in the taking of Keturah as his wife (or concubine) after Sarah's death, fathering six children with her (as insurance of progeny should Isaac and Rebecca continue to be childless, which they had already experienced for twenty years). But somehow, Abraham manages, in the Akedah, to achieve purity of motive and full clarity of belief regarding what God is like and how sure his promises are. I find such an explanation overly optimistic and going beyond what we have textual evidence for, and if we pay attention to the point made earlier that a primary moral of the story is about God's self-revelation of his character to the father of the nation he has chosen, we can see why there is no need to posit such an astonishing change of character in Abraham. What has characterized Abraham from the beginning in his relationship with God stays constant here: when God

---

[5] This view is neither unique nor original, having been endorsed quite widely by others, including Yitzhak Herzog, the first Chief Rabbinate of Israel after it became a state in 1948.

says go, Abraham goes; when God says do, Abraham does. It is the following, the obedience, that is the heart of the faith of Abraham, not some imputed story about motives and beliefs that are somehow both ideal and out-of-character in the most difficult following of all. It is, in a word, a rendering of Abraham's faith in terms of his faithfulness that is crucial to the story, which is the fundamental point made about the affective faith characterized above.

One might worry that this account places too great a weight on the connection between having faith and being faithful. Robert Audi argues against a close connection between the two, claiming that one can have faith without displaying faithfulness:

It should also be stressed that even if a person's attitudinal faith (faith in) is highly compre-hensive, as is faith in democratic institutions, the person might not have the character trait of faithfulness. This may not be widely realized because we so often speak of faith in the context of considering faith in God, and that kind of attitudinal faith is commonly presupposed to imply some degree of commitment to being faithful to what God, at least in the eyes of the person in question, commands or requires. Nonetheless, someone could have faith in God or great faith in other people, yet not be able to keep faith with them and thus lack faithfulness toward them. Having faith in others is mainly a matter of how we view them, and how we are disposed to respond to them, in terms of what we value. Being faithful to others is more a matter of how we act toward them in terms of what they value (though it is not wholly a matter of what they value, since people can be clearly mistaken about their own good).

One way to see this difference is by considering the relation of each kind of faith to trust. If I have faith in you, then I trust you, at least within a certain domain of conduct. If I am faithful to you, you may properly trust me; and if I am faithful to an ideal, I may, in the main, be trusted to live up to it. Neither case of trust implies the other. We can have faith in people, such as foreign heads of state, with whom we have either no relationship or one that does not call on us to keep faith. One way to put the contrast is this: faith is fulfilled when its object meets certain expectations— roughly, fulfills the trust—of the subject; faithfulness is fulfilled when the subject—the faithful person—meets certain expectations, or certain hypothetical expectations, of the object.   (Audi 2011, pp. 296–7)

Audi makes two central points against the idea that faith is always tied to faith-fulness. One idea relies on thinking of faith as connected with trust, relying on the idea that if one has faith in something, one trusts. In the next section, I will argue that there is no such connection, so we can focus here on the other point, which is that faith is an attitude of a certain kind while faithfulness is a disposition of character. As Audi says, "Having faith in others is mainly a matter of how we view them, and how we are disposed to respond to them, in terms of what we value. Being faithful to others is more a matter of how we act toward them in terms of what they value."

Consider first the claim that having faith (in others) is "mainly a matter of how we view them." While this may be true of special kinds of faith, it is not true of faith in general. For one thing, it is primarily cognitive, and hence unable to explain the kind of affective faith displayed by our Little League pitcher and Abraham. Abraham has faith, according to the author of Hebrews. In what does this faith consist? Is it mainly a matter of how he views God (together with some responsiveness to God)? There is no textual evidence for such a claim, and it has a bizarre ring to it. Perhaps if we thought Abraham's faith was a kind of trust, and agreed with cognitive positions on trust, such as Hardin's view that trusting someone just is believing that they are trustworthy, one might come to the conclusion that Abraham's faith was a matter of viewing God as trustworthy. The central problem is that such an account of Abraham's faith is—how shall I put it?—unfaithful to the text. Abraham hears God's command and leaves. He does so by faith. So what is involved in the faith in question? The only textual evidence of what such faith involves is that it provides the explanation of his behavior. It involves a displayed disposition to follow through and the disposition has an affective source, of the sort that provides impetus to the agency of the individual in question. So whatever we might wish to say about some other possible kinds of faith, the distinction Audi is drawing between faith and faithfulness does not apply, or at least does not obviously apply, to the affective faith involved in our examples of Abraham and the Little League pitcher.

Even if we resist Audi's explanation of the distinction between faith and faithfulness, the point he makes remains. Faith, as a disposition, can occur unrealized in faithful behavior. That point, though, is not at issue here, since the view of faith being developed and endorsed here relies on what we might call the "Hebrews inference," the inference from faithful behavior to underlying faith. That inference is all that is needed in order to maintain the account of Abraham's faith noted above.

What of the second point, however, the one relying on the link between faith and trust? I turn to this issue in the next section.

3.4 The Inadequacy of Trust-based Accounts of Affective Faith

Consider, first, the insight of Simpson above, arising out of Baier's important early work on trust: whatever trust is, it involves, or is built on top of reliance. Simpson claims that reliance is Ur-trust, and that a genealogical investigation of trust shows how various human interests will build various uses of the term 'trust' on top of Ur-trust. Baier holds a similar view, claiming that we distinguish between reliance and trust, but that the latter is a special case of the former.

Examples of reliance without trust are easy to find. Spies often find themselves in the position of having to rely on informants, even though they do not trust them. The usual explanation of this possibility is found in the idea that, while trust can be betrayed, mere reliance cannot: when we rely and things go badly, feelings of disappointment and regret are normal and appropriate, but feelings of betrayal are not. It is for this reason that no account of faith can rest comfortably with only the remarks about trust by William Alston:

Here [when discussing faith in a person] the crucial feature would seem to be trust, reliance on the person to carry out commitments, obligations, promises, or, more generally, to act in a way favorable to oneself. I have faith in my wife; I can rely on her doing what she says she will do, on her remaining true to her commitments, on her remaining attached to me by a bond of love.   (Alston 1996, p. 13)

Alston glosses trust in terms of "reliance on a person . . . to act in a way favorable to oneself." Bernie Madoff relied on his victims to act in ways that would be favorable to him—that is what con-artists are good at. But they don't trust their victims, and feelings of betrayal, while appropriate in the case of violations of trust, are not appropriate when scams are uncovered and victims don't play along.

This same deficiency arises in another prominent account of trust deployed in service of understanding faith. Richard Swinburne claims that

To trust someone is to act on the assumption that she will do for you what she knows that you want or need, when the evidence gives some reason for supposing that she may not and where there will be bad consequences if the assumption is false, . . . [where to act on an assumption is] to do those actions which you would do if you believed the stated assumption strongly.

(Swinburne 2005, p. 144)

Once again, shysters and con-artists do not trust their victims, but they rely on them for exploitative purposes. In Swinburne's terminology, they act on the assumption that their victims will do for them what they know is wanted or needed.

Even though their accounts don't fully characterize the distinction between trust and reliance, both Swinburne and Alston agree that trust is a form of reliance, and with this assumption there is nearly universal agreement. Of course, the plausibility of such approaches requires adopting a suitable account of reliance. Accounts of reliance can go wrong by demanding too much in the way of vulnerability: reliance doesn't require likelihood of harm, nor does it require some objective chance of harm. One can be unknowingly immune to the flu, for example, and still rely on one's flu shot to protect one from the disease. Neither does reliance require the possibility of harm, for one can rely on God's good will even if it is impossible for God not to have good will towards one. Moreover, accounts of reliance can err in another direction, by taking a significant chance of harm to be sufficient for reliance. I do not rely on the venomous snake in the grass of which I am unaware (not to bite me) just by walking across the yard. So reliance-based accounts of trust need to be careful not to undermine this approach to trust simply by adopting a ham-fisted account of reliance. We have no reason to suppose, however, that there can't be an account of reliance suitable to the purpose of providing the fundamental determinable of which trust is a particular determinate, so we needn't take the time here to investigate these issues thoroughly, opting instead for the approach that urges us to treat it as a platitude that trust involves reliance when the latter is properly understood.[6]

3.4.1 Trust not sufficient for faith

If we think of trust as appropriately related to reliance (or perceived reliance), I think we know enough about trust to understand why such accounts of faith tend to be inadequate. At least when it comes to the affective faith I am focusing on here, trust-based accounts can be too passive. What is distinctive about affective faith is that it is typically active rather than passive. Abraham is faithful to the command of God to leave, the Little Leaguer is faithful to his resolution to never let that happen again; the disposition in service of an ideal is a disposition toward activity, not a disposition toward passivity. Moreover, in Scriptural contexts, the model of commitment to the Kingdom of God is described in terms of *being a follower*. These examples of faith are not examples of some inclination compatible with passivity. And yet pure passivity, of the sort displayed by the successful achievement of Stoic *apatheia*, can be an expression of trust. Such an attitude toward the universe as a whole can display one's trust in the created order and in whomever or whatever is responsible for that order. But such an inclination toward passivity is not an instance of the kind of affective faith involved in the examples of our Little Leaguer, Abraham, or followers in general. So the first point to note about the view that faith involves trust is that the view will have to be modified to accommodate the fact that some instances of trust do not help us understand faith worth having. In short, we can't identify faith with trust, since trust can involve complete passivity and faith worth having does not. At most, we can only take faith to be a special kind of trust, a kind that involves the characteristically active character of faith not masked or finked, as we find with the faith of Abraham and our young Little Leaguer.

3.4.2 Trust not necessary for faith

Even that much can't be sustained, however. Consider people who have trust issues, people who fail to develop basic trust in early childhood. Such people will have difficulty trusting, and some will never be able to trust much at all. They will, nonetheless, have to rely on others and the world around them, and they will typically come to realize that even though trust is optional, reliance isn't. Could Abraham have been such a person, consistent with the remarks made about him? Yes, he could. He would still have been relying on God in the process of leaving, and his leaving

---

[6] There may also be reasons for abandoning the requirement that trust is built on top of reliance. If so, it will be fine to focus on what is needed over and above reliance or some new surrogate, perhaps something like perceived reliance (to get around the snake example in the text). For discussion of such approaches, see Thompson (2017). Since these issues are ancillary to the main topic, I'll ignore them in the text, and simply assume that we are building an account of trust on top of an account of reliance.

For an account of reliance that offers hope of meeting the above challenges, see Alonso (2014).

would have been by faith. But it would have been questionable whether his leaving would have involved trust. Also noteworthy, as documented in Stump (2012), is the degree of double-mindedness in Abraham's following of God. It is not really clear to what degree he believed the divine promises or trusted in God, as opposing to holding a cherished hope that the path he was following would get him what he wanted—children or heirs if progeny were not in the cards. He brings Lot, a member of his family, with him as a potential heir, even though told to leave his family; he has Eliezer as his heir even after being given the promise of his own offspring; and even after Sarah's death, he fathers more children with Keturah, apparently as an insurance policy against the continuing barrenness of Isaac and Rebecca. Perhaps the preponderance of the evidence here suggests that our question about Abraham's level of trust isn't a hypothetical possibility that he didn't really trust much, but rather the actual situation as described in the story. Such a failure of trust is fully compatible with an exemplary faith. What makes Abraham the father of faith, on this understanding, is the stunningly broad and deep array of circumstances in which his disposition to act in service of an ideal is realized. A disposition can be present and yet fragile, realized only in the most favorable of circumstances.[7] The divine demands on Abraham are extensive and significant. His faith is deep and secure, expressed even under the most trying circumstances, and the exemplary character of that faith isn't threatened by the supposition that it involves a significant degree of failure to trust.

Such a position fits well with the earlier remark by Cunningham about those Reformers who refused to identify faith with trust. Cunningham notes that these Reformers "represent trust and other graces as the fruits or consequences, and not as constituent parts and elements, of faith" (Cunningham 1862, p. 122), and this standpoint is one that we can endorse here. Perhaps fully mature faith is one that involves full trust in God, even though superlative faith of the sort displayed by Abraham needn't. The precise details of the connection between faith and trust need not detain us here, however, for our question isn't one about this connection but rather about the theory of faith that takes trust to be both necessary and sufficient for faith. We have reason to conclude that no such connection exists.

We can see the distance between faith and trust just as easily in the case of mundane faith. Consider those who followed Caesar across the Rubicon. What did they see in him that led to them crossing the Rubicon with him? Never mind those who followed blindly, or as mercenaries, or as conscripts. No emperor survives without a loyal band of devoted aides. And what did this loyal band see in him? What they "saw" wasn't something they cognitively perceived at all: it was their affections at work, an

---

[7] Think here of situationist challenges to virtue ethics, especially the empirical data suggesting strong fragility of virtues we might have expected to see in ordinary humans. Details of the challenge from social psychology can be found in Ross and Nisbett (1991) and philosophical discussion of the significance of the data is found in, e.g., Harman (1999), Doris (1998, 2002), Sreenivasan (2002), Kamtekar (2004), Sabini and Silver (2005), and Prinz (2009).

admiration, or hope, or wish, or affection for the man and the ideal he represents, that motivates. And what is it that their commitment to, their embracing of, an ideal, which in this case is a person and the prospects and hopes he embodies, involves? Their commitment is expressed in the crossing of the Rubicon. So the question to ask of such followers is not what cognitive states they were in at this crucial moment of, perhaps, 10 January in 49 BCE if we want to know whether his followers had faith in him then; it is, rather, whether they crossed the Rubicon with him in a way motivated by the vision they shared. And that they could have done, with the same affective features that led to their initial commitment to the vision for Rome embodied in this Julian band while finding trust difficult and any specific beliefs beside the point.

3.4.3 Metaphysics and epistemology

Given the language I have used to describe and defend this functional account of faith against trust-based alternatives to it, it would not be surprising for the reader to think that the defense of this functional account depends crucially on a fundamental confusion between metaphysics and epistemology. The confusion charge can be generated as follows: "you talk of knowing who has faith and who doesn't and you answer that question by looking to see whether the person in question is faithful. But that's just an epistemological matter of trying to discover who has faith and who doesn't, not the metaphysical issue of what faith itself is. So you can have your inference from faithfulness to faith if you like, but we should still retain the cognitive picture of faith we know and love."

To see why this line of concern is misplaced, begin with a more telling Christian example. Consider the Johannine perspective here on the attraction of Christ: "and we beheld his glory, the glory as of the only begotten of the Father, full of grace and truth." It is clear that what is fundamental to the Johannine perspective here isn't cognitive at all. It is seated in the affections, involving a complex aesthetic, emotional, and attitudinal experience of a sort that resonates with many of us. To try to paint it as fundamentally a cognitive experience involving belief that God exists and is good is simply too cognitive for understanding the experience of beheld glory. As I prefer to characterize this, the experience and resulting attachment to an ideal are fundamentally affective.

So the source of Johannine faith is clearly affective. But the source isn't the faith, for if John and his fellows had beheld the glory in question, and then decided to return to ordinary life, they would have been in the same faithless category as the rich young ruler, who with sadness went back to his wealth when hearing the call to a different life. For faith to be present is for something else to be found here. And notice, what more is needed is not a better understanding of God and his goodness, but rather the orientation of a person in service of one ideal rather than some other. What is needed is a disposition to follow and for that disposition to be displayed in action. The disposition alone, undisplayed, perhaps may be counted as the weakest of faith, and the general defeasibility of dispositions may require us to categorize some persons as people of faith in spite of lack of faithfulness. But such are the extremes, at best, leaving open the barest possibility of faith without faithfulness, where the disposition to the relevant behavior is present but always and everywhere masked or finked.[8] But when we find faithfulness to an ideal, displaying behavior that is an expression of a disposition whose source and identity are found in the affective origins of the attraction of the ideal, we can not only infer the presence of faith, but have located its nature as well.

We may sum up our discussion of the prospects for a trust-based account of faith this way: some kinds of faith might involve trust, just as some kinds might involve belief or some closely-related cognitive feature. In fact, it might be typical or normal or expected that even the affective faith I'm considering involves trust as well as belief or some closely-related cognitive feature. But its core lies elsewhere, and the central explanatory role that affective faith can play both in understanding various religious and secular examples of faith, not to mention the obvious way in which it allows for an explanation of how and why faith is a virtue, should lead us to conclude that at least one central kind of faith shouldn't be understood in terms of trust. Hope for a successful non-cognitive approach to faith worth having will have to look elsewhere.

3.5 Faith and Preferences

One of the most promising ideas for developing a non-cognitive account of faith that looks for some mental state or attitude that isn't a cognitive one is the account in Lara Buchak (2012). The official account she gives is as follows:

A person has faith that X, expressed by A, if and only if that person performs act A when there is some alternative act B such that he strictly prefers A&X to B&X and he strictly prefers B&~X to A&~X, and the person prefers {to commit to A before he examines additional evidence} rather than {to postpone his decision about A until he examines additional evidence}.

A bit later we will look carefully at the details of this account, but what I want to focus on first is the general character of the account. It is an account of faith displayed in action in terms of three preferences. It would thus seem to be accurate to characterize her view of faith as one on which the fundamental nature of faith is given in terms of preferences.

Things are not quite that simple, however, for in discussing her view, she imposes additional constraints on the account that do not appear in the official version and which raise the issue of whether it is correct to classify her account of faith as a preference-based account. She requires that faith is not involved for claims regarding

---

[8] The disposition of a match to light when struck is masked when the striking occurs underwater and no lighting occurs. The disposition of a fragile vase to shatter when struck by a hammer is finked when a watchful magician would make the vase impervious to breaking by eliminating the fragility on any triggering conditions associated with the fragility disposition. For more on the masking and finking of dispositions, see Choi and Fara (2014).

which one is antecedently certain or for which one has conclusive evidence (p. 227). In addition, while officially put in terms of necessary and sufficient conditions for faith in terms of preferences, she also makes claims about faith that sound quite cognitive but do not appear in the official account of faith. For example, in the first footnote, commenting on the claim in the text that faith in a person involves "acquiescing" to some propositional content or other about that person, she writes,

> I speak of acquiescing to a proposition rather than believing it because I am not sure that if I have faith in something, I thereby believe it. While it sounds infelicitous to say 'I believe that ~X but I have faith that X', there may not be anything wrong with saying 'I don't know whether X—I have no idea whether I believe that X or not—but I have faith that X'. So as not to prejudge that issue, I make a weaker claim: that having faith involves taking the proposition to be true, that is, 'going along with it', but not necessarily adopting an attitude we might describe as belief.
>
> (p. 226)

Here, it appears that Buchak is endorsing a claim that there are cognitive elements to propositional faith, even if they are not doxastic elements.[9] So, before looking at the details of her account, we might want to consider whether it is appropriate to cast her account as a non-cognitive one.

For those with an interest in formal decision theory, a slight detour may be useful. For given the satisfaction of certain formal features by a set of preferences, those preferences can be represented as resulting from a unique set of utilities and degrees of belief, relative to which the preferences maximize expected utility.[10] If there were a way to move from "can be represented in terms of" to "actually involve or are", we'd have a straightforward way to generate cognitive elements from any preference-based account. Such a move, however, is simply not available, and for an obvious reason: there is simply no device that, as we might put it, can force logic into the chambers of the human heart. That is, the human capacity for inconsistency, incoherence, irrationality, and downright insanity makes a mockery of any attempt to engage in cross-category deductions of the sort required here. So, we can't rely on claims about representation to generate the relevant cognitive commitments from the official preference-based account, and hence we can't find in such formal results any resolution of the question of the appropriate way to characterize the nature of Buchak's account.

---

[9] I am confident that Buchak is onto something important here about the relationship between faith and belief, but less confident about a further connection she claims between acts of faith and the cognitive state discussed in the quote above. She also maintains that acting on faith involves acquiescing to a proposition. She writes, "For example, if setting down one's own weapons is an act of faith, then this is because setting down one's own weapons involves acquiescing to the claim that the other person will then set down his." (p. 3) To the extent that acquiescing is a cognitive state, this example is not compelling. One might, for example, set down one's weapon, merely hoping that the other person will do so as well.

[10] For discussion of such Representation Theorems and their usefulness in arguments for Probabilism—the thesis that rational degrees of belief must satisfy the probability calculus—see Christensen (2001) and Hájek (2008).

In discussing the details of her account an answer will emerge concerning the purity of her non-cognitivism, but for the present, all we need to note is that it is possible to give a non-cognitive account of faith while at the same time holding that various cognitive elements are involved in any instance of faith. This possibility makes characterizing the difference between cognitivism and non-cognitivism more difficult, however, for presumably one could also be a cognitivist about faith while thinking that no example of faith ever occurs without some sort of affective features being present as well (for example, have a pro-attitude toward the claims that are the objects of faith). Given these possibilities, what makes the difference between a cognitive and a non-cognitive account?

The typical approach among many philosophers is to formulate an account of a phenomenon in terms of necessary and sufficient conditions alone, and this procedure masks whether the account is to be thought of as fundamentally cognitive or non-cognitive, when the conditions include both kinds of features. What we want is an account of the nature of the thing in question, and discussions that focus on necessary and sufficient conditions alone don't address that issue.[11] A set of necessary and sufficient conditions might bypass the nature entirely: think of defining a human being as a featherless biped or a thing inclined to don clothes. Neither account is adequate, but they point toward the reality that what is necessary and sufficient for X might diverge wildly from what the nature of X is.

Typically, those who talk in terms of providing necessary and sufficient conditions intend to be providing an account of the nature of the thing in question, but the metatheory misleads one into thinking that the collection of conditions completes the account of the nature of the thing in question so long as it is counterexample-free. That's a mistake, and a mistake that can be corrected only by abandoning the metatheory that the goal is only one of providing a set of conditions that are necessary and sufficient for the thing in question. Only then will we be able to say, about mixed theories, whether they are fundamentally cognitive or non-cognitive.

In the case of Buchak's theory, however, things are not so difficult to sort out, for the final account has no condition in it in which either belief or acquiescence plays a role. This fact makes it unclear how the official account is related to the claim that faith involves acquiescence, but the strong focus on preferences throughout her discussion shows, I think, that the most charitable understanding attributes to her a fundamentally non-cognitive account of faith that is preference-based.[12] I will

---

[11] For an example of an account of faith of the sort just mentioned, see Howard-Snyder (2013).

[12] The variety of theoretical uses to which the notion of a preference has been put (the theory of risk, preference logic, moral theory, decision theory, rational choice theory, etc.) may give rise to special understandings of this notion that do not imply that preferences are intentional states at all. I have no objection to such special understandings, and if Buchak wishes to elaborate her approach in terms of such a special understanding, the expanded view may no longer involve a commitment to the claim that faith is fundamentally an affective state. None of this should blind us to the obvious point that preferences are intentional, affective states of a person, and I will thus continue to investigate her view on this understanding.

thus examine the plausibility of her approach as a primary example of an attempt to avoid a cognitive understanding of faith by taking faith to be fundamentally a non-cognitive state. As such, it is opposed both to a cognitive approach to faith and to a fundamentally dispositional one.

Let us take a moment to remind ourselves of the dialectic here. We began with a preliminary idea that faith worth having involves dispositions, and it is because it involves dispositions that there is some prospect for defending the idea that faith is a virtue. The question we then ask ourselves is whether the dispositions in question should be explained in terms of underlying mental states, and we first argued against the idea of grounding the dispositions in question in cognitive states. We then turned to non-cognitive approaches, ones that try to ground the generic disposition involved in faith in non-cognitive states of a person, and one leading contender is an attitude of trust, which we examined in the last section. We now consider grounding the dispositions in attitudinal states, such as emotions, hopes, fears, or preferences. We are considering Buchak's preference-based account as proxy for these other theories, for two reasons. First, it is an impressive account in its own right, more impressive to my mind than anything in the literature. But, second, it has the resources and plausibility of modern decision theory behind it. According to such an approach, we can understand human behavior in terms of degrees of beliefs and a preference function, leaving whatever else there is in the mind (including other non-cognitive states such as emotions, hopes, fears, and the like) as explicable elements involved in human behavior to the extent that they are encoded or reflected in the preference function in question. The apparatus of such a decision theory gives an advantage to an account that appeals to preferences because of the success of that theory. In light of these considerations, then, I turn to a comparison of Buchak's preference-based non-cognitivism with the more minimal functionalist non-cognitivism endorsed to this point.

3.6 Preference Non-Cognitivism and Dispositional Non-Cognitivism

As noted earlier, Buchak argues for the following account of faith in terms of preferences:

A person has faith that X, expressed by A, if and only if that person performs act A when there is some alternative act B such that he strictly prefers A&X to B&X and he strictly prefers B&~X to A&~X, and the person prefers {to commit to A before he examines additional evidence} rather than {to postpone his decision about A until he examines additional evidence}.[13]

---

[13] To be formally precise, we'd need to re-formulate the use of the letters 'A' and 'X' in this account. With respect to 'X', we have it used as a schema letter, to be replaced by a grammatical sentence on the left side; and on the right side, we have a name for the proposition expressed by that grammatical sentence. Moreover, 'A' is here both the name of an action and something else proposition-like, since it can be a conjunct of a

An example from Buchak will help us see how the account is supposed to work. Suppose you are thinking of confiding in a friend. Having your confidence violated would be a bad thing, and your action of telling a secret to your friend will involve faith of a certain sort. It will involve faith in your friend, and faith that your friend will keep your secret. So, we can let X=*your friend will keep your secret*, A=*confiding in your friend*, and B=*keeping your secret to yourself.* You have faith that your friend will keep your secret, on the above account, just because (i) you prefer the conjunction of confiding and having your confiding honored to not confiding and having any confiding being honored, (ii) the preference for confiding is reversed when conjoined with having one's confiding violated, and (iii) you prefer to act now rather than wait on additional evidence.

To get the right results here, we need to be careful in our understanding of the "when" claim on the right side of the equivalence. If I say, "I go to the store when it is raining," does that mean that I go to the store every time it rains, or only sometimes? Charity of interpretation should probably lead us to the latter understanding. In the case of Buchak's account, the claim is that there is an action performed when certain strict preferential inequalities hold. Should we understand that to imply that every time a strict preferential inequality holds, the action in question is performed? Probably not. So I propose assuming the weaker reading.

The account can be applied to religious examples as well. Suppose Abraham hears (what he takes to be) the voice of God telling him to pack and go, and Abraham does so, performing an act of faith. In order for such an act of faith to fit Buchak's account, we need to find a proposition that Abraham takes as an object of faith, where such faith is expressed by the action in question. We know some of the story well enough to hazard a guess or two: God says he'll make of Abraham (called "Abram" at the time) a great nation and that all nations of the earth will be blessed through him. So, we might hazard, we are looking for an explanation of Abraham's faith that God will make of him a great nation and bless other nations through him. The account interprets such propositional faith in terms of three preferences, two of which are contrastive (relative to an incompatible alternative act, such as staying in Haran or moving back to Ur) and the other evidential:

For the action A (leaving), there is a a proposition X and an alternative act B (not-leaving), where

   I. Abraham strictly prefers (leaving & X) to (not-leaving & X)
  II. Abraham strictly prefers (not-leaving & $\sim$X) to (leaving & $\sim$X)
 III. Abraham prefers (to commit to leaving before examining additional evidence) to (postponing a decision until he examines additional evidence).

---

conjunction. The idea, I take it, is that the person prefers one conjunction to an incompatible one, where the first conjunct is the propositional correlation of the person's performing of an action and the second is a proposition. Since such technical details do not affect the central points I want to focus on, I will not pursue these issues further.

We'll return to the third preference later, but for now, let's stipulate that it is satisfied, since it isn't relevant to the issue of whether we can explain Abraham's act of faith in terms of propositional faith. A more substantive concern, however, arises from the introduction of the conjunctions in the two contrastive clauses. Presumably Abraham takes an attitude toward each of A, B, and X individually, but it doesn't follow from this fact that Abraham takes an attitude toward the conjunctions in question, whether that attitude is a doxastic one or a preferential one. So, in the abstract, it is possible for Abraham to prefer leaving to not leaving, and also prefer to be the father of a great nation, but not have any conjunctive preferences which combine these preferences. Even so, failure to have such conjunctive preferences doesn't obviously imply that Abraham doesn't have faith that all nations of the world will be blessed through him.

This problem would dissipate if the language of preferences were a mere placeholder for something more generic such as a disposition toward certain kinds of actions. For Abraham's behavior reveals his dispositions, unless we can find some element of masking or finking in the story, which we do not find. So, if we are merely wondering about dispositions involving conjunctions, the problem isn't pressing. But where preferences are actual mental states with content, things are different. It is worth noting that in much of the decision theory literature, the language of preferences can just as easily be understood so as to be merely dispositional and not involve any actual mental state with propositional content. In our context, however, the difference is crucial, since we are looking at Buchak's preference-based account of faith as an alternative to a purely functional, non-cognitive account that refuses to go beyond our minimal starting point of identifying faith in terms of a disposition of some sort. In this context, we only get an alternative of the sort needed if we insist that preferences be understood to require propositional content in some mental state.

It is a vexed question what standard logical operations hold inside of intentional contexts, but with regard to conjunctions, there are two well-confirmed results. The first is that conjunction-elimination is very hard to deny for certain kinds of mental attitudes: if one knows or believes $p\&q$, one also knows or believes p. The second, is that conjunction-introduction is very hard to maintain for such cognitive states: from believing p and believing q, one can't deduce that $p\&q$ is believed. The simplest objection to this idea is the cognitive explosion problem: if you have any two beliefs, and conjunction introduction were correct, you'd have to have an infinite number of beliefs. The same issue arises for preferences: cognitive explosion would result if we embrace conjunction-introduction in preferential contexts.

This problem isn't deep enough to lead us to reject this approach to propositional faith, however, for there are several ways one might address it. For one thing, one might try to distinguish those intentional contexts in which conjunction-introduction holds from those in which it doesn't, and there is no particular reason I see for thinking that such a refinement won't allow the account to stand as formulated. Alternatively, one might replace this talk of conjunctions of preferences with talk of conditional preferences. Instead of talking about Abraham's preferring the conjunction of leaving and thereby fathering a great nation, we might try to talk about his preferring leaving *given that* he will thereby father a great nation. Such a replacement has an additional advantage, for the relevant conditional preferences might be just those toward which the condition in question is one that the agent in question believes or acquiesces to, allowing us to incorporate the footnote cited earlier that seemed a bit out-of-place on Buchak's official account.[14] For what it's worth, I find the conditional preference version a more intuitive expression of the preference-based account, in part because it bypasses the need for addressing the problem of conjunction-introduction in intentional contexts.

Making such a change introduces the need for a further emendation, however, for we don't want to attribute faith that a certain claim is true without the person taking some pro-attitude toward the claim in question. When preferences govern conjunctions involving the claim in question, we perhaps have such a pro-attitude in place already,[15] but when we replace conjunctive preferences with conditional ones, we lose this result. We can get the pro-attitude back by requiring that the claim in question is not only acquiesced to, but is preferred by the person in question.

The resulting changes give us the following alternative account:

For the action A (leaving), there is a preferred proposition X that is acquiesced to and an alternative act B (not-leaving), where

    I. Abraham strictly prefers (leaving|X) to (not-leaving|X)
    II. Abraham strictly prefers (not-leaving|~X) to (leaving|~X)
    III. Abraham prefers (to commit to leaving before examining additional evidence) to (postponing a decision until he examines additional evidence).

Regardless of which approach one takes to the problem of conjunctive preferences, Buchak hopes to show that this account of propositional faith can be used to explain other locutions involving the concept of faith. In addition to propositional faith, there is also objectual faith, typically signaled by sentences involving an 'in' complement. One can have faith in America, in the government, in God, in a spouse, and in one's

---

[14] As a reminder, the footnote reads:

> I speak of acquiescing to a proposition rather than believing it because I am not sure that if I have faith in something, I thereby believe it. While it sounds infelicitous to say 'I believe that ~X but I have faith that X', there may not be anything wrong with saying 'I don't know whether X—I have no idea whether I believe that X or not—but I have faith that X'. So as not to prejudge that issue, I make a weaker claim: that having faith involves taking the proposition to be true, that is, 'going along with it', but not necessarily adopting an attitude we might describe as belief. (p. 226)

[15] Though we might want to question whether conjunction-elimination is valid in preferential contexts. Can a person prefer a conjunction without preferring each conjunct individually? It is tempting to think so, on the basis of facts about defeasibility. Suppose I don't prefer eating certain kinds of food except in certain contexts where the negativity of eating such food is defeated by special circumstances. Stipulate that I prefer to eat when conjoined with such circumstances. But, it would seem, I needn't prefer either eating or the special circumstances individually: I only prefer them together.

horse. We also speak of acts of faith, saying for example that putting money in the stock market in the 1930s was a sheer act of faith. Finally, there is faith *simpliciter*, faith full stop. We speak of people of faith, of the faith of Abraham, and the honor roll of faith in Hebrews 11 repeats over and over that certain things were done by faith.

It is an interesting question which kind of faith is theoretically basic, if any is. To the extent that the first verse of Hebrews 11 is taken as a definition of faith, it is a use of the term that involves no sentential complement or qualifier of any sort—it simply says that "faith is the substance of things hoped for, the evidence of things not seen." Seen in this way, one might think that the Hebrews position is that faith *simpliciter* is basic. But, as is usual, such a specific philosophical thesis is hardly warranted by such a passing characterization, and the verse is not best thought of as a definition in any case. A more literal translation makes this point more obvious: "And faith is of things hoped for a confidence, of matters not seen a conviction." (Young's Literal Translation) The prepositional constructions are central here, showing how to understand the verse without taking it to be a definition, but rather taking it as a description of what faith involves, relative to the contexts of things hoped for and things not seen.

Buchak's account takes an alternative stance, hoping to explain non-propositional faith in terms of propositional faith. As will become clear, I am not optimistic about the prospects for success here, so let's see how the explanations might go.

3.6.1 Explaining non-propositional faith in terms of preferences

Buchak's project is to define other faith locutions in terms of the fundamental locution 'A person has faith that X, expressed by action A': "I propose, then, to make *faith that X, expressed by A* the basic unit of analysis, where X is a proposition and A is an act, and define the other constructions in terms of this one." (p. 228) She then defines faith in a person as follows:

A person P has faith in another person Q if and only if there is some act A and some proposition(s) X that express(es) a positive judgment about Q such that P has faith in X, expressed by A.

And she defines acts of faith in similar fashion:

A person performs an act of faith (or acts on faith) if and only if he performs some act A such that there is a proposition X in which he has faith, expressed by A.

Such an approach appears initially to be a promising one, though some refinement will be necessary. A minor issue here is that the two references to act A do not distinguish properly between the token action performed and the type of action involved in an attribution of propositional faith. Note that in the account of propositional faith expressed in action, the schematic letter 'A' stands for a type of action, one that can be tokened on different occasions by specific token actions. When we speak of a person performing an act of faith, however, we are talking about a token action, so we should not be using the same schematic letter to talk about both it and the action type that appears in the account of propositional faith expressed in action. What we should do, instead, is talk of a token action which is an instance of the type in question. This refinement might seem trivial, but it is not, for it raises the possibility of performing a specific action which is of the relevant type, but where the performance of the specific, token act is unrelated to the propositional faith in question. Suppose, for example, that Harry has faith that Sally will keep their lunch appointment, as expressed by him going to the restaurant where they are supposed to meet (and, we assume, this is a favorite restaurant and they have met here many times). As lunchtime rolls around, Harry has forgotten the plans with Sally, but decides in favor of going to this same restaurant because he wants a burrito and they have the best burritos in town. His token action is an instance of the relevant type, but his going to the restaurant is not an act of faith. It is not an act of faith because he doesn't choose the restaurant on the basis of his faith that Sally will keep their appointment. So, once we notice the need for a type/token disambiguation in the account of what it is to perform an act of faith, we'll need to replace Buchak's account with one that invokes the relevant basis from which the token act arises. Doing so gives us:

A person performs an act of faith (or acts on faith) if and only if the person performs an instance of some act type A, and performs it on the basis of the person's faith in some proposition X, expressed by A.

Second, the account given here attributes faith in a person too broadly, and the literature on the *de re/de dicto* distinction contains the relevant concerns. A proposition can be about a person in very indirect ways, and a person can have an attitude involving that proposition without any direct acquaintance or causal connection to the person at all. For example, one can believe that the tallest spy is a spy quite easily, but it is a much different thing to believe of the tallest spy that he or she is a spy. To make this point relevant to the definition above, let the proposition in question be the proposition that the most talented person is courageous, and let the person in question have faith in this proposition, expressed by averring publicly that the most talented person is courageous. We also stipulate, however, that this devout witnessing is not accompanied by any acquaintance with the most talented person, but only by the strong conviction that the most talented, whoever he or she is, *must* be courageous—the world could not be right without it! Suppose, then, that there is a most talented person, and her name is 'Mary'. In such a case, our devout witness does not have faith in Mary. Mary is completely unknown to said person.

This difficulty would be a deep one if the literature on the *de re/de dicto* distinction showed that such cases undermine the possibility of defining the former in terms of the latter, but the standard view is that such is not the case. The standard view is that such a definition merely requires the addition of some acquaintance or causal relation between the subject of the proposition and the person taking the attitude in question, and that same view could be endorsed here. In such a case, we would need to find a proposition that expresses a positive judgment about Q, where the required acquaintance or causal connection of the person in question to Q obtained, in order to define faith in a person in terms of propositional faith. Perhaps the following will work:

A person P has faith in another person Q if and only if there is some act A and some proposition(s) X that express(es) a positive judgment about Q such that P has faith in X, expressed by A, and P is in the right sort of acquaintance relation to Q.[16]

Once we have a successful account of this sort, we can generalize the account to explain, not only faith in a person, but faith in an object more generally, using the same device of identifying a proposition about the object in question and requiring the right kind of acquaintance relation to that object. One can have faith in Obama, and one can also have faith in the government (though it is sometimes hard to see why one would), and an adequate account of objectual faith should include all such objects and not just persons.

Even given success on these fronts, however, two problems remain. One problem concerns the notion of propositional faith itself, where the faith in question is dormant and thus not expressed in action. I will postpone this issue, though, to focus first on the notion of faith *simpliciter*, as is indicated when we say that Abraham was a man of faith, or that faith is, of things hoped for, a confidence. Buchak gives no account of such uses, so the question arises whether her approach can be extended to these cases as well.

One way to do so would be to resist the idea that these constructions are different in kind from the ones already considered. Instead, one might hold that such constructions are always elliptical for other uses, uses which attribute either propositional or objectual faith, or some acts of faith (which I'll call "praxical faith"). As a matter of syntax alone, there is no basis for such a position. The clearest evidence for this claim is that, in ellipses, the full statement is easily recoverable in any context of assertion in which the elided sentence is used. Such a point is clearly seen in a wide variety of ellipses:

- Ben does epistemology and Chris metaphysics. (gapping)
- Gary does ethics, and Linda, too. (stripping)
- Anyone who wants to read Dewey can. (verb phrase ellipsis)
- Who reads James? John and Gregory. (answer ellipsis)

---

[16] A further complication here is that *de te* awareness, awareness of persons, is different from the more generic *de re* awareness of objects, and both of these are clearly different from *de se* awareness of self. For discussion of some of these issues regarding second-person awareness, see Stump (2010) and Darwall (2009). I assume that the differences between these types of awareness will be a function of different acquaintance relations to the object in question, so to bypass them in the text, I make the vague reference to "the right sort of" acquaintance relation. (Much the same can be said about *de se* awareness, awareness of oneself as oneself. It is one thing to have faith in someone who just happens to be oneself, and another thing to have faith in oneself as oneself. Again, I will assume here that the acquaintance relation will be different in such cases, and so will bypass further discussion of this issue in the text.)

- When I don't know, but Michael will show up. (sluicing)
- The department chair, leader that she is, served on three onerous University committees because everyone else in the department served on two. (nominal ellipsis)
- Do you know whether Elizabeth will take the job? No, I don't. (null complement anaphora)

Compare, then, some of the claims of faith *simpliciter*, all from Hebrews 11:

- By faith, Abel brought a better offering than Cain.
- By faith, Enoch was taken from this life.
- By faith, Noah . . . built an ark.
- All these people were living by faith when they died.
- These were all commended for their faith.

Careless classification is required to lump the latter together with the former. That is, none of the constructions in the second list are instances of anything in the first list, and full statements to replace these supposedly elided ones are not recoverable from the context. In short, faith *simpliciter* constructions are not syntactically elliptical.

Another proposal would be to hold that there is a semantic basis for thinking of such constructions as identical in meaning to some complex of propositional and objectual and praxical faith. That suggestion is not promising, even if it is plausible to think of faith *simpliciter* as requiring some combination of propositional and objectual faith. For note that faith can go undisplayed: Abraham was a man of faith even when not acting on it. So, we can't endorse that faith *simpliciter* requires praxical faith, and the idea that some combination of propositional and objectual faith implies faith *simpliciter* looks like the same mistake as trying to infer a character trait such as courage from some combination of actions and mental states of the person in question.

A more promising view can be gleaned from one of Buchak's remarks about faith. She writes:

Along the same lines, having faith typically involves an action: a person's having faith in something should make a difference to her behaviour. However, this needn't be an actual action. It would be enough for faith that if a person were put in a particular situation, she would then manifest the relevant behaviour (assuming that there are no forces that would stop her). Faith is thus linked to a disposition to act. (p. 226)

Buchak notes that faith is linked to a disposition to act, and if we replace this claim with the somewhat stronger claim that faith *simpliciter* is a disposition toward acts of faith—toward praxical faith—we have the resources to develop a unified account of faith, even if we can't define faith *simpliciter* solely in terms of propositional, objectual, and praxical faith. We begin by defining faith *simpliciter* in terms of a disposition toward acts of faith, and then define acts of faith in terms of objectual and propositional faith, as before. We thus have an approach that shows some promise in clarifying faith *simpliciter* within the strictures of Buchak's framework.

There remains the other concern, for Buchak doesn't give us an account of propositional faith, but rather an account of *propositional faith expressed by action A*. That is, as formulated, it isn't quite an account of faith-that, since it includes a restriction involving the expression of such faith in an action. One might conclude, then, that it only informs us about propositional faith relative to a restriction, rather than propositional faith itself.

One might hope to be able to transform the account into one of propositional faith itself, putting the reference to actions on the other side of the central connective of the account. We might try, for example:

A given mental state S of a person is an instance of faith that X for that person if and only if for any action A that the person in question performs that expresses state S, that person performs act A when there is some alternative act B such that there is a strict preference for A&X over B&X and a strict preference for B&~X over A&~X, and the person prefers {to commit to A before he examines additional evidence} rather than {to postpone his decision about A until he examines additional evidence}.

This formulation is not quite adequate, however. Notice that it quantifies over every action that expresses the state in question, and we noted earlier that such an interpretation of the account is uncharitably strong. More charitable is to replace the universal claim with one involving the existential quantifier instead:

A given state S of a person is an instance of faith that X for that person if and only if for some action A that the person in question performs that expresses state S, that person performs act A when there is some alternative act B such there is a strict preference for A&X over B&X and a strict preference for B&~X over A&~X, and the person prefers {to commit to A before he examines additional evidence} rather than {to postpone his decision about A until he examines additional evidence}.

If we assume the background requirement that the state in question has to be a cognitive state involving at least acquiescence to the claim in question, together with other changes considered above to avoid other problems for Buchak's initial formulation, it looks like we have found a way to explain propositional faith in terms of Buchak's fundamental locution. What remains, then, is an evaluation of the plausibility of this package of claims as a theory of faith. To that issue I now turn.

3.6.2 The adequacy of the account of propositional faith

A central concern about preference-based accounts of faith is the way in which they need to rely on preferential contrasts between circumstances in which the faith claim is true and those in which the faith claim is false. In many cases, and perhaps in the most important cases, the preferential contrasts under the assumption of falsity may not be present. Let X be a claim that Abraham is so fully committed to that his life can make no sense to him if it isn't true. For many people, there are such central truths. The future makes no sense apart from that assumption. For example, for many after years of marriage, imagining how to carry on with one's life apart from one's spouse renders one catatonic. It is of the essence of such cataclysmic events that preparation for them can be unimaginable. There is no set of plans or attitudes or goals to drive reflection on how to go on with one's life in the face of them. In keeping with the etymology of the word, all is washed down to nothing by the contemplation of such events.

The absence of such conditions would create crisis, and imagining what one would do or think, prefer or avoid under such circumstances, leads nowhere. In such a case, it is easy to imagine a person being aware of how catastrophic such an event would be and having this awareness reflected in their preferences. So it is easy to see how the first condition above can be satisfied for such a proposition while the second condition is not: the first strict preference is a matter of life proceeding normally, but the second involves such cataclysm that preferential differences are simply not present at all.

Yet, some such absolutely central claims to the life of a person are just the sorts of claims that are properly described as objects of propositional faith. For some, the existence of God or the reality of Jesus are just such cataclysmic elements, and the people for whom they are, are people who have faith that God exists or that Jesus is their Redeemer. Here, the story of Jesus and Peter in John 6 is instructive. People abandon Jesus after his "hard sermon," the sermon in which he requires the drinking of his blood and eating of his flesh. The claims leave the audience flabbergasted, and many leave. Jesus asks the twelve whether they too will leave, and Peter replies, "Where would we go? You have the words of eternal life."

Peter's response may signal an attitude of the cataclysmic nature of his understanding of Jesus and the promise he brings for the future. To leave would be to abandon that attitude, and Peter's response indicates that he finds doing that unimaginable. Some see in Peter's response an affirmation of his deep confidence in who Jesus is, but I suspect otherwise. It could just as easily be, and I suspect it is, a cry of hope and despair—Peter is noting what his life has become and how unimaginable a future is apart from the promise Jesus embodies (however he understands that). So Peter has faith in Jesus, in spite of not being in a position to make sense of the hard sermon, and though he understands why others are leaving, he cannot fathom it for himself. By Buchak's account, to have faith in Jesus requires propositional faith of some sort, perhaps faith that Jesus is the promised one. And the cataclysmic status of that claim in the life of Peter could easily involve no preferential difference between leaving and continuing to follow, under the assumption that (or in conjunction with the claim that) Jesus isn't the promised one.

The same could be true for Abraham and his faith in God and faith that God exists. There is no reason to suppose that Abraham strictly prefers not leaving under the assumption that there is no God to staying under that same assumption. His faith is, perhaps, too central, too deep, too significant in his life for such a preference to be present.

Note as well that a more generic, functional account doesn't face any such problem. On such an account, we leave open what precise mental attitudes would be involved, allowing different combinations of substrate involving mental states with content to underlie a given instance of functional faith. We thus have some reason for preferring a functional account to a preference-based one that involves such contrastive preferences.

Our starting point regarding faith worth having identifies it in terms of a disposition to behavior aimed at an ideal of some sort. One way to preserve this starting point is to find more specific conditions that imply such a disposition, but another way to preserve it is to view the starting point as the account itself, treating the item in question as a functional one and allowing for its realization in a multitude of ways. A functional account holds that the identity conditions for faith are at a functional level, and even if this functional entity must be grounded or realized in certain, more basic ontological features, the functional account maintains that the realizing ground can vary while the functional entity remains the same. So, for example, in discussing trust, we noted that some examples of faith can be exemplary even if the level of trust involved is minimal, while other examples of exemplary faith might involve full and complete trust. Note that the same variability arises when in Buchak's preference-based account: faith can be present when the preferences are as articulated, but also when those particular preferences are absent. On this score, a functional account of faith differs dramatically from the cognitive and non-cognitive accounts surveyed to this point, accounts which allow that faith involves dispositions of some sort, but see these dispositions as being generated by an underlying feature involving belief, preference, trust, or some other item, where faith is identified with the relevant substrate that grounds the dispositions, rather than allowing faith to be identified with the dispositions and be realized in different people by different substrata.

A useful example in this regard is with the nature of belief. If we adopt a functional account of belief, we will hold that the identity conditions for belief are functional ones, and if we also hold that such functional entities must have a categorical basis (which I will assume for this discussion), then any particular belief will have an underlying substrate in which the functional entity is realized. But the substrate is not the belief; it is, rather, that in which the belief is realized. Perhaps, for example, beliefs in human beings are realized in certain brain state patterns, and maybe the same belief can be in two different human beings and be realized in different brain state patterns. This possibility mirrors the basic argument for identifying belief with the functional level rather than with the more basic, categorical level in that the same beliefs can be realized in radically different cognitive architectures. Some are realized in the cognitive architecture that is distinctively human, involving brain states and the like, while others are realized in, perhaps, artificial life forms, other species of animal, and even divine beings.

Just so with a functional account of faith. If we hold that functional entities must bottom out at the categorical level, we will view the functional entity which is faith as something that can only exist when realized in more basic entities. Moreover, we might hold that the grounding of this functional entity is multi-level: faith is grounded at the first level in various conative, cognitive, and affective elements, some of which are themselves functional entities, and so grounded as well in deeper, categorical elements which also ground, at the second-level, the faith that is grounded in items at the first level.

The value of the investigation of cognitive and non-cognitive approaches to faith discussed to this point is this: that investigation provides the same kind of argument for a functional account of faith that is at work in defending a functional account of belief. In discussing cognitive requirements for faith, a topic that kept recurring was the possibility of faith without the specific cognitive elements proposed by various approaches to faith, and in discussing non-cognitive approaches, the striking thing to note is the way in which faith worth having can still be present in spite of divergent underlying combinations of preferences, desires, levels of trust, and so on. The investigation thus provides a strong argument for identifying faith with the functional level itself, rather than looking for a substrate of the disposition that is the faith in question.

The functional account thus resists the temptation to identify the precise attitudinal components that might be involved in having such a disposition, even though it is fairly clear that the disposition in question is one that involves some combination of affective, cognitive, and conative elements. Not all dispositions to behavior are so grounded, of course, for some operate at the submental level. In this latter category are pain-response behaviors: we pull our hand away quickly from a hot stove, displaying a certain pain-avoidance disposition. But the response is so quick that the parts of the brain involved in mentation can't be involved. Engaging them would take more time than would be advantageous from an evolutionary perspective, and thus mechanisms to allow a quicker process evolve to minimize the damage from the heat source. Clearly, however, the disposition to behavior that is involved in the kind of faith worth having isn't that kind of disposition, for behavior that expresses such faith is clearly of the sort that involves mentation of some sort or other.

Endorsing a functional account of faith has pleasing implications concerning how to treat those with different ways of thinking, feeling, and seeing the world from our own. Once we see the wide variety of ways in which the same functional faith can be realized in different substrate combinations, and once we see the value to focus on in terms of the faith itself rather than in the substrates, we might find ourselves being more tolerant of those who are not mirror images of ourselves. One might find oneself in solidarity with those with whom one disagrees, and one might be more tolerant of those who live lives of faith that are different from one's own life of faith.

I don't want to exaggerate the reach of such benefits, though, since solidarity and tolerance will have their limits even on a functional account. But the lessons of history regarding how matters of faith lead to horrendous evil should lead us to see this benefit as an important one, even if it isn't a panacea for all the evils of the world resulting from incompatible faiths, sacred or secular.

3.6.3 A major difference

Even if we endorse this functional account, there is an important element of Buchak's account that needs to be addressed and accommodated within the functional framework. To this point, all we have noted is that faith must involve a disposition to behavior in order to be a virtue and something worth having, and the last two chapters have provided the needed background for seeing the basic argument for adopting a functional account of faith that identifies it with the disposition to respond in service of an ideal of some sort. What this account doesn't include, however, is anything like Buchak's third condition, involving a disposition to act without seeking further evidence. We should consider whether to endorse such a requirement within our functional framework.

Here is one reason to resist including this dimension in a functional account. A person of faith who has a certain disposition, will act in a characteristic way in the triggering conditions for that disposition, unless the disposition is masked or finked. Once one notices the role played by masking and finking in the story of realized dispositions, we can appreciate the role that masking and finking can play in the creation of a new disposition as well. The triggering conditions for a disposition might also be triggering conditions for the creation of a new disposition with precisely those triggering conditions. In such a case, the disposition wasn't present prior to the occurrence of the triggering conditions. Perhaps faith is an instance of this phenomenon, so that it is a disposition to act in service of an ideal, where the disposition itself has identity conditions that make it be the kind of thing that in certain triggering conditions leads not only to action but also to the formation of additional dispositions, such as the disposition to act without first seeking additional information. Moreover, it is at least somewhat plausible to see this feature as part of what it is to embrace an ideal of some sort. To do so involves an attachment or attraction to a thing or idea or person that has some degree of resilience in the face of events or circumstances that incline one to abandon the ideal. The antagonistic event might be something as simple as a sneer by a friend, or an evoking of sympathy for an alternative way of life, but it might also involve the presentation of evidence against some of the claims involved in the life of faith involving that ideal. In each such example, we needn't suppose that there is already present a disposition to resist such intrusions, for it could be that the resistance is itself generated by the original disposition toward service of an ideal together with the antagonistic event. If so, faith worth having doesn't involve a disposition to act without seeking additional evidence (nor does it involve a disposition to act in the face of other antagonisms), but does involve a disposition that is sometimes realized in a way that produces these additional dispositions.

If one thinks about the Little Leaguer example, this resistance to Buchak's third condition may be exactly right. The Little Leaguer is likely to be a bit young for it to be sensible to attribute to him any combination of mental states needed to ground a disposition to act without seeking additional evidence, though once the issue of seeking additional evidence is raised (say, by a concerned parent worried that too much obsessing about sports might not be in the best interests of the tyke), the Little Leaguer may then develop a disposition to display the characteristic behavior without seeking additional information on whether doing so is a good idea.

The same could be said of Abraham, I believe. The ordinary human experience is to trust and act on information gathered, and the moments of sophistication where character traits involving skeptical concerns are developed, such as those that would counsel seeking additional information before acting, are but the tip of the iceberg of human experience rather than the bulk of it. In the usual case, no dispositions need to be present regarding what to do or think about the possibility of seeking additional information (or what to do in the face of other antagonistic occurrences). But, of course, once the question is raised, the very question itself can trigger both the creation of a disposition and its characteristic display, and this fact makes it look as if the disposition were present all along. It is part of being a realist about dispositions, however, to recognize the possibility that such looks are misleading.

I thus conclude that the more generic description, in terms of a disposition to act in pursuit of an ideal, is to be preferred to a more specific description in terms of acting in pursuit of an ideal in a way that includes an aversion toward examining additional evidence. The more specific account may be an accurate description of sophisticated or reflective faith, but not of faith itself in all its forms and varieties.

3.7 Conclusion

The culmination of our inquiry over the last two chapters is instructive in that it provides a general argument for taking the dispositional starting point regarding faith worth having at face value. That is, the difficulties and failures of the accounts surveyed in the last two chapters give us a reason for identifying faith worth having with the functional level itself, rather than trying to find something in the substrate for the dispositions in question with which to identify the faith in question.

Moreover, this functional approach has rather straightforward resources for explaining not only what faith worth having is, but also the variety of locutions that Buchak's account was designed to handle. On a functional account, acts of faith are acts which express the disposition in service of an ideal, and having faith in X is best thought of in terms of having a disposition in service of an ideal, where X is an integral component in an account of the ideal in question. Finally, propositional faith can be understood in terms of faith itself, where the faith has a substrate involving mental states that have the proposition in question as their content.

Some of these are in need of careful articulation. Regarding propositional faith, we might wonder whether the mental state with content has to be an affective state, or a cognitive state, or both. Suppose, for example, that a person has faith that Gandhi is a saint, with a high degree of felt attraction for this idea. To have such faith, does the person also have to be in a cognitive state with *Gandhi is a saint* as propositional content? Here the functional nature of our proposal counsels against legislation. We should expect that lowering the degree of commitment along cognitive dimensions, for the claim in question, can be compensated for by raising the degree of commitment along affective and conative dimensions; and vice versa. So, on a functional account, we should expect no positive requirement except one that involves finding the proposition in question among the mental states that constitute the substrate in question (leaving open the possibility of including purely negative requirements such as not simply believing or endorsing the denial of the claim in question, or preferring its falsity). Moreover, in keeping with the evidence presented to this point, the crucial element in identifying a collection of mental states that are capable of constituting the requisite substrate for a given instance of propositional faith, the central mental elements will be affective and conative rather than cognitive. Hence, there is a good case to be made for the idea that we must start with propositional content rooted in the affections, adding cognitive elements as needed to avoid attributing propositional faith regarding claims, for example, known to be false.

Another aspect of this approach requiring elucidation concerns acts of faith. We often use the language of the virtues even when the action in question is one done out-of-character. For example, cowards sometimes perform acts of courage, in spite of obviously lacking the virtue in question. Just so, we might expect it to be possible to perform an act of faith even when one does not possess the faith in question.

There are two ways one might approach this issue. In considering acts of courage by those lacking it, it might be that we are confusing the total absence of courage with a very minimal amount of it, so that the minimal amount of courage is hardly ever on display but manages to come to the surface in the case at hand. On this approach, it is not possible to perform an act of courage and be totally lacking in the virtue, though it is possible to have a very minimal amount of a virtue so that any acting on it still counts as being out-of-character.

The other way is to try to identify the acts in question in terms of the characteristic behavior of people who have the virtue in question. Thus an act done by a person totally lacking in courage could still be an act of courage because it is the kind of act that courageous people typically do in the type of circumstances in question. Accounts of this sort have an advantage over the prior proposal because they don't need to assume even a minimal level of courage in those performing acts of courage.

The difficulty faced by this approach is the obscurity of the key elements of the account. First, there are lots of different types of courageous folk, and identifying what the courageous typically do in a set of circumstances may not be possible. Perhaps if we specify which courageous person we are talking about, we can specify what that person typically does in various kinds of circumstances, but then the problem is to say which particular person is the one to use to explain any particular instance of acting out-of-character.

Another version of this approach would be to identify the kinds of motives and reasons for which a courageous person acts when performing an act of courage, and then call an act by a coward an "act of courage" when the performance of that act is based on those kinds of motives and reasons. This approach avoids the need to find something that courageous people typically do in a given set of circumstances. One may worry that there is a similar problem here, in that there may be no generalizations available concerning the kinds of motives and reasons for which virtuous people act, but perhaps all that is needed is to see the act of a coward as having a basis on which a virtuous person might act. Even if there are no generalizations available about how a virtuous person acts or would act, we can still identify the kinds of motives and reasons that conform to the virtues.

Each of these approaches can be applied as well to acts of faith, but there would be no need for such unless there can be acts of faith by the totally faithless. I take it to be clear and uncontroversial that there can be acts of courage by cowards, but the idea of an act of faith by the totally faithless, when the kind of faith in question is a kind worth having and is a virtue, is less clear. For one thing, it is not clear what it would be to be a totally faithless person, though it is clearly possible to be totally faithless with respect to some given ideal. A person can have no faith in democracy, or in equality, or in humanity, or in God. But in such a case, we are not talking of acts of faith in those who are faithless, but rather about acts of faith in X, where the person in question has no faith in X. I, for one, don't understand what that would be. What would it be like to perform an act of faith in humanity while having no faith in humanity? If there can't be examples of that sort, they pose no special challenge to the capacity of the functional account of faith to explain the varieties of faith locutions there are when we delimit the topic to faith worth having.

I do not pretend here to have given anything close to a fully general theory of faith, one which treats faith *simpliciter* as the basic kind of faith and uses this basic kind to define and explain other types of faith, such as propositional, objectual, and praxical faith, in terms of it. What I have provided points in the direction of a theory of faith that is fully general, but does little more than that. The reason for resting content with such has to do with the nature of our current inquiry, which is to uncover the fundamental character of faith worth having, and to elucidate its connection to the virtue of humility. It is sufficient for such a project to indicate the direction to look for a fully general theory of faith, but it would be too much of a lengthy diversion to pursue such a theory when the direction indicated looks promising enough even without the full details. We can thus proceed with our inquiry without being sidetracked by an issue that is important and interesting in its own right but not crucial for the results sought here.

We thus have good reason to provisionally endorse this functional view of faith, according to which the basic kind of faith worth having involves a disposition to act in service of an ideal. The intellectual heritage of this view of faith is found in the work of John Dewey, and we can make progress on elucidating the slogan for this functional account of faith (a disposition in service of an ideal) by examining his account and seeing where it falls short. We thus turn to Dewey's account in the next chapter and to needed enhancements and revisions of it.

4

Dewey, Epistemic Fetishism, and Classical Theism

4.1 Introduction

An account of faith in terms of the slogan of being disposed to act in service of an ideal is found in John Dewey's *A Common Faith*, given as public lectures in the Terry Lecture Series at Yale University during the 1933–4 academic year. Dewey does two things relevant to our inquiry in the first chapter of this work. One part involves a denigration of religious ideologies, lamenting the focus on doctrinal elements found in organized religions. The other part involves an identification and characterization of a central feature of human life, characterized sometimes in terms of the language of the religious in human experience and other times in terms of the notion of faith. Throughout, however, he registers an antipathy toward the kind of cognitive systems that characterize organized religion, insisting that the relationship between the religious and religions is one involving a kind of enslavement from which emancipation is needed.

Dewey's discussion deserves attention, much more attention than it has received in the dominant kind of academic philosophy in Europe, Australia, and North America in recent history. In the present context, the motivation for looking carefully at what he says about faith is that it is a sustained attempt to develop a functional account of faith. It is also interesting in another more troubling way. The working hypothesis governing our inquiry is that faith worth having is something that appears in both sacred and secular contexts, but Dewey's development of a functional account of faith is strongly antithetical to the idea that it has sacred expressions. So we will also be testing this negative thesis in conjunction with developing an account of functional faith that is at least Deweyan in spirit if not in letter. I will be arguing that we should affirm something very close to Dewey's account of faith, but that the antipathy toward organized religion can be mitigated by careful attention to the details of the functional account in question. To these ends, we begin with Dewey's account of faith.

4.2 Dewey on Faith

Dewey's account of faith proceeds through an account of the religious, distinguishing that phenomenon from religion in general and from any particular religion.

The heart of my point...is that there is a difference between religion, *a* religion, and the religious; between anything that may be denoted by a noun substantive and the quality of experience that is designated by an adjective. (Dewey 1934, p. 3)

Crucial to Dewey's approach to the religious is that it involves an attitude. He writes:

To be more explicit, a religion...always signifies a special body of beliefs and practices having some kind of institutional organization, loose or tight. In contrast, the adjective "religious" denotes nothing in the way of a specifiable entity, either institutional or as a system of beliefs. It does not denote anything to which one can specifically point as one can point to this and that historic religion or existing church. For it does not denote anything that can exist by itself or that can be organized into a particular and distinction form of existence. It denotes attitudes that may be taken toward every object and every proposed end or ideal. (Dewey 1934, p. 9)

It is clear, then, that Dewey's approach to the religious and the faith involved in it is attitudinal. Moreover, Dewey informs us early on in the discussion what the general category of attitude involved is:

Let us then for the moment drop the term "religious," and ask what are the attitudes that lend deep and enduring support to the processes of living. (Dewey 1934, p. 14)

So, we should expect to find that the religious attitude, the attitude of faith, is found as a subtype of those attitudes that lend deep and enduring support to the processes of living. He begins his discussion of the more general phenomenon by describing various types of adjustments we make in the process of experiencing the world around us. He first identifies passive accommodations we make to our environment, and then speaks of more active adaptations we make as well. Both of these count as adjustments, but the kind of adjustment that is more interesting in our context is an adjustment that is both more general and deeper:

But there are also changes in ourselves in relation to the world in which we live that are much more inclusive and deep seated. They relate not to this and that want in relation to this and that condition of our surroundings, but pertain to our being in its entirety. Because of their scope, this modification of ourselves is enduring. It lasts through any amount of vicissitude of circumstances, internal and external. There is a composing and harmonizing of the various elements of our being such that, in spite of changes in the special conditions that surround us, these conditions are also arranged, settled, in relation to us. (Dewey 1934, p. 15)

It is the claim of religions that they effect this generic and enduring change in attitude. I should like to turn that statement around and say that whenever this change takes place there is a definitely religious attitude.... [W]hen it occurs,...there is a religious outlook and function.
(Dewey 1934, pp. 15–16)

The kind of adjustment in question involves this general and deeper change in attitude, which involves a "composing and harmonizing" of things. Even when special conditions continue to change, there is a deeper sense in which things are "arranged" or "settled". Thus, even though adjustments can be more local and particular, when the adjustment is more general in this way, it involves the taking on of a religious attitude.

Dewey's task, then, is to say exactly what is involved in making such a general adjustment in attitude, one that pertains to our being in its entirety and is enduring. To characterize this attitude change, one which involves a harmonizing of the self, Dewey employs the notion of an ideal.

> The connection between imagination and the harmonizing of the self is closer than is usually thought. The idea of a whole, whether of the whole personal being or of the world, is an imaginative, not a literal, idea. . . . Neither observation, thought, nor practical activity can attain that complete unification of the self which is called a whole. The *whole* self is an ideal, an imaginative projection. (Dewey 1934, p. 17)

I will return to the appeal to the imagination here, but the first point to note is the central role played by the notion of an ideal. The attitude adjustment that is crucial for faith involves the entire person, harmonizing the self in its relation to all of reality, and this harmonizing of the self involves a posit, a projection of sorts, one which Dewey terms an "ideal." We can get a sense of what this appeal to an ideal involves by noting its use by Dewey in moral contexts:

> Apart from any theological context, there is a difference between belief that is a conviction that some end should be supreme over conduct, and belief that some object or being exists as a truth for the intellect. Conviction in the moral sense signifies being conquered, vanquished, in our active nature by an ideal end; it signifies acknowledgment of its rightful claim over our desires and purposes. Such acknowledgment is practical, not primarily intellectual. It goes beyond evidence that can be presented to *any* possible observer. Reflection, often long and arduous, may be involved in arriving at the conviction, but the import of thought is not exhausted in discovery of evidence that can justify intellectual assent. The authority of an ideal over choice and conduct is the authority of an ideal, not of a fact, of a truth guaranteed to intellect, not of the status of the one who propounds the truth. (Dewey 1934, p. 19)

Note first that Dewey is at least slouching toward a non-cognitivist position regarding moral obligations: believing that some end is supreme over conduct is quite different from believing that something is true. Second, note that the former involves being "vanquished" by an ideal end. It is the authority of an ideal rather than a fact that controls moral obligation as opposed to intellectual assent. It is this submission to the authority of an ideal that constitutes moral faith, for Dewey.

Such moral faith, however, is not sufficient for faith in the sense involved in the religious attitude:

> What has been said does not imply that all moral faith in ideal ends is by virtue of that fact religious in quality. The religious is "morality touched by emotion" only when the ends of moral conviction arouse emotions that are not only intense but are actuated and supported by ends so inclusive that they unify the self. . . . The religious attitude signifies something that is bound through imagination to a *general* attitude. (Dewey 1934, p. 21)

Apart from the tip of the hat to Matthew Arnold,[1] the key element in moving from mere moral faith to the religious are ends or ideals that are "so inclusive that they unify the self."

Such faith is not unique to religion, however:

Any activity pursued in behalf of an ideal end against obstacles and in spite of threats of personal loss because of conviction of its general and enduring value is religious in quality. Many a person, inquirer, artist, philanthropist, citizen, men and women in the humblest walks of life, have achieved, without presumption and without display, such unification of themselves and of their relations to the conditions of existence.... [T]he claim on the part of religions to possess a monopoly of ideas and of the supernatural means by which alone, it is alleged, they can be furthered, stands in the way of the realization of distinctively religious values inherent in natural experience. (Dewey 1934, p. 25)

The essential components of Dewey's account of faith, then, are these. Faith involves an ideal, an end of some sort. Moreover, that end or ideal must be all-encompassing, so inclusive that it unifies or harmonizes the self. More restrictive types of faith are possible when the ideal is not quite so all-encompassing, and the more generic attitude is possible independently of commitment to any particular religion, available to all in any pursuit of a life that involves pursuit of an ideal against difficulty and threat of loss. Dewey summarizes this account as follows: "I should describe this faith as the unification of the self through allegiance to inclusive ideal ends, which imagination presents to us and to which the human will responds as worthy of controlling our desires and choices." (Dewey 2008, p. 23)

The proper form of the phenomenon in question is identified progressively. We begin the attempt to say what faith is by considering examples of temporally localized, purposive behavior. Some of our behavior is intentional and purposive, but is also local and particular. One gets hungry and seeks something in the kitchen to satisfy the urge; one wants to sit in the sun and so leaves the house for the backyard. The explanation of such behavior is teleological, in terms of desires, purposes, and intentions. But the teleology here is quite local and episodic. Such local and episodic teleology can be more extended in time, as when hunger leads, in hunter-gatherer societies, to some hunt that might take hours or even days. But the teleology involved is still local and particular.

We then imagine a life filled with nothing teleological other than the local and particular. No long-range planning occurs, and no attempt is ever made to make one's behavior fit into some overall larger plan. We can think of a life filled with nothing more than the local and particular as a life showing no hints of the kind of faith that Dewey characterizes. Hints of faith appear only when longer-term planning occurs or

---

[1] See Arnold (1924 [originally published in 1873]). The significance of the quoted phrase seems to be Dewey's agreement with Arnold that morality and whatever good there is to be found in religion are not in conflict, but that the latter is, in some sense, "heightened" morality.

when some overall larger plan is developed to guide the local and particular choices that a person makes. We can understand the reference to ideals in Dewey in terms of such longer-term, overall plans or goals. In pursuing such goals, the goal itself is experienced as worthy of pursuit, as a good of some sort. It is here that we find the first hint of the kinds of attitudes that "lend deep and enduring support to the processes of living."

Dewey's account then turns to the distinctions between accommodations to one's environment and adaptations that are more active. Both of these categories are, however, too shallow to be examples of the kind of faith Dewey seeks to characterize. He looks for changes that are "more inclusive and deep seated." Such changes "pertain to our being in its entirety," Dewey says, and the changes are "enduring." He writes, "There is a composing and harmonizing of the various elements of our being such that, in spite of changes in the special conditions that surround us, these conditions are also arranged, settled, in relation to us." (p. 15)

This "composing and harmonizing" can be characterized using the psychological language of integration. As we develop longer-term and large plans and purposes, we move from the more local and particular to the more general and inclusive. Merely moving away from the local and particular, however, doesn't mean that we've achieved the kind of full integration of which Dewey speaks. Instead, we progress toward such an optimal state in fits and starts. Moreover, the optimal state, we should suspect, is rarely if ever achieved. Instead, the ordinary lot of humanity moves from one semi-integrated state to another in response to the vicissitudes of experience. In all such experience, however, there is the hint of a better possibility, which is the possibility Dewey describes. It is a state in which one's plans, purposes, intentions, heart, soul, and mind are all organized, integrated in a fully settled way so that no matter what changes occur in the world around us, the full integration and settledness of attitude and intention remain.

The typical existence, however, involves a less inclusive organizational scheme, and it is far from clear that the total unification that Dewey envisions is really optimal. For the most part, we live in the land of incommensurables, never resolving how the conflicts between our larger purposes, goals, and intentions are to be harmonized, nor needing them to be. In some cases, the result is a flitting between fates, but in more admirable cases, we find a life with a nice variety of interests and purposes. An adequate response here will have to distinguish between the kinds of motives and interests, desires and preferences, that drive ordinary life, and some grander scheme or plan or stable orientation of a person regarding the possibilities of conflict between the more basic driving forces of ordinary life. Even the most saintly and heavenly-minded often still enjoy a good meal with friends, without any explicit motivational structure that brings this activity to serve more eternal purposes. Nonetheless, such saints may still be characterized by an orientation toward all of life that makes the eternal purposes trump having a good meal with friends when conflict between the two arises. This orientational feature doesn't, and needn't, play any causal role in the activity of enjoying a meal with friends, and this fact remains ubiquitous in the relationship between grand plans and visions and the local, episodic grit of causation in everyday activities. Such disengagement often causes consternation in those who recognize it in their own lives, but it is hard to see the full integration to which Dewey points as anything more than an unrealistic idealization which might guide a life in some weak sense, but not in a sense that requires all of life to be causally affected by it.

Some may sense some pressure on the notion of unification from another direction as well. Not only is such unification unrealistic and hardly compelling, even approximations toward it have been challenged in recent years by the empirical data in support of situationism. The challenge of situationism is that character traits of the sort that unification or integration would involve do not enter into the best explanations for how people behave (see, for example, Sreenivasan (2002), Kamtekar (2004), Prinz (2009), Merritt (2000), Adams (2006), Milgram (1963, 1974), Harman (2003, 1999), Ross and Nisbett (1991), Doris (1998, 2002), Kamtekar (2004), Darley and Batson (1973), Hartshorne and May (1928), Isen and Levin (1972)). One thus might conclude that any talk of composing and harmonizing, of integrating in service of a fully unified self, is chimerical, and that no decent account of anything should be given in such terms. One might conclude, that is, that if two people behave differently, the difference in their behavior needs to be explained by differences in their situations rather than differences in their personalities or character (see, for example, Harman (1999), Doris (1998, 2002) and Alfano (2013)).

Such a conclusion overreaches, however. First note that it would be a bizarre exaggeration to hold that human behavior is a product only of external circumstances and never internal traits of character of any sort. Such a view would be as objectionable as a view that claimed that human behavior followed exceptionless and necessary laws that predicted that no matter what internal differences one finds between two people, if they are placed in the same external situations, they will always behave the same.

The concern, then, cannot be about whether situational or characterological considerations are relevant to human behavior, but rather about which particular elements from each category are involved. On this score, the most disturbing data is that which shows that non-rational situational factors, such as whether one is smelling the wonderful odors coming from a bakery or whether one has just found money in a phone booth or whether a noisy leaf blower is in the vicinity, affect one's likelihood of being helpful to someone in need. Such factors are "non-rational" because the mood one is in would never be a reason one could give to oneself for why helping or not helping was an appropriate thing to do. Instead, learning that our behavior is at the whim of our mood is a cause for chagrin, and prompts a desire to try to become a better person. These non-rational, situational factors are significantly different from temptations to weakness of will, for in such situations, there is some rational factor, some good, the attractiveness of which swamps better judgment about what to do. In the case of non-rational situational factors, the factors in question are ones to which the agent is oblivious.

These concerns raise problems for defenses of a virtue-theoretic approach in ethics, but in our context are less pressing. For they do not show that a fully integrated life of faith is impossible, but incline us toward a realization that even the most integrated of human lives tend to fall far short of the full integration that is the Deweyan ideal. Such a realization is part and parcel of the enduring attraction of Gnosticism, growing out of a realization, a resentment, that biology and spirituality are at odds with each other, leading to a metaphysical demotion of the one in favor of the other. Regardless of that point, however, the role of ideals in human life is not undermined by noting the rarity of realization, and thus the situational challenge is just another among a variety of ways in which the realities of existence impinge on any optimistic portrayal of the degree to which the spiritual aspect of human beings, expressed in the functional faith that is worth having, explains our experience and behavior.

The proper response to the situationists' challenge, then, is not to despair of the possibility of faith in Dewey's sense, but rather to supplement that account with a degree'd notion of faith (or, rather, note the ways in which the account already includes such variability), one which can account for both the first hints of faith and the developments toward full and complete faith that involves the harmonization, the integration of one's purposes, intentions, affections, and thoughts. The ideal here is fully integrated singlemindedness of heart and mind, of which we all fall far short, but which remains the ideal of a fully integrated character (though always qualified so that there is no expectation or demand that the integration in question plays a causal role in ordinary, mundane activities).

4.3 The Functional Character of the Account

Such an account, as already noted, is a functional account of faith, identifying the phenomenon in question in terms of the role it plays in a person's life rather than a substantive, structural realization of the phenomenon in terms of some combination of mental states that constitute the phenomenon in question. This approach to the phenomenon might raise the concern that we are leaving out what we really want, telling us only what faith *does* and not what it *is*. A functional account of water, for example, would leave out its chemical composition, focusing on its uses for drinking and washing, for example, and would leave us unsatisfied if it is our goal to understand the nature of water. Shouldn't we think the same about any functional account of faith?

Drawing this conclusion requires ignoring the fact that lots of things are really functional entities, even if the function can't exist without being realized in some substrate or other. A heart, for example, can't be characterized in any intrinsic way apart from the functional role of pumping blood, and any physical description beyond that functional one will apply only to some hearts and not others (actual or possible). Moreover, specific descriptions of faith, such as that faith is the belief that God exists and is good, are, as we have seen, subject to the same problems as arise when characterizing a heart as something with four chambers: in both cases, there may be examples of the phenomenon in question that meet the description given, but there are also other examples that don't. The point here is, then, that we should not bar functional accounts, but should rather focus on whether the phenomenon in question is best characterized in that way or in terms of something more substantive.

Moreover, the phenomenon being characterized functionally by Dewey appears to identify a phenomenon that has apparently unlimited substantive realizations. It could be realized by many different combinations of cognitive, conative, and affective features of a person, just as hearts can be found in a quite wide array of physical arrangements. In light of this point, a point developed at length in the preceding chapters, we should be unsympathetic to the idea that the kind of faith in question can be characterized by any particular combination of mental states, and instead lending credence to the idea that a functional role account is better suited to the phenomenon in question, even if there are difficulties attending Dewey's specific functional account.

One concern about Dewey's particular functional account is whether it is too broad. Such a functional account, built on the idea of a fully integrated life, may appear to catch more in the net than is really desired for an account of faith. For such a life can be lived in service of a *telos* that is purely self-serving, limited to the interests and purposes of the individual alone. Such persons may exhibit no interest in or attachment to the community or any other element of importance other than themselves, displaying a decided distancing toward others except insofar as they are means to private ends. In doing so, such individuals may have no interest in the prospects for others to succeed in pursuing their goals, or may be cynical about humanity and the community they are part of. For want of a better term, they are narcissists, and one may wonder whether a fully integrated, narcissistic life can really be a life of faith.

A Deweyian approach can try to accommodate a negative response to such a suggestion by emphasizing the difference between a disposition to act in service of an ideal and a disposition to act in service of a goal or purpose. In the case of the narcissist, the goal or purpose in question, Dewey could maintain, is not an ideal. It unifies a life, to be sure, but it fails to do so in a way that functions in service of an ideal, on grounds that the self cannot, strictly speaking, count as an ideal of any sort.

Such a maneuver will handle the problem raised, though it replaces a descriptive, functional account of faith with one that is both functional and normative. For such a view will now need to say what makes some goals or purposes ideal and others not. On a fully descriptive account, the ideality in question is completely perspectival, constituted by whatever perceived goods function to unify the self in the requisite way. Once we require a constraint on such integration, we introduce a non-descriptive element into the equation, requiring that the integrational functioning in question only counts as faith when it integrates toward something on our approved list of ideals. Such a move replaces a clearly descriptive account of the nature of faith with an account of faith that adverts not only to the functional elements in question but also to the demand that the unifying in question count as valuable. Such an account, mixing function with value, abandons the simplicity of a purely descriptive functional account, and that loss should lead us to wonder whether the issue in question is a strong enough consideration to force such a change in approach.

The question to ask, then, is whether we should resist the implication of a purely descriptive functional account that narcissistic faith is possible. Here is an analogical argument that we should not resist this implication, for such faith may be viewed as no more objectionable than the possibility of displaying other virtues, such as courage, in service of bad ends. For example, pursuing Nazi goals in the face of considerable danger is certainly odious behavior, all-things-considered, but the question is whether it can nonetheless involve a display of courage. To this question, some philosophers answer "no."[2]

This negative response, however, romances. One should be able to approve the character trait while disapproving the end pursued, and it provides no advantage to insist that there is no virtue here when it is obvious that the behavior is admirable in certain respects. Just so, if one views the ends of someone lost in self as worthy of disfavor, that in itself should not be sufficient to keep the behavior from being admirable in some other respect, and perhaps in precisely the way that counts as a display of the virtue of faith, however distorted that faith may be. That is, we should keep separate our assessment of the virtues that are present from our assessment of the quality of one's goals and purposes. In so doing, we leave intact the simplicity of a descriptive functional account of faith, explaining away the disvalue of narcissistic self-absorption, not in terms of a lack of faith, but rather in terms of objectionable ends.

4.4 Affective Faith and Ontological Commitment

Besides developing such a functional account, Dewey also aims to distance this account of faith from religion. He begins by constrasting the two:

[T]he moment we have a religion, whether that of the Sioux Indians or of Judaism or of Christianity, that moment the ideal factors in experience that may be called religious take on a load that is not inherent in them, a load of current beliefs and of institutional practices that are irrelevant to them. (Dewey 1934, p. 8)

The difference between an experience having a religious force because of what it does in and to the processes of living and religious experience as a separate kind of thing gives me occasion to refer to a previous remark. If this function were rescued through emancipation from dependence upon specific types of beliefs and practices, from those elements that constitute a religion, many individuals would find that experiences having the force of bringing about a better, deeper and enduring adjustment in life are not so rare and infrequent as they are commonly supposed to be. (Dewey 1934, p. 13)

---

[2] See e.g. Philippa Foot (1978).

In these passages, Dewey claims that the functional nature of faith does not need the enhancements of that faith that play a role in organized religion. Such remarks are surely correct, if for no other reason than that functional faith can be completely mundane. It can occur in the form of faith in democracy or faith in humanity. Dewey's attitude, however, is more strongly anti-doctrinal than this point alone implies. Not only does Dewey think that the beliefs and practices of organized religion are not essential to the proper function of faith in the life of a person, he thinks there is opposition to be found here.

The intimate connection of imagination with ideal elements in experience is generally recognized. Such is not the case with respect to its connection with faith. The latter has been regarded as a substitute for knowledge, for sight. It is defined, in the Christian religion, as *evidence* of things not seen. The implication is that faith is a kind of anticipatory vision of things that are now invisible because of the limitations of our finite and erring nature. Because it is a substitute for knowledge, its material and object are all intellectual in quality. As John Locke summed up the matter, faith is "assent to a proposition . . . on the credit of its proposer." Religious faith is then given to a body of propositions as true on the credit of their supernatural author, reason coming in to demonstrate the reasonableness of giving such credit. Of necessity there results the development of theologies . . .   (Dewey 1934, p. 18)[3]

Moreover, Dewey is skeptical about the epistemic credentials of such developed theologies:

In reality, the only thing that can be said to be "proved" [by religious experience] is the existence of some complex of conditions that have operated to effect an adjustment in life, an orientation, that brings with it a sense of security and peace. The particular interpretation given to this complex of conditions is not inherent in the experience itself. It is derived from the culture with which a particular person has been imbued. . . . The determining factor in the interpretation of the experience is the particular doctrinal apparatus into which a person has been inducted.

(Dewey 1934, p. 12)

Dewey thus contrasts a properly attitudinal and functional approach to faith with a cognitive one, and blames organized religion for substituting the latter for the former. In the process, he at least hints at two quite different kinds of arguments for these claims, one a more metaphysical or conceptual sort and the other more epistemological. As we will see, the particularities of Dewey's discussion cloud the issues a bit, and my goal here is not to investigate the distinctively Deweyan forms

---

[3] I should note again that, even though the understanding of Hebrews 11:1 that Dewey refers to in this passage is common and nearly ubiquitous, it is a mistake. A more literal rendering, from Young's Literal Translation, makes this clear: "And faith is of things hoped for a confidence, of matters not seen a conviction." The prepositional construction reveals that what is being endorsed is something about what faith amounts to in certain specific contexts, the contexts of things hoped for and things not seen. It tells us something about faith, *relative to these contexts*, which is a quite different claim than what is involved in giving a definition of faith. Relative to the context of drawing a geometric figure with a pencil on a piece of paper, a circle is composed of graphite, but such a remark sheds no light on a proper definition of the term 'circle'.

of these objections, but rather to use his discussion to find and consider the best versions of these concerns for trying to distance the value of faith from organized religion.

4.4.1 The metaphysical opposition

We get a hint of such an argument when Dewey considers the theistic elements of typical organized religion, where the ideal toward which functional faith is directed would be most obviously characterized in divine terms. Dewey's initial volley against such faith is to resist taking the term 'God' at face value, as referring to a divine being (if it refers at all):

> On one score, the word can mean only a particular Being. On the other score, it denotes the unity of all ideal ends arousing us to desire and actions. Does the unification have a claim upon our attitude and conduct because it is already, apart from us, in realized existence, or because of its own inherent meaning and value? Suppose for the moment that the word "God" means the ideal ends that at a given time and place one acknowledges as having authority over his volition and emotion, the values to which one is supremely devoted, as far as these ends, through imagination, take on unity. If we make this supposition, the issue will stand out clearly in contrast with the doctrine of religions that "God" designates some kind of Being having prior and therefore non-ideal existence.
>
> The word "non-ideal" is to be taken literally in regard to some religions that have historically existed, to all of them as far as they are neglectful of moral qualities in their divine beings. It does not apply in the same literal way to Judaism and Christianity. For they have asserted that the Supreme Being has moral and spiritual attributes. But it applies to them none the less in that these moral and spiritual characters are thought of as properties of a particular existence and are thought to be of religious value for us because of this embodiment in such an existence. Here, as far as I can see, is the ultimate issue as to the difference between a religion and the religious as a function of experience.   (Dewey 2008, pp. 30–1)

Dewey claims that religions confuse ontology with ideality, cognition with imagination. The source of ideals is not cognition but imagination, and if God is somehow central to a life of faith, it must be because the term 'God' is standing for, or representing in some way, the ideal ends that one acknowledges as having authority over one. Religions with ontological commitment to a Supreme Being are always non-ideal, and therefore not a suitable vehicle for a life of functional faith.

We thus get a glimpse of the kind of reasons in favor of the conclusion that the ontological commitments involved in religion are not only unnecessary, but antithetical to functional faith. To the extent that religions provide a source of unity and ideality that is central to functional faith, it is not the metaphysics and a cognitive grasp of it that drives the machine but rather something imaginative and ideal instead. In short, God is the central object of faith in religion (or at least in the religions Dewey is thinking about in this passage), and no life of functional faith can have such a focus, since only something imaginative can provide that. So, not only is religion unnecessary for a life of faith, it is antithetical to it.

It would be unfortunate, however, to try to sustain anything like this argument in terms of the ordinary notion of semantic content and an associated notion of semantic reference. For it is perfectly obvious that an adequate semantical treatment of the word 'God' does not assign to that word anything about the unity involved in the notion of an ideal. Rejecting Dewey's position on these grounds alone, however, would be uncharitable, for he is clearly right that the concept of God plays two quite different roles in theistic religion, one an ontological role and another that is action-guiding and moral.

Even so, such a point is surely insufficient to get to the conclusion about religion and faith being antithetical. Lots of things play multiple roles in people's lives, without making this world an impossible one or one involving tensions that can only be relieved by eliminating some of the roles. To get to that stronger conclusion, we need not only that there are two different roles played by the concept of God in organized religion, but that somehow the two roles conflict. What would be required is to find some analysis on which we can distinguish between ontological and imaginative components involved in the idea of God, and then insist that a functional account of faith advert only to the imaginative, maintaining that the ontological elements generate a clash of some sort with the more fundamental role arising out of the imagination or affections.

What premises would generate that conclusion are hard to imagine, and apparently not to be found in Dewey's presentation. What Dewey seeks is an explanation of the ideality of the ideal, and finds the source of that in the imagination. Yet, it is compatible with that explanation that the ideal itself has both an imaginative source or central aspect and also involves cognitive elements, using religious faith as the obvious example of such (though faith in one's family and friends will equally involve cognitive elements of one sort or another). Dewey may insist that it isn't in virtue of the ontological commitments involved in the content of the ideal in question that the ideal has the action-guiding and moral significance that it has. Note first, however, that such a claim is questionable in its own right (how could faith in family and friends not be action-guiding at least in part because of the cognitive awareness of who one's family and friends are?). Yet, even if we grant the claim, it is a further and unlicensed step to insist that the presence of ontological commitments interferes with the ideality of the ideal so as to undermine it in some way. It is one thing to say that an explanation of the value of theistic faith begins in the same way as any explanation of the value of faith worth having. It is quite another thing to conclude or add that the value of the faith in question is preserved only when nothing beyond the source of such faith (in the imagination or affections) is involved. The attractiveness of a Deweyan account of faith is that it identifies a common feature of instances of faith that is also a good-making feature of it, thereby helping with the task of explaining why faith can be faith worth having. It is a further step, however, to the conclusion that the only kind of faith worth having is that kind of faith that includes only those elements appealed to in the explanation of the fundamental source of that kind of faith.

Moreover, it is a step that generates incoherence. For, in many cases, the elements that explain value also entail the existence of other things not mentioned in the explanation of value, and so can't exist without these other things. The value of the heart is in its pumping function, but there would be no such function without some underlying physical substrate responsible for the structure of the heart that allows it to perform the function in question. In other cases, there are explanatory and causal links between the value elements and the presence of other features so that, without these other things, the value elements would never have come into existence in the first place. To insist that we eliminate the role of these background conditions entails preferring a world with much less value in it.

It is also a mistake of a rather basic sort to move from the idea that it is in virtue of X that Y is valuable to the conclusion that all examples, or valuable examples, of Y are those involving nothing more than the presence of X. Honesty is valuable for the way in which cooperative engagement depends on truth-telling, but every instance of honesty is accompanied by additional features beyond those that explain the value of honesty (for example, the feature of involving the particular claim or content regarding which one is being honest). Theistic faith as well as faith in family and friends would seem to be examples of the same sort.

It is useful to direct one's attention to a particularly compelling example of a (secular) faith that involves elements that go beyond the imaginative and affective source of the value in question. Such faith can be heard in the voice of Marcus Aurelius in the movie *Gladiator*, portrayed by Richard Harris, talking about Rome:

Yet you have never been there. You have not seen what it has become. I am dying, Maximus. When a man sees his end ... he wants to know there was some purpose to his life. How will the world speak my name in years to come? Will I be known as the philosopher? The warrior? The tyrant ...? Or will I be the emperor who gave Rome back her true self? There was once a dream that was Rome. You could only whisper it. Anything more than a whisper and it would vanish ... it was so fragile. And I fear that it will not survive the winter.

What we can hear here is an instance of the kind of unification of the self that faith worth having involves: "a dream that was Rome." Essential to this unification, however, is ontological commitment. We might be able to abstract out the imaginative from the cognitive, but that is a quite different claim than that the faith itself involves no ontological commitment at all or that we could somehow keep the value of the faith in question while purging it of its cognitive soul.

The functional account of faith developed here shares a feature with Dewey's account, since both make the unifying, focusing function of a given character trait fundamental to it. In doing so, it places heart over mind, affection and conation over cognition, in a proper understanding of faith. For the conviction attendant on an ideal, especially "the acknowledgment of its rightful claim over our desires and purposes" is a function of the affective side of a person, not (solely or primarily) of the cognitive side.[4] Dewey's own account includes a further element, however, one which involves not merely a demotion of the centrality of cognition to faith but rather an outright hostility to standard assumptions about the cognitive aspects of religious faith in particular. We have just considered Dewey's metaphysical attempt to sustain this hostility and have seen that it fails, but Dewey has another, more epistemological way to the same conclusion. In order to see whether his hostility can be sustained, we need to examine the epistemological route as well.

4.4.2 The epistemological opposition

Because we have already seen the failure of the metaphysical attempt to disbar religious faith, we will be assuming that Dewey isn't claiming that no ideal can involve any substantive metaphysical commitments nor that the kind of unification and integration constitutive of functional faith never involves such commitments. Instead, we will embrace what should strike us as obvious: that ideals that can guide a life of faith include such things as great teachers (Buddha, Jesus, Socrates) and social causes (democracy, equality, liberty) and involve some substantive intellectual commitments or other (perhaps, for example, that Buddha is wise, that Socrates is admirable, that Jesus is good, that democracies involve everyone having a voice, that slavery is incompatible with the ideals of equality and liberty, etc.). So concerns about the mere existence of intellectual commitments is not an issue to distract us at this point.

Even if the metaphysical argument fails, there remains the Deweyan concern that the cognitive commitments involved in some such faith will come into conflict with appropriate epistemological constraints on such commitments. Dewey makes clear that "the issue does not concern this and that piecemeal item of belief, but centres in the question of the method by which any and every item of intellectual belief is to be arrived at and justified." (Dewey 2008, p. 23) What is this method? It is the method "conveyed by the word 'scientific' . . . " (Dewey 2008, p. 23). So Dewey's second concern is that as soon as metaphysical commitments intrude into a legitimate attitude of faith, the appropriate methods of inquiry, the scientific attitude that constitutes the way in which responsible individuals arrive at and justify their beliefs, will be abandoned. The result is that functional faith needs to be purged of the intellectual commitments of religion:

[T]he positive lesson is that religious qualities and values if they are real at all are not bound up with any single item of intellectual assent, not even that of the existence of the God of theism; and that, under existing conditions, the religious function in experience can be emancipated

---

[4] I here assume that we can understand the mental life of a person as divided into the cognitive and the non-cognitive, where the latter involves affection and conation. It is a further step to think that these three elements exhaust the mental life of a person, and I make no such assumption here.

only through surrender of the whole notion of special truths that are religious by their own nature, together with the idea of peculiar avenues of access to such truths.

(Dewey 2008, p. 23)

This constraint on admirable faith is worthy of reflection. I begin with some minor points. First, the appeal to the scientific method is simply incapable of carrying the weight needed here, for it is clear that any kind of functional faith, whether in the God of Abraham or in humanity or in the ideals of liberty and equality, will involve intellectual commitments of one sort or another. Among these intellectual commitments may be found ontological commitments and category commitments (for example, that God exists and is supernatural, that there are human beings and that they compose a natural kind, etc.) but also normative and evaluative claims (for example, that all humans are, by nature, equal, that human beings are moral agents deserving of respect as persons, etc.). An appeal to the scientific method is both too strong and too weak to handle the diversity of possible intellectual commitments involved in functional faith, the kind of faith that unifies the self and sustains us in the process of living.

It is too weak, since the normative and evaluative claims are as much in need of epistemic propriety as are the ontological and category commitments, and it is a gross exaggeration to hold that any entitlement to normative and evaluative claims comes through use of the scientific method, no matter how broadly conceived. One might wish to note here the Humean point that an "ought" never follows from an "is," though that claim is contentious and certainly not decisive (since not all epistemic support comes in the form of deductive derivation). One might note as well, however, that there are no ethics labs running experiments to determine whether, for example, waterboarding is wrong or whether forests are legitimate objects of moral concern. Though empirical information is certainly relevant to normative and evaluative conclusions, no adequate epistemology can rest content with the idea that what is good and right, what is beautiful and why, is to be ascertained by employing the same method we employ to calculate the contours of the perihelion of Mercury. Finally, appeal to the scientific method cannot sustain the very claim made for it, that reliance on the scientific method is required for adequate belief. Whatever the credibility of various philosophical doctrines, their defense has to be found elsewhere than by some appeal to the scientific method.

Appeal to the scientific method is also too strong, for it embraces an objectionable kind of *a priori* unrevisability regarding the ways in which epistemic rationality can arise. This point requires elaboration, and one feature that must be noted in developing such an elaboration is the manifold nature of normative evaluation. Human beings are, in Ernest Sosa's memorable phrase, "zestfully judgmental" (Sosa 2007, p. 70), and the same can be said not only of appraisal in general but also of the sort of cognitive appraisal relevant in the present context—epistemic appraisal. Cognitive commitments can be unjustified, irrational, unreliable, unwarranted, and lacking in entitlement, and they can also be inapt, incorrect, bizarre, fishy, dubious, off-base, ill-advised, far-fetched, half-baked, quixotic, preposterous, strained, abnormal, and even out of character. This "blooming, buzzing confusion" of ways to complain about cognitive commitments forces on us a need to find some way of limiting the scope of evaluation, since the variety of possible criticism is not only extensive but seemingly open-ended. If it's not what you say or believe that is the problem, it's probably the tone with which you say it or the particular way in which you embrace the claim in question. If the goal of theorizing here is to find some way of being immune from criticism of cognitive commitments, I recommend concluding that the task is hopeless.

There is a better way to proceed here, and it involves identifying some important human need, interest, purpose, or intention relative to which we assess various possible cognitive commitments. In the context of evaluating an account of functional faith, however, it is easy to see that an important, perhaps singularly important, perspective to take here, one which makes manageable the kinds of criticism that might be appropriate, is that of the egocentric predicament regarding what to do and think, what to be and become. This predicament is intensely personal, and any account of the functions that unify the self in addressing this predicament so as to sustain us in the processes of living must address this fundamental predicament.

Once we have identified this predicament as the need or purpose relative to which we assess various cognitive commitments, the central issue is that of assessing various resolutions of this predicament. What makes a resolution appropriate, and why? We will still have a multiplicity of evaluations here, for a resolution can be appropriate from a practical point of view but inappropriate from a moral point of view. Fortunately in our context, we can limit this multiplicity somewhat, since the only point of view in question is epistemic. What is the, or an, epistemic point of view? It is a purely intellectual or theoretical point of view, abstracting from all other concerns or interests, including practical, moral, aesthetic, social and political concerns. An epistemic judgment thus arises from noting that from such a point of view, some resolutions of the egocentric predicament are appropriate or reasonable and some are not.

Which resolutions are to be approved here is thoroughly perspectival, adverting to the perspective of the individual subject to the predicament in the first place. No God's-eye point of view is appropriately imposed on such resolutions, since from the perspective of the individual in question, such an imposed resolution might make no sense whatsoever. It might be true, for example, that the best thing for me would be to eat no vegetables from my fridge today (perhaps, for example, they are, unknown to me, tainted with a deadly virus), but our criticisms of any resolution of the egocentric predicament should acknowledge a distinction between good and best ways to proceed and the ways to proceed from the point of view of agents themselves. In other words, the account of rationality that we adopt relative to the interest or need of resolving perplexity concerning what to do and think should acknowledge the difference between the theory of value and the theory of obligation: what is required of one, what is permissible for one to do or think, must be kept distinct from what is best for one to do or think or good for one to do or think.

Once we approach the issue of the rationality of intellectual commitments in functional faith from this fully perspectival way of addressing the egocentric predicament regarding what to do or think, we are in a position to see why Dewey's appeal to the scientific method for delineating the range of acceptable intellectual commitments is too strong. It is too strong since it imposes a constraint on rational opinion that is *a priori* unrevisable, demanding application of a method that, even if it is the best available method for getting to the truth and avoiding error, may not appear to be so from the perspective of any given person. The complaint I want to lodge against such a position is that all such constraints are fundamentally anti-intellectual, imposing the same constraints on fully articulate, reflective knowledge that it imposes on the knowledge of the beasts. It thereby treats the change of perspective that results from such reflection as if it makes no difference whatsoever to the rational status of the target beliefs in question. The simple fact is that the perspectivality platitude—that rationality is always and everywhere sensitive to change in first-person perspective—undermines any and every attempt to give substantive rules or methods required for, or even appropriate for, generating positive epistemic status. Such an *a priori* rationalism about epistemic rules is incompatible with a thorough-going perspectivalism demanded by any theory driven by the concerns of the egocentric predicament.

The best way to understand the inadequacy of such anti-intellectualism is that rationality is not merely a function of what evidence or experience one has. In a slogan, there is both the evidence and what we make of it. Even if there is a beastly dimension of rationality, one that applies when no reflective efforts have been made with respect to experience and what it shows, there is also the reflective dimension, and only an objectionable anti-intellectualism can insist that the same rules and principles and methods apply to the reflective situation as apply to the beastly situation.[5]

One might be concerned that I'm merely substituting an empiricist appeal to experience for a rationalist appeal to necessary truths, but that's not the way in which my use of the language of experience is to be understood. My use of the language of experience reflects my own sense of what is relevant from a purely intellectual point of view, and the view I've articulated allows alternative conceptions of what is relevant from a purely intellectual point of view that remain compatible with full and reflective epistemic rationality. So the argument is not one between empiricism and rationalism, but rather a dispute between those who deny the epistemic significance of reflective ascent and those, such as I, who insist on it.

---

[5] For full elaboration and defense of these points, see Kvanvig (2014).

We thus should resist the idea that there is a method that is *a priori* unrevisable and relative to which epistemic adequacy is determined. In fairness to Dewey, however, this appeal to the scientific method, though oft-repeated in the chapter in question, isn't actually required to raise his concerns about the cognitive aspects of religion. He writes:

> For scientific method is adverse not only to dogma but to doctrine as well, provided we take "doctrine" in its usual meaning—a body of definite beliefs that need only to be taught and learned as true. This negative attitude of science to doctrine does not indicate indifference to truth. It signifies supreme loyalty to the method by which truth is attained. The scientific-religious conflict ultimately is a conflict between allegiance to this method and allegiance to even an irreducible minimum of belief so fixed in advance that it can never be modified.
>
> (Dewey 2008, p. 28)

Though reference to the scientific method is prominent in this passage as well, what is important is not some fixation on that method, whatever it is, but rather the contrast between dogma and doctrine on the one hand and cognitive commitments that remain revisable in light of new information. These latter are claimed to be what we get from applying the scientific method carefully, but a defender of Dewey could easily admit that this focus on the scientific method was unwise while still retaining the spirit of the view that involves an attachment to ever-present, in principle revisability in light of new and better information.

4.4.3 Unrevisability and anathemas

It is worth attending to this concern about the unrevisability of dogma and doctrine in religion, for the attitude Dewey criticizes is surely common in religion. Careful articulation of the concern will show, however, that there is no conflict here between religion and the religious attitude central to functional faith. To see this, note Dewey's gloss on the cognitive commitments identified: doctrine is "a body of definite beliefs that need only be taught and learned as true," a body of belief "so fixed in advance that it can never be modified." Both phrases involve strong modal notions: doctrine *need* only be taught and learned, and *can never* be modified. It is important to appreciate the motivation for such strong claims, but also to see that even within theologically conservative religious perspectives, there are grounds for resisting such strong claims and even weaker claims involving full universality. Let's consider first, however, the motivation for such claims.

We can begin by reminding ourselves of the language of the Athanasian Creed: "Whosoever will be saved, before all things it is necessary that he hold the catholic faith. Which faith except every one do keep whole and undefiled; without doubt he shall perish everlastingly. . . . This is the catholic faith; which except a man believe truly and firmly, he cannot be saved." The type of necessity here is clearly that of salvific adequacy. Without believing the correct doctrines, a person cannot be saved, and religious faith, if it is to be worth anything at all, had better be a kind of faith contributing to salvation.

Dewey's concern is about this move from functional faith worth having to saving faith that involves doctrinal requirements that trigger anathemas of the sort involved in this Creed. Moreover, it would seem that the history of Christianity, if not other religions, embraces such a transposition, for the emphasis on doctrine forms the key ingredients for the major schisms and divisions within the Christian religion. The emphasis is not always accompanied by anathemas, but it is often enough to trigger concern of the sort Dewey expresses—that saving faith has unrevisable doctrinal components and that the solution is simply to believe them, regardless of the epistemic impropriety of doing so.

A bit of historical understanding can help alleviate some of this concern. The language of anathema is found both in the New Testament and in some early Church synods, but the focus of such anathemas was practical rather than theoretical. St. Paul anathematizes those who call for the circumcision of early converts, and the canons of the Synod of Elvira include the language of anathema for the practices enjoined. But the application of such language to theoretical disputes becomes central and significant after the Council of Nicaea in 325 AD. Theological discussion and dispute were common in the centuries between the time of Jesus and this Council, but disagreement and dispute are one thing, and damnation another. What is new, after this Council, is condemnation for theological stances that are no longer to be tolerated. What we find in the Athanasian Creed is an exaggerated expression of a practice emanating from that early Council: one focused on theory, rather than practice, and one to be condemned with the language of anathema.

Moreover, the impetus for this Council is political in nature: Constantine had converted to Christianity and was troubled by the unrest arising from disputes about the nature of the Trinity and the nature of the Incarnation, and he called the Council in order for the Church to come to unity about such matters. There is thus much more at stake here than the purely intellectual issue of the truth of the matter and the quality of arguments and evidence for various positions. Prior Councils had condemned various groups, such as the condemnation of Montanism in the second century and the excommunication of adherents from certain churches, but the specific aspects leading to such condemnation are murky at best. But after Nicaea, uniformity is at a premium, and anathemas are flung freely.

It is worth comparing this political influence with the similar influence on language during the rise of modern nation states. One of the primary tools for unification in such contexts is the imposition of a common language, and the power of the state is impressively displayed in its capacity to generate such uniformity. Not only is the imposition successful, it becomes so successful that ordinary citizens internalize the normative conception of language, coming to view as less intelligent and capable those who speak and write ungrammatically or spell poorly! One can see the same power at work in the political influence on doctrinal conformity after Nicaea. Not only is agreement required, the language of anathema is used so as to generate the internal correlates of outward documents endorsed by the Councils. Instead of saying with Luther, "Here we stand, we can do no other," the political influence leads to a claim more like, "Here we stand, *you* can do no other." That is, it is only when the power of the state comes into play that we find exaggerated demands for theological conformity of the sort found in the anathemas of the Athanasian Creed. This point should make us suspicious, at the very least.

A second point is equally important. The Church came to view such language in much subtler terms than we find in the Athanasian Creed. To be anathematized was to be cut off from the Church, to be excommunicated, which is not the same thing as being subject to eternal damnation. To be cut off from the Church need not imply that one is no longer a member of the Church, just as a severed ear is still that person's ear. Moreover, even the anathema attached to the statement coming out of the Council (the anathema is dropped when the official Nicene Creed is adopted at Constantinople in 381 AD) is more subtle than that of the Athanasian Creed. Where the latter speaks of the connection between belief and salvation, the former speaks only of the relationship between what one says and salvation: "But those who say . . . are condemned by the holy catholic and apostolic Church." Does this language signal a recognition of the possibility of outward unity that doesn't require doctrinal conformity? That isn't clear, but it raises such a possibility.

In light of these points, it is worth noting the contortions required to insist on Athanasian anathemas. It is one thing to insist that there are various truths that are distinctively religious and central to particular religious traditions—that, for example, God was in Christ reconciling the world to himself—and quite another to insist that believing such truths is required for salvation. One needs only the slightest sensitivity to anthropological considerations to question which such beliefs could plausibly be attributed to the Patriarchs,[6] for example, and it is uncomfortable to read the history of doctrinal disputes in the first few centuries of Christianity in terms of a distinction between who will be redeemed and who will be damned. In addition, the stories describing the ways in which these figures secured their favor with God do not advert to beliefs or intellectual commitments, but rather to actions which display the kind of functional faith that Dewey admires, as we have seen in prior discussion. Finally, it should be noted that the language of being a believer is not central to the earliest Gospel accounts: nowhere in the Synoptics are the disciples described as "believers." Instead, they are referred to as "followers," making it a pressing question exactly what

---

[6] I recall making this point to my parents while home during a semester break as an undergraduate, to which they replied by quoting John 8:56: "Your father Abraham rejoiced to see my day: and he saw it, and was glad." While this rejoinder deserves a direct response, it is worth noting that whatever we make of Abraham's cognizance here, there is no basis for making similar claims about the other Patriarchs. Moreover, regarding the claim itself, there is seeing and there is understanding what has been seen, and only the latter can generate the kind of cognitive commitments that the Athanasian Creed demands. You can see a UFO, but if you understand what you've seen, it is no longer an unidentified flying object! A similarly modest approach to Jesus's remark can allow Abraham to have seen something about which he had hardly any understanding, but it is also worth mentioning the love of hyperbole that characterizes Jesus's rhetoric.

they believed or affirmed in the process of displaying the functional faith involving whatever ideality they saw embodied in this man from Nazareth.

These points put pressure both on doctrinal requirements imposed after the fact by the Church Councils, but also on the idea that what one must believe in order to be saved evolves in tandem with doctrinal stances developed as the Church is established. For those who wish to rain down damnation on heretics, those who reject teachings officially adopted, but not on those who erred prior to such official adoption, an explanation is needed concerning the difference. Here, the central features cited are those of being in open rebellion against the Body of Christ, resisting through stubbornness and hardness of heart. That is, such disagreement is never innocent but always a failure to take the proper measure of one's own cognitive limitations and sinful pride, the remedy for which is the humility of submission to the teachings of the Church.

I expect there is more than a grain of truth in these claims, but not enough to justify Athanasian anathemas. First, nothing in this description shows the impossibility of honest, blameless disagreement. Second, such descriptions, to the extent that they ring true, do so in the way that statistical generalizations ring true: smoking causes cancer, bad company corrupts, love is blind. Perhaps disagreement is so highly correlated with being disagreeable that sermons against theological disputes are justified, but we aren't here giving practical advice about how to live one's life, but trying to ascertain the truth of the matter. And that truth is that there are no grounds here that are adequate in a fully general way to tie faith worth having, where in religious contexts such involves saving faith, to doctrinal requirements. By contrast, we should maintain instead that faith worth having has to be part of an authentic life, both practically and intellectually. There is no substitute for love of truth, but we should also note that Dewey's concern about the role of doctrine in religious faith can't be sustained by noting that it requires abandoning this fundamental intellectual motivation.

Consider more carefully an attempt to tie resistance to doctrinal formulations to open rebellion against God. Such an attempt might be developed, for example, so that disagreement is an analogue of the failures that repeatedly occur in Greek tragedies, where mistakes are disastrous and the protagonist has no idea where the land mines are to be found. In the context of damnatory clauses, the tragedy results whether or not the one who is damned has "seen the light" concerning the theology of the Church and its legitimate authority, and such a defense of the damnatory clauses should be found wanting. There is not the space here to go into the details of the failure of this conception of wrongdoing and justly deserved punishment, but it is worth at least a pointing in the direction of such a detailed account. One problem is that such an account has no hope of offering a solution to the problem of hell, as I argued extensively in Kvanvig (1993). If Oedipus deserves punishment, it isn't for killing his father and marrying his mother. He's not blameworthy for *that*. The more general problem is that the kind of responsibility that generates the possibility of such tragedies is simply not the fundamental sort of responsibility that undergirds explanations of moral wrongdoing, personal responsibility, blameworthiness, and justified punishment. A notion of responsibility that connects to these latter concepts requires a focus on what the person in question knew and intended—expressed in legal terms as *mens rea* requirements.[7] That is why, whatever are Oedipus's flaws and just deserts, they don't include any fundamental responsibility for killing his father and marrying his mother. In the same way, the language of damnatory clauses could only be justified by a kind of responsibility that is quite different from that which forms the core ingredient of tragedies.

A more promising way to use the concern about legitimate intellectual authority to undergird the damnatory clauses is to notice the way in which the human will can interfere with the operations of cognition, often in a way that is in conflict with the love of truth and the intellectual integrity that demands such love. To succeed along this path, however, it is not enough that there be an adequate theology of the Church and its authority in creedal matters. Instead, what would be required is that it is impossible for any Christian inculpably to fail to recognize the adequacy of that theology. For if such recognition is lacking, we are back with a sense of responsibility that is an analogue of that which arises in Greek tragedies.

Once this recognition requirement is acknowledged, however, it is not difficult to see that a better understanding is achieved by replacing the damnatory clauses with something else. One could, for example, note the way in which maturity in the faith could be tied to a proper recognition of the Church's authority in such matters, and point out as well the proper role for intellectual humility in the life of the mind when it comes to such matters. One could also remind readers of the creed that being stiff-necked and prideful is one central way in which our intellect is corrupted, and that focusing on such vices can help prevent rejecting positions which have the weight of evidence in their favor. In addition, one could remark that there is a legitimate suspicion that those who have seen the creed and know of the efforts involved in crafting it show themselves to be full of arrogant pride and other vices, and that such a condition is not one to be complacent about. So there are many quite serious warnings that might be included (and I'm not endorsing any of the ones I mention), but the actual warning that is included is one that is probably better explained in a way that doesn't rely on the truth of the claim. I am thinking, for example, of things parents say to their children that are quite obviously false but which express quite well the anxiety parents often feel. Parents tell toddlers not to play in the street because they'll get run over by a car; they tell adolescents that failure in school will mean you'll be digging ditches for the rest of your life; that failure to practice means you'll lose your starting position with the team; and so on. Snakebites will kill you, smoking cigarettes will give you cancer, unprotected sex will result in pregnancy; drink drive go to jail. The warnings should be taken seriously, but the claims themselves are simply not true.

---

[7] I argue this point at length in the opening chapters of Kvanvig (2014).

Moreover, once the preceding discussion concerning the nature of faith has been digested, defensive maneuvers aimed at rescuing the accuracy and legitimacy of such damnatory language seem strained at best. In particular, there is a significant lack of fit between this doxastic and doctrinal turn and the sensible account presented and defended here concerning what could possibly make faith such an important part of life, both religious and mundane. Faith matters because it involves the setting of one's heart on things that matter. It involves a commitment to a way of life and an organizing and prioritizing of what one cares about and values so as to further the ideal in question, whether that ideal is an abstract entity such as democracy or equality of opportunity or something less generic such as the kingdom of God and the reconciliation of all things to God through Christ. In the latter context, the value of faith should not be assumed to transmute into something that is fundamentally a matter of having true beliefs of the sort demanded by Athanasian orthodoxy, but rather remains a matter of loyalty and commitment to a cause. Such loyalty and commitment can surely be present in people with vastly different cognitive stances regarding the implications of any very generic characterization of the Christian message, such as that God was in Christ reconciling the world to himself.

4.4.4 Religious fundamentals

Such a conclusion often sends defenders of anathematizing off in search of a short list of fundamentals that demand agreement. Instead of the exaggerated demands for agreement on picayunish matter of doctrinal minutiae, such an approach looks for items of agreement among all of the redeemed, hoping to find there some central components that are non-negotiable. Such a requirement, however, is difficult to sustain as well.

In the discussion above, I revealed my own commitments: that God was in Christ reconciling the world to himself. But I make no pretense of insisting that every instance of Christian faith requires endorsement of this claim. In fact, I doubt the early Christians endorsed this claim, at least not before they'd learned of and heard the content of the last of the known letters from Paul to the Corinthians. Moreover, this point generalizes: when you defend a claim as being one of the fundamentals of the Christian faith, full stop, as opposed to something that is central to your own particular instance of Christian faith, you must be able to defend the claim that all of the redeemed, from the saints of the Old Testament onward, actually endorsed the claim in question. On this score, it is fairly clear that none of Abraham, Isaac, or Jacob endorsed the specific claim that I have voiced.

Once this point is acknowledged, one can either opt for further retrenchment concerning the fundamentals or one can simply deny that there is any common core, fundamental claims that are soteriologically required. What would further retrenchment look like? Taking this path involves finding some generic content that all true believers endorse, perhaps something as generic as that God is for us, that God is redemptive, or something like that. The problem with any such attempt is that it demands representational content in the cognitive region of the mind, and it is more plausible to think of generic claims such as those just noted as being entailed by what is actually present rather than what is actually present. For example, I doubt that Abraham believed or otherwise endorsed the claim that God is redemptive or that God is for us. But I think it is obvious that, among his cognitive commitments can be found claims that entail that God is redemptive or that God is for us. As I see it, the proper way to accommodate this point is to reject the idea of fundamental cognitive commitments for the religion, in favor of the idea that religious faith, like other kinds of faith, is fundamentally non-cognitive, though involving cognitive elements in some way or other.

Nothing I say here should be understood to undermine or cast doubt on the legitimate role that intellectual authorities play in authentic and responsible religious lives. While religious authorities often seem to favor mindless following rather than disbelief, there is no good reason to think that such mindless following is essential to religion. Instead, religious authority can play the same sort of testimonial role that explains most of our understanding of the world and our place in it: most of what we know or believe comes through testimony, originally that of our parents, but also that of other teachers and mentors. Such a role for intellectual dependence is compatible with full intellectual autonomy, both in religion and elsewhere. Even the most mindless, rote learning of what we are told still leaves open a variety of rational options regarding what to believe and endorse. With only rare exceptions, anomalous experience can intrude in a way that leads a responsible intellect to question even the most deeply-ingrained attitudes, and religious attitudes and beliefs are no different in this regard. In the face of such, religious authorities are often unhelpful, often counseling blind endorsement of creedal formulae. Even so, anyone acquainted with the widespread ineptitude of humanity to comfort and encourage each other through disability, depression, misery, and death shouldn't be surprised to find the advice of the caretakers of our souls to be similarly inept in the face of intellectual doubts. Perhaps there is a special disposition among religious authorities to resort to the hyperbole of anathema in the face of an inability to convince others of a truth perceived and embraced. Instead of coming to loathe such responses as objectionable and either essential or unique to religion, a more understanding attitude would be to see this behavior as merely a particular instance of a more general human phenomenon. As every parent knows from experience, our attitudes, beliefs, and habits, even when formed in the most fully reflective way, forget their origins, and when questioned by our children or others, often cannot account for themselves. It takes immense patience and good judgment in such circumstances to recognize the phenomenon for what it is and to sit with the questioner to think through the issues all over again. Much more common is irritation and impatience at the question and one's inability to dredge up a good explanation, often resulting in appeals to authority; and it is easy to see how this pattern could be writ large in the history of religion. Even so, the legitimacy of the criticism shouldn't be extended to religion as such, no more than to an opposition to human parenting, but should rather be taken as motive for all authorities to recognize their foibles and try to do better.

This emphasis on a proper acknowledgment of the open-endedness of our attempts at making sense of the world and our place in it must be combined, both in religion and elsewhere, with an accompanying recognition of the legitimacy of closure of inquiry, if we are to understand a proper role for cognitive commitments in a life of functional faith. Inquiry comes to an end, and often legitimately so, both from a practical and theoretical point of view. Of special interest here is justified closure of inquiry on a topic, where the information available to one makes it rational to conclude that further investigation is no longer needed. In such a case, one's commitment to the claim in question can be rational in a way to make further investigation unnecessary from a purely theoretical point of view. Those in such a position have no theoretical reason to inquire further into the matter, and can thus seem to have become (objectionably) dogmatic on the topic in question. But is a poor epistemological psychology that can't distinguish between full conviction involving legitimate closure of inquiry and dogmatism of the sort Dewey finds problematic.

It is also worth noting that cognitive commitments come in a wide variety of types. In Dewey's discussion as in much of contemporary epistemology, everything cognitive is talked about in terms of belief.[8] Recent discussion, both in epistemology and philosophy of science, indicates the possibility of a broader epistemological psychology: in addition to belief, we see discussion of acceptance, assumption, disposition to belief, degree of belief, presupposition, supposition, opinion, affirmation, confidence, and mental assents, and we could enlarge our list of states to consider by including suspicion, speculation, and expectancy along with the attitudes of taking a stance on an issue or cause, making an intellectual commitment, and the notion of judgment itself. When we speak of cognitive commitments involved in a given instance of faith, we thus should not assume that the only possible commitment is doxastic. Moreover, whatever standard of epistemic rationality we endorse for belief, we cannot assume that this same standard is appropriate for every possible cognitive state or commitment.

These points about cognitive commitment have only rarely been acknowledged in discussions of theistic faith. But once we see the attractiveness of a functional account of faith, it is worth considering carefully what would be involved in a functional faith involving a theistic ideal. The issue is what is required for one to be committed to the propositional claim that God exists, for example, when that content is the specific content referred to by the tetragrammaton. Any reasonable understanding of Frege's puzzle[9] shows how opaque can be the propositional content of an attitude. Lois Lane

---

[8] Though more recent epistemology also includes discussion of degrees of belief, reflecting the beauty and power of Bayesian epistemology, and leading to the important issue of whether degree of belief is to be understood in terms of belief. For discussion, see e.g. Sturgeon (2008).

[9] See Salmon (1989).

is in love with Clark Kent, though not under that description; a person can believe that London is pretty while also believing that it is not (by believing the second as expressed by the sentence 'Londres est jolie').[10] Once we appreciate the reach of Frege's puzzle, one can no longer limit the class of theists to those willing to endorse a theistic claim transparently expressed by sentences such as 'God exists', 'Yahweh exists', etc. For example, perhaps there is fodder in Frege's puzzle for allowing that a commitment to the Good and the Right is sufficient for theistic commitment, and certainly there is room within the panoply of varieties of pantheism and panentheism for certain commitments regarding the universe itself to count as theistic commitments.[11] So a commitment to theism may be much easier to come by than Dewey's opposition to intellectual components in functional faith takes into account.

To sum up, then, we have good grounds for resisting Dewey's doctrinal character-ization of religious commitments. Rote and mindless belief might be present quite often, and may even be statistically normal, in certain religious groups. But even in conservative Christianity, where we tend to find more than a grain of truth in Dewey's characterization, there are good, internal grounds for rejecting any such connection between faith worth having and such doctrinal requirements. So, at the very least, Dewey's concern about religious faith will have to be grounded in something a bit more subtle than would be involved in merely pointing out the central role of Athanasian anathematizing in the history of Christian thought.

4.5 From Deweyan Faith to Classical Theism

Even if we distance ourselves from a conception of faith that involves doctrinal commitments of the sort described above, it remains true that the development of religious faith will involve some theological commitments, even if no uniformity is required here in order for religious faith to be saving faith. Even if there need be nothing rote or mindless about such commitments, we might wonder with Dewey whether, given the actual nature of religious experiences and the correct explanations of them, it is simply impossible for the laudable religious attitude to be anything but inhibited by the theoretical commitments of organized religion. Is it possible to get from affective faith of the sort that characterizes what Dewey calls "the religious attitude" to doctrinal positions of any sort, including those of Classical Theism, without being condemned to an intellectual life that is not suitably scientific or experimental or empirically sensitive, in the way Dewey claims?

---

[10] See Kripke (1979).

[11] As an aside, these points lead to an interesting taxonomical question about what separates anti-religious naturalists/physicalists/materialists from theists, given that pantheism is a version of theism. Perhaps endorsing that all there is to reality is the spatiotemporal continuum (or whatever other slogan these anti-religious positions wish to endorse) is no different from what pantheists claim, leaving these anti-religious positions in the uncomfortable position of finding it difficult to avoid an identification of their views with certain theistic ones.

It will be useful to approach this issue with a bit of historical fiction, aimed at characterizing the way in which Classical Theism might have arisen from an initial affective orientation toward an itinerant preacher from Nazareth. The story will be a fiction, since the cultural presuppositions of the time and place in question are ones that I want to abstract away from in order to give Dewey's objections a fair hearing.

My goal here is not to use the fiction to undermine Dewey's complaints. Instead, my goal is to paint a realistic enough picture of how things might develop, with enough detail to provide a setting for addressing directly the kinds of concerns that Dewey raises. It is unfortunate that too much discussion of the rational credentials of Classical Theism is devoid of context, except for the joyful celebration by critics of the embarrassing details of Christian Fundamentalism. What is needed is a minimal narrative about how Classical Theism could arise from affective faith and be sustained across generations, described in a way that will make rational some sense of what it would be like to move from the kind of faith worth having to the doctrinal commitments in question. Such a sense-making narrative will present the development as charitably as possible, aiming to describe a context and a kind of development that give some hope of answering Dewey's concerns, but the narrative itself is not intended to be an answer to those concerns. Instead, as we will see, it will merely provide as neutral a context as possible for raising the concerns in question and seeing whether they have the strength some have thought them to have.

The aim, then, is to articulate a sensible path from fundamental faith to Classical Theism, one that arises in the process of sense-making that is at the heart of worthwhile theorizing about ourselves and our place in the universe. In this regard, a first step to notice is that out of the affective origins of Christian faith is the wonder, awe, adoration, and resultant worship central to such affections. Jesus is not only taken to be one-to-be-followed, but comes to have a place in the wonder, awe, and adoration that is central to religious expression of every sort.

Such expressions are easy to anticipate to be verbal as well as emotional, and in giving verbal expression to the underlying emotions and affections, we should expect to find honorific expressions of adoration that are probably best viewed as hyperbolic, at least initially. We see the same phenomenon in loyalty to sports teams and the admiration, praise, and veneration of our athletic heroes: they are not only great athletes, we want them to be the greatest ever. It is also much like the kind of exalted characterizations we give of each other when first falling in love. What we find here is not to be thought of as pretense of any sort. Instead, what we find is a product of enthusiasm for a life to be pursued and the elements involved in it.

What begins as enthusiastic acclaim on behalf of an ideal, whether a person or something more abstract, moves from an entertained thought or idea, together with attendant affective engagement, toward something more cognitive and more committed. Moreover, whatever cognitive elements are present will be elements that go beyond experience. They will involve the more theoretical and metaphysical aspects that are parts of the normal human patterns of understanding, explaining, and making sense of experience, both one's own and that of those around us. What gets posited at this stage is tentative and affectively infused, however, not even remotely like the kinds of cognitive attitudes we might expect of a person motivated solely by a disinterested concern for truth.

As a result, these first stages of cognitive formation along the path I'm envisioning are probably not best thought of in terms of belief or degrees of belief, at least not when these things are conceived of as purely cognitive. We don't have a good vocabulary to talk about such states, so perhaps we can do no better than what Tamar Gendler does in inventing the term "alief" (Gendler 2008a,b). Here is one of her examples:

The same phenomenon occurs when I set my watch five minutes fast. The effectiveness of the strategy does not depend on my *forgetting* that the watch is inaccurate, or on my *doubting* that it's really 9:40 rather than 9:45, or my *deceiving* myself or others into thinking that it's five minutes later than it is. Rather, as with the glass-bottomed Skywalk, when I look at my watch, input to my visual system suggests that I am in a world where the time is t+5. This visual input activates a set of affective response patterns (feelings of urgency) and motor routines (tensing of the muscles, an overcoming of certain sorts of inertia), leading to the activation of behavior patterns that would not be triggered by my explicit, conscious, vivid, occurrent belief that it is actually only 9:40.

The activation of these response patterns constitutes the rendering occurrent of what I hereby dub a *belief-discordant alief*. (Gendler 2008a, pp. 640–1)

The point to note about Gendler's discussion is the complex disposition which is the target of her term 'alief'. The presence of alief involves various feelings and motor responses, triggering various behavior patterns, and doing so in a way that is seemingly distinct from the doxastic realm. In our context, we can employ such a possibility to help avoid the impression that the initial theorizing that moves from enthusiastic hyperbole to something more cognitive and theoretical can only be understood in terms of belief formation of an epistemically suspect form. Instead, we should expect that the stage of loyalty inculcation and initial sense-making doesn't have well-defined doxastic elements, but also isn't simply affective, conative, and behavioral. It is a way for initial hyperbolic expressions of enthusiasm and other underlying affective elements to filter into the way in which a person begins to see and experience the world, leading to further inclinations to adopt various theoretical postulates in the attempt to make sense of such an evolving experience. As noted already, these early speculations and postulations do not require actual belief, though of course they may, but are rather better understood as some combined state of the individual somewhere near the logical space of Gendler's notion of alief, involving possibly a hunch, a posited shot in the dark, a predilection to believe, a perhaps tentative conjecture, or a sneaking suspicion that amounts to little more than a hope-filled guess.

A central objection to Gendler's thesis from those wanting to preserve a more standard view of cognition and its relationship to behavior is that alief is not really a distinct kind of mental state, but is rather a dynamic relationship between dispositions toward behavior and other, more standard mental states.[12] In fact, Gendler describes alief in terms that suggest such: it is representational, affective, and behavioral, with causal relationships between the three. Since we already have an ontology populated by lots of representational states, including perceptual experience as well as beliefs and degrees of belief (on the cognitive side), it is natural to view alief as merely a name for a complex that is not really itself a mental state.

Note however that in our context it doesn't much matter whether we side with Gendler or the critics. The crucial thing to note is that if we acknowledge the dispositional and affective nature and origins of faith, there is no reason to treat the initial cognitive and theoretical stages of faith in the early disciples of Jesus in terms of a model focused on belief. We might quite justifiably describe it in somewhat the same way in which Gendler talks about alief, embracing the idea that there is no determinate answer to the question of exactly what doxastic dimensions are involved in such early stages of faith.

4.5.1 From affection to theory

The relevance of the notion of alief in our context is that there is something a bit off-target in describing the enthusiasm and fervor, the animation and intensity, of overt expressions of affective faith in terms of the language of belief. Especially, when one listens to the language voiced publicly, declaring allegiance to causes, purposes, and persons, it is often hard to see doxastic commitments tracking with any precision the attitudes being expressed. If one shouts, "Democracy is utopia!" as a way of expressing one's commitment to a cause, there may be some doxastic commitments present that help explain the utterance, but it is implausible to insist that those commitments include the claim that democracy is utopia. Certainly we should not think that there needs to be such a belief with whatever content is expressed by a literal use of the sentence, "Democracy is utopia!", and if we think the remark is obviously figurative (as we should), it would be philosophically incautious to insist on the presence of such a figurative belief. For one thing, we might want to take seriously the possibility that there are no such things as figurative propositions, and hence no beliefs with figurative content. Even if there are beliefs with non-literal content, however, we should recognize that sincere avowals, prompted by affective faith, need not be underwritten by belief, even if we want to insist that there is some generic type of cognitive commitment to the content in question. A bit of self-awareness by we philosophers should make it clear to us that we often sincerely avow things that we don't actually believe. We are, perhaps, inclined to believe them, we think the claims make better sense than opposing claims, we may even be willing to take some substantial bets on whether the claim can survive scrutiny. Even so, if we grant that much of what we endorse isn't something we know to be true, we should also grant

---

[12] For useful discussion here, see Gendler (2012b), Nagel (2012), Currie and Ichino (2012), Doggett (2012), Gendler (2012a).

that we can sincerely assert a claim that we don't actually believe. For it is possible to behave as philosophers behave while regulating our mental lives by the idea that you shouldn't believe what you don't know to be true.

Some of the above is controversial, but all I want for the present is to refuse to make assumptions. I won't here sign the pledge of allegiance to the claims needed to draw the conclusion that sincerity requires belief, and will present an account that doesn't require them. Instead, I want to pursue the idea that the exclamatory nature of expressions of fervor for a cause is not best understood as an expression of belief combined with some emotional element. They can be such, but need not be. The enthusiasm and fervor may only be part of a process that leads to belief formation, of the sort we might find in Thomas's response to encountering Jesus after having expressed some skepticism about the experience of the other apostles. He exclaims, "My lord and my God," and even if the language is decidedly anti-Sabellian and anti-Arian in content, it would be an indefensible hermeneutic to think that Thomas had to be embracing this part of orthodoxy in order for his exclamation to lack pretense. Instead, it may describe an inclination of heart and mind toward a certain theological position, one that over time may blossom into one that embraces, both affectively and doxastically, the full divinity of Jesus. But an explanation of a surprise encounter that ignores the way in which surprising joy can be accompanied by disbelief and confusion is simply not adequate to the experience.

Consider, for example, an unexpected encounter with a cherished friend whom one hasn't seen for decades. The rush of excitement and the hope involved are regularly accompanied by some measure of incredulity: "is that really you?" The process begins from emotional and affective elements and proceeds rather quickly to full belief, but it is simply a mistake to require the presence of full belief when the initial proclamations of identity are voiced: "Sam, it's you; I can't believe it, it's really you! Where have you been, I've been wondering what happened to you!" Instead, the language of alief or some close cousin of it is more fitting, as the process is one moving from affective patterns and associated behavior patterns—the kinds of items characteristic of Gendler's notion of alief—to belief in relatively short order.

Such speed of identification is predictable in cases of perception, whether prompted by positive emotions such as joy or by negative affective states such as fear of predators. The affections are triggered by a perceptual input that presents an appearance of a certain sort, leading to behavioral responses and perhaps finally to belief formation. But belief formation follows rather than leads, or at least it can; it is just that in perceptual cases, the process is very quick. We should expect things to move more slowly when dealing with non-perceptual cases.

The process, when occurring in the normal way, does not show the signs of uniquely intellectual interests and motives central to typical theories concerning the epistemic rationality of doxastic formation and sustenance. Instead, we find significant degrees of cognitive penetration, of the sort generating much discussion in the recent literature on perception (see, for example, Siegel (2005, 2013)). In cases of ordinary perception, a person's strong desire for finding gold might penetrate the cognitive system so that a particular rock is perceptually taken to be a piece of gold when without that strong desire, that rock would be perceptually taken to be fool's gold. In such cases, we have a legitimate question as to whether the perceptual seeming in question can play its usual role in supporting the epistemic rationality of belief formation. In our context, however, not much turns on the question of whether epistemic rationality can be sustained through processes involving cognitive penetration by affective and conative elements. For unlike the simple perceptual cases, the process of fixation of belief in cases of affective faith can be clearly rational in a broader, more pragmatic sense even if the beliefs that result are not, at least initially, epistemically rational according to theories that have stronger requirements concerning purely truth-related motivations.

Paradigm examples of such processes involve allegiance to political causes and movements. Attraction to the ideas of equality, fairness, and human dignity for all often results in joining particular organizations; and in the process of working in service of an attractive ideal of this sort, one may easily come to have opinions about certain actual political structures in various parts of the world that are, from a more neutral affective standpoint, less than realistic. Supporters of the Russian revolution, for example, often allowed attraction for the ideals it embodied to color their opinion of the regime that resulted, and the opinions of that regime would likely count as epistemically irrational opinions even if the entire process from attraction to an ideal through the process of belief fixation counted as rational in an all-things-considered sense. Consider, for example, the experience of Jack Reed, as chronicled in the 1981 Warren Beatty movie *Reds*. Reed, inspired by the ideals of the Russian revolution, travels to Russia and participates in the events of 1917. The views and opinions he comes to hold initially are both laudable (concerning the ideals in question) and naive at the same time (thinking that the result of a revolution will bring in something resembling Utopia). There is, of course, a real question about when the voicing of such claims involves something closer to alief than belief, but it is clear that the process aims toward fixation of belief and finally results in it. And when such fixation is achieved, it is questionable the degree to which such beliefs will be epistemically rational. In spite of any such defect, however, it would be a mistake to view the entire process from commitment to an ideal to its outworking in both mind and behavior as one that is somehow irrational, all-things-considered. Fixation of belief is the normal, expected outcome of the bravado and enthusiasm present at the initial stages of commitment to a cause, and should be tolerated in our assessments of rationality much as we (should) tolerate youthful lack of caution more generally. Perhaps such tolerance should lead to fewer findings of epistemic irrationality in the process (as opposed to other intellectual vices or mistakes), but even if we retain such findings, we shouldn't display such epistemic fetishism that an overall evaluation is swamped by such defects.

One may question this claim by noting that such a conclusion involves a finding of rationality for a feature that may not be best for the person in question to display. That point is correct, but it is not an objection that should lead us to balk at the conclusion. What is rational to do or to believe quite regularly departs from what is best to do or believe. We often resort to kicking ourselves when we realize that the choices we have made have not been for the best, but the proper response here is to give oneself a break: what is reasonable to do in the circumstances, given the information available to us, is not guaranteed to have the best results. It is regrettable when rationality and optimality part company, and though lament may be an appropriate response, reproach, chastisement, and blame are not. Those troubled by the lack of optimality here should note it as a feature not to be ignored, but grant the point that such a lack doesn't require abandoning the claims made about the case.

To return to the point about the possibility that cognitive penetration generates epistemic irrationality even though it does not always generate all-things-considered irrationality, we should note as well that findings of epistemic irrationality as a result of the penetration of cognitive processes by various affective and conative elements, however, may overreach. Hardcore defenders of Phenomenal Conservatism will be unmoved by worries about the source of our seeming states, whether intellectual or perceptual, and they may be right.[13] But we needn't settle that dispute here to reject the idea that the process from affection to the adoption of a system of understanding that satisfies the sense-making urges that drive human cognition can be fully satisfactory, all-things-considered, even if subject to criticism from more particular points of view. The explanation of how to get from functional faith of an affective sort to a mature Christian faith that involves the metaphysical commitments of Classical Theism is thus aimed at Deweyans who approve of the affective, functional faith in question but are inclined to think that such faith is in conflict with the metaphysical commitments of Classical Theism. What I have been arguing is that it is quite easy to see how a fully experimental approach to the universe and our place in it can take one from affective faith in a person such as Jesus to the kind of cognitive expression of such faith that is found in the Classical Theism of traditional Christianity. This point holds even if one insists that the lack of purely intellectual motivations in the process somehow disturbs or prevents the possibility of epistemic rationality of the sort claimed to be required for knowledge.

4.5.2 Reversing the process: from belief to faith worth having

This part of our story regarding how the cognitive dimensions of Classical Theism could arise in a non-coercive way in the early history of Christianity leaves untouched the issue of how the actual or purported wisdom of one generation is passed on to the next. Our discussion of the move from affective faith to Classical Theism cannot be complete without addressing this issue.

---

[13] For an excellent collection on the prospects and difficulties for Phenomenal Conservatism, see Tucker (2013).

Note first that there is nothing unique to religious contexts here. Successful living, for human beings, depends in large part on an understanding of the world and one's place in it that is not a result of one's own direct experience of the world. Instead, it is mediated learning through the phenomenon of testimony in its various forms, including the tropes of culture and the allusions that surround us in any human civilization. Such figurative elements direct our minds and hearts toward that which is (taken to be) most important and central to our joint flourishing (from flags and mottos to aesthetic dimensions in public art and architecture which yield a sense of *gravitas* for certain cultural institutions over others, a sense that goes beyond the aesthetic beauty of the things in question). The understanding— the picture of reality—derived in this way has a structure, with certain parts of it more central and fundamental than other parts of it, with other parts more peripheral and easier to abandon. Such a recognition is common to all the major players in the mature epistemologies of the twentieth century, including the coherence-infused foundationalism of Chisholm, the web of belief metaphor of a Quinean coherentism, or the bedrock metaphor of a Wittgensteinian assumptionalism.[14] These elements of coherence that are both descriptively and normatively relevant to our understanding of the world are also inherently conservative, functioning in part to make vivid to all what is significant and what isn't. So one needn't be a foundationalist to grant the point that conservative principles form a large part of the story of human cognition, both from an explanatory and also a normative perspective.

Once we recognize this dimension of human life, and also recognize the way in which faith of whatever variety is a force for unification of the various dimensions of life, we have a sound basis for seeing a strong tendency for functional faith to receive expression in terms of some propositional content or other and for whatever propositional content results to come to be deeply entrenched in cognitive life. Perhaps it reaches the foundationalist's nirvana of incorrigible belief (I mean the term as used in ordinary speech, referring to the incapacity for change, as when parents exasperatingly exclaim to young children, "you are just *incorrigible*, aren't you!"— an exclamation that would be more useful, perhaps, if the children knew what the word meant!), but even if it falls short of such, it will still be deeply resistant to

---

[14] In fairness to Quine and Chisholm (not to mention other luminaries of the epistemology of the last century, such as Wilfrid Sellars, Nelson Goodman, Keith Lehrer, and Laurence BonJour), one on the above list is not quite like the others: assumptionalism, like infinitism, has only the barest outline of a response to the regress argument, in comparison with the more developed responses by foundationalists and coherentists. There is, of course, the other of the twin towers of motivation for epistemological theorizing, the underdetermination argument aimed at showing that our opinions are generally fallible, but in our context, it is the regress argument that is most important, since it is that argument that forces one's hand to describe the structure of a system of understanding that might survive rational scrutiny. It is for that reason that my discussion in the text ignores recent versions of externalism, such as those of David Armstrong, Fred Dretske, Alvin Goldman, Alvin Plantinga, Ernest Sosa, Robert Nozick, and even Timothy Williamson, since those theories are more at home as responses to underdetermination arguments, aimed at showing why skepticism isn't the inevitable consequence of our fallibility.

revision, in the way that the central features of the web of belief are revised only rarely. We should expect, that is, that cognitive elements become deeply resistant to change, whether they are present in doxastic form or in the form of a cognitive stance that is something a bit different from belief. We can find evidence of such in philosophical stances, an example already noted earlier, where philosophers tend toward ossification of stance and attitude, even if these stances and attitudes do not count as belief.

Nonetheless, the goal of inculcated belief is attractive, with the ideal of full certainty the gold standard, when it comes to the kind of influence that individuals and institutions wish to have over future generations. The reason is relatively simple: the influence of cognition on behavior is unsurpassable when doxastic components are compared with non-doxastic ones. It is not that it is impossible to duplicate the effect of belief on behavior by cognitive stances that are not doxastic (though I think we don't know enough to rule either way on this score), but belief is always as useful and typically more effective than other cognitive stances (when we have in place the appropriate controls, such as not allowing different degrees of commitment between different types of stances). Moreover, it is, perhaps, the natural cognitive condition, whereas cognitive stances that are non-doxastic tend to require levels of reflective sophistication that may not be widespread and even if widespread, require levels of maturity that make belief a better target when it comes to intergenerational pedagogy.

The descriptive story of a focus on belief is thus fairly straightforward. Even so, it leaves us with a serious question about the normative status of the cognitive dimensions of functional faith, whether they arise as the result of a sense-making project prompted by the affections or whether they arise first, or in concert with, those affections. Here the questions are whether such dimensions can be rational, and whether the kind of rationality is the right sort. These questions derive from the accusation that there simply is no possibility of the cognitive underpinnings of a given instance of affective faith surviving rational scrutiny. This question of whether such cognitive underpinnings can have the right kind of rational standing can be put in the form of a dilemma. If the kind of rationality found, assuming there is one to be found, is something other than epistemic rationality, there will be strong pressure against the maintenance of these commitments, and such strong pressure will be resistible only through mechanisms of belief fixation that exploit non-epistemic factors. In short, if the kind of rationality is non-epistemic, the cognitive elements in question will be paradigm examples of *bad faith*, rather than innocuous accompaniments of a kind of faith worth having. If we think of good reasons as the kinds of things that motivate normal individuals toward what they are reasons for, it is easy to come to the conclusion that those lacking epistemic warrant for their cognitive commitments must be "true believers" in the sense found in Hoffer (1951), those who somehow manage to go to whatever length it takes to maintain a point of view, even in the face of objections and incoherencies that are obvious to us or to any good therapist. Such faith is bad faith, even if it falls under the same kind of functional faith defended here.

4.6 Types of Appraisal and Epistemic Fetishism

I believe this residual concern can be assuaged if we can attain a more general understanding of what is legitimately involved in normative assessments. The particular
example of such that interests us here is that of religious faith, which we might
assess only from a special perspective, as when we assess it in terms of its political
usefulness, or whether writing the story of such a life makes for good literature.
More generally, one might also ask whether such a faith is morally acceptable, or
practically rational, or involves only intellectual commitments that are epistemically
justified or epistemically rational or are known to be true. Here the categories are
manifold, in a way that calls out for systematization. What we really want to know
is not some piecemeal story about which dimensions of normative propriety and
impropriety a given element of human life displays. Instead, we want some all-
things-considered judgment about whether to view that element as appropriate or
acceptable or permissible. On this score, we need an approach that requires an
inclusive normative response that speaks with a single voice. To the extent that a
response merely identifies ways in which a given instance of faith is propitious and
other ways in which it is regrettable, we hear the sound of cacophony.[15] In order
to secure an account that speaks with a single voice, we pursue some function on
the individual rationalizing factors that enter into an all-things-considered evaluative
conclusion about a given aspect of human existence such as the presence or absence
of faith.

At the extreme, we find proposed functions that are fetishistic.[16] Fetishism involves
an exaggerated weighting of particular dimensions, whether epistemic, moral, practical, social, political, aesthetic, or whatever other dimensions one thinks play a role in
an all-things-considered evaluation of some aspect of human life. A Fetishist singles
out one particular way of evaluating the overall status of the item being evaluated,
giving it overriding importance. So a Practical Rationality Fetishist insists that the
all-things-considered adequacy of functional faith requires practical rationality: no
functional faith can be adequate if it doesn't survive scrutiny by our best decision
theory. One kind of Moral Fetishist insists that functional faith is only adequate in
this way when it is morally required of one to have it.

A version of Fetishism of special interest in our context is Epistemic Fetishism.
Epistemic Fetishism assesses a given instance of faith by looking at the intellectual
components of faith and insisting that the faith in question is adequate when and

---

[15] This same issue arises within each local, particular domain of normativity. For example, within
the domain of epistemic normativity, many hold and some argue that there are multiple dimensions of
normative adequacy. Perhaps, for example, there is a primary norm requiring that one believe only what
one knows to be true, but also a secondary norm that makes it OK to believe something that one rationally
but mistakenly takes oneself to know. For arguments against such approaches, and an account of how to
avoid them, see Kvanvig (2014).

[16] My use of the term 'fetish' derives from Smith (1994), though his use of the term and my use of it are
different.

only when the intellectual components survive epistemic scrutiny. A particularly noteworthy endorsement of such a position occurs in an interview with Bertrand Russell in an interview from 1959.[17] Russell first denies that there is evidence for religious beliefs, which leads the interviewer to ask about other possible reasons for belief. She asks, "Do you think there is a practical reason for having a religious belief?", to which Russell replies,

"Well, there can't be a practical reason for believing what isn't true . . . at least I rule it out as impossible. Either a thing is true or it isn't. If it is true, you should believe it. If it isn't true, you shouldn't believe it. It seems to me a fundamental dishonesty and fundamental treachery to intellectual integrity to hold a belief because you think it is useful and not because you think it is true."

There is much to question in Russell's remarks. First, even for epistemic rationality, the connection between truth and what one should believe is more vexed than what Russell claims. It is simply false that one should believe the true and disbelieve the false, at least if the 'should' in question is that which encodes the kind of epistemic rationality or justification central in the history of epistemology. There is some epistemic connection between truth and falsity and what sorts of beliefs are epistemically appropriate—there is something to the idea that the governing idea regarding epistemic rationality is the goal of getting to the truth and avoiding error— but the means–ends connection between the goal and the proper thing to believe in service of the goal is far from as simple as Russell suggests. One simple reason for rejecting his claim is that if we accept it, the distinction between a true belief account of knowledge and a reasonable true belief account of knowledge would disappear.

Second, Russell's remarks elide another important distinction. One issue is whether there can be non-epistemic reasons for belief, and another issue, distinct from the first, is whether one is permitted to believe on the basis of whatever non-epistemic reasons for belief there might be. Note that Russell first claims that it is impossible for there to be non-epistemic reasons for belief, but then backtracks to a weaker position, one according to which it is "dishonest" or "treacherous to intellectual integrity" to believe on the basis of non-epistemic reasons. Note, however, that the question of basing belief on non-epistemic reasons is a different question from the question of whether there are adequate practical reasons for belief: reasons are one thing, basing belief on reasons another.

It is a little unfair, however, to treat the casual setting of a conversation with a journalist by the standards of rigor appropriate to an evaluation of published work in philosophy. So I don't want to press any further these particular points against Russell, nor give the impression that these are his settled views on these epistemological issues. The relevance of the quote is elsewhere, for Russell expresses quite clearly an endorsement of Epistemic Fetishism, the position that maintains that

---

[17] There is a YouTube video of the interview here: https://www.youtube.com/watch?v=Il7Kxw9TDBc.

epistemic considerations swamp all other considerations when it comes to intellectual commitments. So, when the question is what is rational in this arena, all-things-considered, the answer is that it is always and everywhere and necessarily, that which survives epistemic scrutiny.

Of course, this scrutiny comes in a variety of epistemic personages: those who insist on knowledge, those who insist on justification, those who insist on rationality, etc. But the feature they have in common is more interesting in our context than what separates them, for it is easy to detect the odor of Epistemic Fetishism in Dewey's remarks. When Dewey claims that "the issue . . . centres in the question of the method by which any and every item of intellectual belief is to be arrived at and justified," it is easy to sense a requirement that no faith can be adequate, all things considered, if it does not pass epistemic scrutiny first (ignoring for the moment the particular kind of epistemic scrutiny in question). If failure along epistemic dimensions is sufficient for failure of all-things-considered adequacy, however, we have the substance and not the mere scent of Epistemic Fetishism.

Moreover, as the name suggests, there is little to recommend such Fetishism.[18] It would be surprising to find one particular kind of reason to have such power over all other kinds of reasons, regardless of context.[19] There is good reason to reject Epistemic Fetishism.

If Epistemic Fetishism were true, the charge of bad faith above could be bypassed, since there would be no need for any additional criticism of the cognitive commitments of affective faith beyond arguing that they don't pass epistemic scrutiny.

The charge of bad faith, however, can be leveled without relying on Epistemic Fetishism. Once we see the truth in the idea that the natural or normal state for cognition is in terms of tracking (appreciated) evidence, when we find a person holding a belief but having no epistemic basis for such a belief, a realistic assessment of such a situation is that it will be quite unstable, requiring serious effort and expense to maintain. Given this tendency to instability, there will be reasons to try to find non-epistemic factors to contribute toward fixation of belief or other intellectual commitments, and then the charge of bad faith is quite natural. The argument here can thus be summarized as follows: even if the nature of reasons shows that Epistemic Fetishism is false, normalcy in cognitive function gives confounding evidence that nothing other than epistemic reasons is likely to yield the kind of stability of cognitive commitment that is efficient enough to make for all-things-considered rational allegiance to a cause

---

[18] There is one caveat here, and it concerns whether moral evaluation of an act or characteristic is itself the same thing as all-things-considered evaluation. Though this claim is controversial, if it is true, then Moral Fetishism is not a form of Fetishism (or, perhaps, even if it is a form of Fetishism, it is not an objectionable form of it).

[19] For further discussion of the demerits of the kind of intellectual impartiality toward all things that would be required of a generalized Epistemic Fetishism, see e.g. Parfit (2001), Rabinowicz and Rønnow-Rasmussen (2004), D'Arms and Jacobson (2000), Keller (2004a), Stroud (2006).

or point of view. So, one doesn't have to be an Epistemic Fetishist to make the charge of bad faith here. It is enough to have the simple decency and concern of a therapist.

Even though Dewey's concerns are often expressed in a way that appears to embrace Epistemic Fetishism, I do not think the problems that concern him require that endorsement. Instead, the concerns are, as above, two-pronged: religious faith doesn't meet the standards of epistemic propriety, and in part because it doesn't, such faith must be counted as bad faith. It is this two-pronged attack that needs to be addressed. My focus will be on the second prong, but before turning to it, I want to cast at least a small bit of doubt about whether the first prong can be sustained.

4.6.1 Functional faith and rational commitments

In some cases, the therapeutic concern is misplaced because of an unsound epistemology, and it is worth noting that it is much harder to sustain the charge of epistemic irrationality than is commonly thought. A common assumption in such arguments is that epistemic rationality is a function of bodies of information, so that if two people have exactly the same body of information, the same things will be epistemically rational for them. Once we note that it is rare for lives of faith to involve evidence or information to which the concerned therapist isn't privy, it is easy to see how the argument will go. The mantra is that either private experience or public evidence is needed to generate epistemic rationality, and absence in both areas will strongly confirm the existence of bad faith even when bad faith is not entailed by a failure of epistemic rationality.

A more careful epistemology, however, reveals flaws in this line of thinking. I cannot here delve into this issue as deeply as it deserves,[20] but the broad strokes painting will be useful nonetheless in rebutting the line of thought above. In short, I will suggest that the story of epistemic rationality is a story involving a myriad of complexities that the line of thought above ignores.

The complexities involve the following factors. First, order of inquiry matters: two people can come to the same total body of information and yet only one of them does so in an order that makes rational belief possible. Second, there is both information possessed as well as the way in which a given piece of information is embedded in a given cognitive system, and all of these factors affect epistemic rationality. Third, the lesson of the Quine–Duhem problem is that there is significant optionality in epistemic rationality, both diachronically and synchronically. Finally, the mantra that results from a proper appreciation of all of these features is this: when it comes to rational opinion, there is both the evidence and what we make of it. A corollary of the mantra is that we learn from experience, not only what the world is like, but also what confirms what. The epistemic connections that control rational opinion are

---

[20] I have done so elsewhere, especially in Kvanvig (2014).

a posteriori, even though the theory of epistemic rationality is a matter of epistemic principles that are necessarily true and probably *a priori* as well.

Some clarificatory remarks about each of these points may help. We can begin with the last point. Any genuinely experimental attitude toward the world around us has to recognize that we are often in the dark, not only about what the truth is, but also about what significance to attach to our experience of the world and what we learn about it. A simple example here involves the difference between second-person awareness by those suffering from autistic spectrum disorder and those without such a disorder. Those with autistic spectrum disorder have to learn what a given facial expression *means*, whereas those without the disorder can just see what it means. The difference, however, isn't one impugning epistemic rationality in either group, but rather a difference affecting the ability to discern the truth easily. Moreover, in other cases, we learn not to trust our intuitive and non-inferential inclinations toward belief-formation. The lesson is clear: the significance of experience, what to make of it in terms of what to believe and how strongly, is something that we master if things go well for us, intellectually speaking, and something that hounds us for life when things do not go well for us. And whether we are related to experience as master or prey, the entire life can be one of full epistemic rationality.

Second, the lesson of the Quine–Duhem problem is that experience doesn't require any given change of opinion, nor is any given opinion typically required by a given body of information. Relative to any body of information, there will typically be a variety of intellectual responses all of which are rational. Does the vase on the table look red to you? Yes? So you believe that the vase on the table is red. I doubt it is red, wondering whether the lights are abnormal, or whether I'm subject to trickery. Or I don't believe it is red at all, since I don't think colors are real. The list goes on and on about the kinds of attitudes one can hold in light of experience, compatible with full epistemic rationality of opinion.

One corollary of this point is that commutativity of experience is indefensible. It is tempting to think that if two persons X and Y begin from the same intellectual starting point, and X has experiences E1 and E2 successively, and Y has the same experiences but in the opposite order, the final opinion of each, assuming the same background information, must be the same if they are to be epistemically rational. Once we grant the optionality point and the more general point that there is both the evidence of experience and what to make of it, we must deny commutativity. Cases of this sort will arise when one rational effect of E1 is both to change one's picture of the world and one's theory of evidence of what significance to attach to various future experiences, resulting in a different rational significance for E2 than one would have had if one had experienced E2 first. Careful attention to the phenomenon of transformative experiences, religious or otherwise, confirms that they are precisely the kinds of experiences to expect to have such features.

This point is worth discussing a bit further because of the literature in Bayesian epistemology that takes denials of commutativity to be problematic. The literature began with the recognition that Jeffrey conditionalization—the needed fallibilistic replacement for Strict Conditionalization—does not preserve commutativity on input distributions.[21] The notion of an input distribution, however, is not the same as the notion of experience, and the question of the relationship between inputs and experiences allows a defender of Jeffrey conditionalization to preserve commutativity of experience even though commutativity of input distributions is abandoned. The basic point against commutativity, however, can be made in the context of Strict Conditionalization, which is well-known for preserving commutativity. It preserves commutativity, however, only when the relevant conditional probabilities on which updating occurs remain constant. In our context, the right way to think about these conditional probabilities is that they encode the theory of evidence for the person in question, and to the extent that the theory of evidence is something we learn about in the process of experience, to that extent the conditional probabilities should not be thought of as incorrigible. If there is both the evidence of experience and what we make of it, we should expect the updating to sometimes affect unconditional probabilities and sometimes to affect conditional ones, and if the relevant conditional probabilities change, commutativity on successive experiences is lost, independently of whether Jeffrey conditionalization can be understood so as to preserve commutativity of experiential learning. The upshot, then, is that it matters at what point in life one has had a given experience; not simply that one has had it.

If we continue to think in Bayesian terms here, the lesson to learn is that we can't assess the epistemic rationality of a given life of faith with reference only to private experience and public evidence. We also must address the issue of how information is embedded in the relevant system of information, and such embedding is at least partially a matter of what conditional probabilities are present in the system: the more deeply embedded in the system, the less susceptibility to change of opinion by Strict Conditionalization as revealed in the conditional probabilities.[22]

As a result, it is significantly more difficult for those wishing to defend the charge of bad faith against a given life of faith to show the needed presupposition that the cognitive elements in question really are inadequate from a purely epistemic point of view. The basic problem is that it is difficult to raise such an objection without also being guilty of substituting the perspective of the critic for the relevant perspective and life experience of the person of faith. The point of this brief sketch of the relevant theory of epistemic rationality is to reveal how easy it is to fail on this score, much easier than has been widely recognized.

---

[21] Recognition of the problem is found in Skyrms (1975) and in van Fraassen (1989), with discussion of how to avoid the problem and whether it is in fact a problem in Field (1978), Garber (1980), Christensen (1992), Lange (2000), Wagner (2002), and Weisberg (2009).

[22] But embedding is not measured only by the conditional probabilities, for the conditional probabilities themselves can be more or less deeply embedded in a system, revealing how fixed the theory of evidence is for a given person.

Even so, if the only route toward answering the concern about bad faith was by showing the greater complexity of the story of epistemic rationality, we would have an answer that would mirror the standpoint of the Epistemic Fetishist: faith is fine as long as it is epistemically rational faith; otherwise all bets are off. That is not the position I intend to argue for, however, and the rest of the story involves needed limitations on the reach of epistemic rationality into the kind of full and rich life we legitimately hope for. So I turn to the second prong, the one that claims that if religious faith doesn't survive epistemic scrutiny, it will be bad faith.

4.6.2 Sense-making and bad faith

Notice that the charge of bad faith here is an all-things-considered negative judgment. It would not be enough of a concern if it were merely *pro tanto*. Some people use inefficient rubrics for solving the mathematical problems that arise in ordinary life, and their doing so is questionable, for if there is no consideration that outweighs this inefficiency, the practice will be all-things-considered irrational. The charge of bad faith, however, is not of this sort. One can't say, as we can in the case of the math example, "Yes, but this is how I was taught and changing my ways at this point would be too time-consuming to be worth the effort." Such a response would reveal a failure to appreciate the gravity of the charge being made. What is needed is not a response to counter a *pro tanto* consideration against the faith in question, but rather a response that shows that the critic's perception is mistaken: that any *prima facie* badness disappears once we look more closely.[23] This part of the story involves the phenomenon of cognitive penetration and, for want of a better term, the partiality of much of our experience of the world.

Cognitive penetration involves a generalization of the old worry in the philosophy of science concerning the theory-ladenness of observation. Whereas the latter issue concerns the worry within cognition itself that what we see is a function of prior theoretical commitments, and thus not a suitably passive and given aspect upon which to build a foundational theory of knowledge, cognitive penetration generalizes to other mental states as well. For example, suppose I am more likely to visually experience a certain rock as a piece of gold if I really want it to be gold; suppose I seem to remember only disturbing things for people I dislike; etc. It is clear, and clearly good, that experts can see more in an X-ray than I can, but it is not always good if one's belief that someone is angry causes one to experience an ambiguous

---

[23] Here I echo Shelly Kagan in distinguishing *pro tanto* reasons from *prima facie* ones: "A pro tanto reason has genuine weight, but nonetheless may be outweighed by other considerations. Thus, calling a reason a pro tanto reason is to be distinguished from calling it a prima facie reason, which I take to involve an epistemological qualification: a prima facie reason appears to be a reason, but may actually not be a reason at all." (Kagan 1989, p. 17 n.) While Kagan's way of taking these terms is correct linguistically and is also the use found in W. D. Ross (1930) (since Ross also calls a *prima facie* duty a "conditional duty"), it is not the use of the term in the epistemological literature deriving from Chisholm (1957), in which the notion of a *prima facie* reason is what Kagan describes as a *pro tanto* reason.

facial expression as hostile. My fear of snakes makes me more likely to detect them in certain contexts, and that is a good thing; your supreme self-confidence inclines you to experience love and affection from everyone you meet, and while that makes you happy and is good in virtue of that, it's also a bit discouraging to see you so out of touch with reality. As Carly Simon sang, some people are so vain they probably think this song is about them, though perhaps their vanity could equally be expressed in not thinking the song is about them.

The difficult questions here are two-fold. The first is a descriptive one, about the extent to which perception is cognitively penetrable and whether there is some early vision system in place that is encapsulated from penetration, that is modular in the sense of Fodor (1983). Once the descriptive task is complete, however, there is still the normative task of saying what effect the penetrability in question has on the epistemic standing of the resultant beliefs. At one end of the spectrum are the hardcore Phenomenal Conservatives, who think that it doesn't matter one whit where your seemings come from, all that matters is which seemings you in fact have. At some distance from this view, but maintaining some affinity with it, are those who discriminate among seemings in terms of the reliability of the mechanism involved, or on the basis of the sensitivity of the system for getting to the truth and avoiding error.

An alternative that I favor doesn't treat all seemings the same but doesn't sort them teleologically in terms of likelihood for getting to the truth. Instead, I favor an approach that adverts to a kind of Kantian autonomy when it comes to the epistemological story. What matters for epistemic rationality is the degree to which one is motivated by, to speak with the medievals, a love of truth. Such motivation comes in degrees, and the degree to which one's cognitive attitudes are epistemically rational is at least partially a function of one's motivation. It is precisely the motivational issue that underlies the deep concern over cognitive penetration. It is for this reason that Jerry Fodor, in Fodor (1984), took it to be wonderful epistemological news that our perceptual mechanisms are modular in the sense he specifies: their operation is not sensitive to the beliefs, desires, and other mental features of the larger organism of which they are a part.

Sad to say, but the truth must be told: the perceptual system as a whole is simply not modular in that sense. That is what the facts about cognitive penetrability show. Of course, it may still be that there is some subpart that is modular in the required sense, but even if that is true, it won't free us from the epistemological consequences of cognitive penetrability, since the fact of cognitive penetrability remains substantiated whether or not there is a subsystem that is motivationally untouched by outside forces.

Instead of lamenting cognitive penetrability and seeking ways to diminish or eliminate it, however, a better approach is to embrace it for what it is: a legitimate component of many full and rich human lives, the kinds of life the ancients sought as philosophy arises in hopes for a better life. The fact of cognitive penetrability might be found not only in purely theoretical areas, but in the elements central to the good life itself. For a full realization of the good life is to a great degree a matter of having the right cares and concerns, friends and loved ones, and there is simply no escape from the fact that what one loves and adores, who one cares about and who one despises, colors one's experience of the world in ways that are fairly easy to detect in others and in ourselves if we pay sufficient attention. In the first-person case, it is not difficult to find that one's interpretation of experience is often not driven solely by a disinterested concern for the truth. This point is easily appreciated by attending to the way in which the allegiance that is central to friendship plays a role in our intellectual lives. The significance of such allegiance, such standing by, is voiced nicely by Ryan Preston-Roedder:

Standing by people in the sense I described is morally admirable given the following view, which is both plausible and familiar, about the role that morality plays in human life: conforming to moral ideals enables a person to live in a kind of community with others, even though their interests and aims may differ considerably from her own. In other words, the world is teeming with people, and their various interests and aims can come into sharp conflict. On the one hand, each of these people devotes special attention to her own private aims, and according to this view, it is appropriate for her to do so. But on the other hand, there is a sense in which each person is just one among others, and no one is any more or less significant than anyone else. These two judgments are deeply plausible and central to the living of our lives, and conforming to moral requirements enables a person to live in a way that gives expression to each. Roughly, a virtuous person may pursue her own private aims in some cases, but she limits her pursuit of these aims, adopts new aims, and adopts attitudes in ways that bring her into a kind of community, or harmony, with everyone else. Standing by people, as when one has faith in them; adopting others' interests as one's own, as when one has the virtue of benevolence; and limiting one's pursuit of one's own aims so that others can pursue their aims as well, as when one has the virtue of justice, are all ways in which a morally virtuous person escapes her solitude and enters into this form of community. (Preston-Roedder 2013, p. 684)

The central point to note here is the kind of partiality that faith in humanity and friends involves, a kind of partiality toward attitudes that reflect our loyalty toward them and our continued desire for and commitment to community with them. This kind of partiality conflicts directly with the kind of disinterestedness that a purely intellectual motivation for getting to the truth and avoiding error involves, and often results in attitudes and opinions that would not be present apart from the partiality in question. What is most important in our context is to note how impoverished a life it would be if we were to agree to oppose such faith, thinking of it as bad faith and such partiality and loyalty as an all-things-considered defect in a person. Preston-Roedder remarks about such partiality and its value:

A third consideration that makes faith in humanity morally admirable is the fact that having faith in people's decency, despite reasons for doubt, is a way of standing by them, in roughly the sense in which one might stand by a decision, an ideal, or a friend to whom one is committed, despite reasons to abandon or denigrate her. The cognitive element of faith works together with the volitional to account for this link between having faith and standing by. Someone who has such faith is not just disposed to view people in a favorable light, but also invested in their confirming her favorable expectations. She roots for people to lead morally decent lives, even in the face of reasons to doubt that they can, or will, do so.   (Preston-Roedder 2013, p. 683)

Preston-Roedder describes the way in which purely mundane relationships, such as friendship, can both cause and rely on epistemic biases that are part and parcel of the phenomenon of cognitive penetration.[24] Our interpretation of the behavior of our friends often treats that behavior as innocuous, when other, less partial interpretation takes a more negative tone. One can try to explain away such partiality by appeal to better background information about the individual in question, but such an explanation is easily recognized to get things backwards: our greater familiarity is a function of the way in which friendship works, not the other way around. We often become friends quickly, generating the partiality in question much earlier than can be explained by an appeal to better information through long spans of familiarity.

Another way to appreciate this point is to think of what it would be like to be motivated only by a disinterested concern for truth in dealing with those around one. Such motivation is in tension with the kind of loyalty to friends and family involved in standing by them when questions arise, for one rational option in the face of such evidence is to walk away, and one motivated only by a disinterested concern for truth can just as easily walk away as not.

Such cases are the central focus of the case for epistemic partiality in friendship made by Sarah Stroud and Simon Keller. Keller writes:

It can sometimes *feel* as though loyalty to a friend pulls you in an opposite direction from your better epistemic judgment. Suppose that your friend is denying an accusation, and that the evidence against her is strong but not conclusive. You might find yourself believing your friend's story, while having the nagging realization that, did she not happen to be your friend, you wouldn't. . . .

The thesis that the norms of friendship can clash with epistemic norms offers one explanation of these observations.   (Keller 2004b, p. 331)

Along the same lines, Stroud writes:

Similarly, our friendships function as commitments. To be someone's friend is to have cast your lot in with his and, indeed, with his good character; and this properly affects how you respond to new situations and new data. . . . A commitment to your friend's merits is more something you bring to the various situations which confront you than something you take away from the information you receive. This is reflected in our epistemic partiality toward our friends.

(Stroud 2006, p. 512)

If this picture of the moral life is correct, then it is possible to have morally appropriate and perhaps required beliefs even in the absence of adequate evidence for them. Questions will remain even after granting this point, for there are stronger and weaker versions of the thesis of epistemic partiality that one might opt for. At one

---

[24] For defense and discussion, see Keller (2004a) and Stroud (2006).

end is the position that no one can have friends without being subject to epistemic partiality. Such a claim strikes me as too extreme, and so here I've been endorsing only the weaker claim that it is possible for epistemic partiality to be fully justified, in an all-things-considered sense, as part of a full and flourishing human life, so that the partiality is not itself a defect to be overlooked in such a life, but an integral component of it that helps to explain why such a life is a life worth living.

Once this point about the epistemic scandal of particularity is appreciated, it is easy to see why the portrayal of epistemic inadequacy in matters of faith does not invariably lead to bad faith. What needs to be shown, to sustain the charge of bad faith, is not just that epistemic rationality is absent from some (or even all) lives of faith, but that the faith in question inhibits the good life rather than making it possible. Recognizing the great variability of the good life should lead us to conclude that there simply will be no general line of argument from epistemically deficient intellectual commitments to bad faith, but should lead us to acknowledge instead that the biases involved in the epistemic scandal of particularity are often central to the good life, even if that good life is not epistemically ideal.

4.7 Conclusion

Where does all of the above leave us? For some, what will stand out is the variety of criticisms of religious faith that are not addressed, even when the kinds of criticisms allowed are restricted to those of a purely theoretical or intellectual nature (as opposed to political, aesthetic, moral, and practical types). We can point out that nothing in the above discussion tends to show that traditional Christian beliefs are sensitive to the truth in the way competent perception is (we hope and assume), or alethically safe in the way sophisticated statistical inferences are. We can note that believing things that you don't know to be true is as *pro tanto* objectionable as confidently asserting claims that you don't know to be true, so in the absence of a defense of the claim that traditional Christian belief counts as knowledge, a problem remains.

My response to all of these complaints begins by acknowledging that the above account is guilty as charged, but it does not end there. I believe it is important to resist the idea that the goal of normative theorizing is to show what it takes to be immune to criticism. I suspect, instead, that the varieties of intellectual value we find when we engage in epistemology from the kind of value-driven perspective I have argued for[25] will result in competition among values rather than a utopian vision that would make possible full immunity from intellectual criticism. In the face of such a pessimistic induction about epistemic value, the strategy I counsel is to begin theorizing about a particular kind of intellectual value only after explaining the importance of that value, relative to other kinds of intellectual value. I have argued elsewhere that the kind of

---

[25] See, especially, Kvanvig (2003) and Kvanvig (2014).

intellectual value addressed by the theory of rationality involved in the discussion above is perhaps the most important intellectual value, addressed as it is to the fundamental and inescapable egocentric predicament of what to do and think, what to be and become. I would thus ask those who wish to remind us of the remaining criticisms to engage in the metaepistemological value theory needed for explaining why the criticisms that remain are so worthy of consideration, rather than being akin to criticizing the President of the United States, not for his foreign policy or for a flagging economy, but for his boring wardrobe.

Once we reach this conclusion, what remains is to investigate the role that functional faith can play in religious contexts, especially within the context of historic Christianity. For, to many, this kind of faith will seem alien to the language of faith in Scripture and tradition, so much so that it might be thought that even if our inquiry is successful in identifying a kind of faith worth having, it can't be of much help in understanding the language of faith within the Christian tradition. The task of the next chapter, then, is to show how wide, broad, and deep is the reach of this approach to faith.

5

Functional Faith in Religious Contexts

5.1 Introduction

Our inquiry to this point has focused on the following ideas. We began by noting that the language of faith is used in a multitude of ways: faith in humanity, being a person of faith, having faith that the economy won't collapse, the catholic faith, etc. Faith is sometimes used as a synonym of trust, sometimes of belief. Those familiar with the linguistic turn in philosophy may seek semantic or conceptual systematization, and those of a different methodological persuasion may prefer conceptual genealogy, attempting a historical or perhaps mythical account of where our current concept comes from or might have come from (hoping to elucidate the phenomenon in question in the process). I have here articulated and adopted a different strategy, one focused on faith worth having. One might think of such an approach as one that mixes metaphysics and value theory, thinking of the idea of fundamentality here in terms of axiological fundamentality. For a basic tenet regarding faith is that it is not like being snub-nosed, which is true of some and not others though not in a way that is deeply significant for our understanding of the structure of reality and our place in it. By contrast, faith worth having is purportedly a virtue and somehow central to a well-lived life. While some might prefer to bracket axiological questions in the interest of first giving a systematic treatment of the ways we use the language of faith (or of the variety of conceptualizations of this phenomenon), my approach puts axiology first, leaving open the possibility that a substantial portion of the logical space of the language of faith and the conceptualizations involved can be written off as uninteresting or unimportant.

Such an approach begins at the functional level, characterizing the role that faith plays in the lives of people of faith. One pre-theoretic possibility is that a characterization of the functional role of faith will force it to be significant only for some lives and only in certain contexts. Such is a fairly common understanding, relegating the value of faith to religious contexts and individuals, especially those involving the faith-based religion of Christianity. Such a picture of faith is easy to paint, especially when developed from a methodological standpoint involving linguistic or conceptual analysis. From our alternative methodology of looking for what is axiologically fundamental, we discover that the functional nature of faith finds a natural home outside of religious contexts, playing a central role in a quite broad range of human pursuits and interests. In fact, it is fair to say that a primary goal of the preceding chapters is to reveal the extent to which faith worth having is not a distinctively sacred topic. Faith worth having is intimately linked with the psychological phenomenon of integration of a personality and thus also an ingredient in the kind of integrity that is a hallmark of a life that takes morality seriously.

The danger of such a focus, however, is that it can make it seem that this kind of faith is one that doesn't fit well in sacred arenas, where the standard assumptions about faith require substantive doctrinal commitments. I intend to argue that this perception is mistaken, and that the language of faith in Sacred Writ is driven largely if not completely by this same kind of faith. I cannot, of course, argue that succeeding developments in the history of Christian thought involve a notion of faith that is largely free of doctrinal commitments, and those who favor a picture of the Christian religion that views the language of Scripture as displaying an understanding only of Christianity in its infancy and not its full maturity will find this discussion unhelpful for establishing the desired conclusion that fully developed versions of Christian faith are best understood in terms of functional faith. For alternative perspectives which place greater authority in Scripture itself, however, there is a story to tell, I maintain, about why the language of faith in Scripture is fundamentally in concord with the account developed here of faith worth having. Moreover, as hinted in the last chapter, there is reason to conclude that more doctrinal conceptions of faith result from an undesirable intrusion of political dimensions into the history of theology, rather than from some essential component of the faith from which such discussions spring.

These conclusions will require some backfilling regarding the language of faith in Scripture, since these conclusions are so at odds with standard interpretations of sacred texts. As we will see, however, there is good reason in favor of, and no reason from the data in question to oppose, the view that what is axiologically fundamental here is a kind of faith that involves dispositions toward responses in service of an ideal.

This conclusion is also a centerpiece in the attempt to show that the kind of faith that is fundamental in religious contexts, especially Christianity, isn't of a different and less defensible variety. On this issue, I will press several points. First, I will argue that there needs to be a defense of any faith-based enterprise, including faith-based religions such as Christianity. Second, I will show how the received view of faith in the Christian tradition, on which faith is fundamentally doctrinal, makes it susceptible to the charge of being defenseless. We have already seen above some reason to question the credentials of the received view, and I will press this concern further by considering and rejecting the two strongest arguments on behalf of the received view. That will leave us with the option of adopting the received view or showing how to extend the above account of faith to religious contexts. I will turn to that issue after examining the received view of religious faith.

5.2 Faith and the Christian Tradition

In the Christian tradition faith is supposed to be central to salvation and thus of utmost significance. That makes it important no matter what kind of faith is involved, but not in the right way. If we wish to think about fundamental faith from an axiological perspective, we want faith to get its significance from the inside rather than the outside, so to speak. We want an answer to the question of what makes faith important that is more internal to the faith in question. For notice that things that are completely uninteresting and nearly useless in themselves can come to be deeply significant at the whims of a powerful despot who demands that they be collected and treasured. So the centrality of faith to salvation doesn't by itself yield the right kind of defense of it, but rather only shows that the religion in question is faith-based (in some sense or other). In order to assess the significance of the kind of faith in question, we begin by asking "Why?" Why would it be that this particular phenomenon is so central to eternal salvation?

One might resist the question, insisting that we are not in a position to question the standards God adopts or suggesting that there needn't be any explanation here. In response, I note two things. First, I doubt that a proper theology makes God out to be defensive when it comes to questioning by human beings. Note, for example, the serious questioning and resistance that both Abraham and Moses show. I'm thinking, especially, of Moses' resistance when God proposes to put an end to his chosen people[1] and Abraham's resistance to God's decision to destroy Sodom and Gomorrah.[2] Second, it is also to be noted that questions can be asked for purposes of resisting a viewpoint or challenging it, but they can also be asked in hope of achieving understanding. There should be no objection to seeking understanding.

---

[1] See e.g. Exodus 32:9–10,

> "I have seen these people," the LORD said to Moses, "and they are a stiff-necked people. Now leave me alone so that my anger may burn against them and that I may destroy them. Then I will make you into a great nation" (NIV)

and Numbers 16:41–5,

> But when the assembly gathered in opposition to Moses and Aaron and turned toward the tent of meeting, suddenly the cloud covered it and the glory of the LORD appeared. Then Moses and Aaron went to the front of the tent of meeting, and the LORD said to Moses, "Get away from this assembly so I can put an end to them at once." (NIV)

[2] In Genesis 18, verses 20–5:

> Then the Lord said, "The outcry against Sodom and Gomorrah is so great and their sin so grievous that I will go down and see if what they have done is as bad as the outcry that has reached me. If not, I will know." . . . Then Abraham approached him and said: "Will you sweep away the righteous with the wicked? What if there are fifty righteous people in the city? Will you really sweep it away and not spare the place for the sake of the fifty righteous people in it? Far be it from you to do such a thing—to kill the righteous with the wicked, treating the righteous and the wicked alike. Far be it from you! Will not the Judge of all the earth do right?" (NIV)

Once we ask the question (perhaps insisting on doing so with the right attitude), we face the possibility that there is no answer to it—that the focus on faith is just a matter of divine fiat, with no underlying rationale of any sort. Such a result would be deeply disappointing, and would present a challenge to every theology that falls short of the strongest universalism (the view that necessarily, in the end all will be saved). For if one's eternal destiny turns on the issue of satisfying some arbitrary matter of divine fiat, it is hard to see how eternal destruction could be an appropriate response to failure on this score.[3] Consider, for example, other possible arbitrary standards. Perhaps the standard is that you have to cut off your little toe on your right foot or have a tattoo on your right forearm, on pain of eternal destruction. A first problem with "lose the toe" theology and "tattoo" theology is the unfairness to those who never hear the demand until it is too late. A very clear demand of justice is that just laws have to be publicized to the point that if you don't know about the law, it's your own fault. But standards of justice go further: a just law typically involves some point to it, some goal or consideration that counts in favor of that law in comparison with other laws. This point doesn't imply that there typically exists a full justification for, for example, why the speed limit is exactly 70 miles per hour rather any other number among the infinity of possible alternatives to a 70 mile-per-hour speed limit—an explanation need not be a contrastive explanation to be a good one. This point lies at the heart of an adequate understanding of the Buridan's Ass Paradox, where we can get an explanation for the ass's eating from the left bale even if we can't get an explanation of the ass's eating from the left rather than from the right bale.[4] When there is such a contrastive justification available, we might say that there is a complete defense available for it, but even laws lacking a complete defense typically have a rationale of some sort or other. Beyond a minimal requirement of consistency with other laws, we should expect some point to a law. For example, in the case of speed limit laws, the point of the law is a concern for public safety, yielding a range of possibilities for such laws within which the actual law falls, and the same principle holds more generally. In the particular case of faith, perhaps there is some purpose or interest or concern that is worthy of attention, and having faith is the, or a, fitting vehicle for such.

Philosophers often live to fray the fringes of a generalization, and the same is to be expected here. "Why can't there be arbitrary foundations for a life well-lived?" one might ask. If the question is intended to indicate resistance to any need for full, contrastive justification of the foundations, we can agree. If the question, however, is intended to signal the possibility of foundations for which there is no rationale at all, we should resist. Such a stance certainly doesn't fit well with any major religion, and certainly not with Christianity, which grounds the life of faith in an account of the problems of sin and misery plaguing the created order. Moreover, the Christian story about how a life of faith is a suitable response to these problems is certainly

---

[3] For detailed discussion of this problem, see Kvanvig (1993).
[4] For discussion and defense, see Kvanvig (2009b).

not presented in Scripture in terms of an arbitrarily selected mark to identify the redeemed, but rather as part and parcel of a story about God's redemptive and reconciliatory purposes for all of creation. From this perspective, an account of faith in terms of dispositions to respond in service of an ideal is easily seen as being internally related to a process of reconciliation when the ideal itself is or involves the coming of the Kingdom of God and what it represents, and we should want to see something similar from any alternative proposal about why faith is required for salvation. A response to the effect that that's just the way it is should strike us as too absurd to take seriously, a response that shows the inadequacy of the theology in question and a serious misrepresentation of a religion that has played such a central role in a wide variety of flourishing lives and civilizations.

So, at least as a methodological stance, we should begin by assuming that there is a point to the requirement of faith beyond mere divine fiat, and we should investigate the nature of faith (worth having) in terms of this assumption. Once we do so, however, the received view concerning the nature of faith, an approach that treats faith as fundamentally doctrinal, is easily seen as inadequate. For the idea that the difference-maker regarding one's eternal destiny is simply a matter of being in the right cognitive state is no better than the idea that the difference-maker regarding one's eternal destiny is a tattoo on the right forearm or a missing little toe on the right foot.

This point deserves clarification and commentary, since the language of belief is so common in English translations of Christian Scripture. Situated where we are in human history, when we think of belief we do so primarily in terms of claims that are true or false. We thus notice the false beliefs of the past: that the earth is flat, that the sun revolves around the earth, etc. And we focus in the present on beliefs that we wish no one held: beliefs that vaccinating children causes harm, beliefs that human behavior isn't responsible for (some of) global warming, etc. So when we hear the call of the television evangelist to "just *BELIEVE!*" we wonder "believe *WHAT*?" The injunction and the question form such a natural pair that the answer is going to have to be in terms of a truth-claim of some sort, and that is just what we get: "believe that God loves you, believe that Jesus died for your sins, that you need to repent of your sins, and that you will thereby be forgiven and enter the Kingdom," etc.

Yet, if we take all of these quite common steps—beginning from the centrality of faith to the Christian story, to a connection between faith and belief, and to an understanding of belief that involves a complement clause that makes a claim which is either true or not—we end up portraying a theology of faith that is not better off than "lose your toe" theology. If this theological picture weren't so common, it would immediately strike us as absurd and nonsensical, in the same way we respond when reading in *The Hitchhiker's Guide to the Galaxy* that the number 42 is the answer to the ultimate question of life, the universe, and everything. Of all the concerns God might have about human beings and the lives that they live, how could it come down to something like a true/false checklist that you fill out honestly, and the answers determine your destiny? Why not whether you have a mole on your right cheek? Why not whether you want to eat M&Ms for breakfast? My point is not that there will be no place for doxastic commitments of some sort when the theology of faith is properly developed, but only that the picture that goes straight from faith to propositional beliefs is one that turns the theology of faith into a hopeless disaster.

Defenders of the received view, the view on which faith is fundamentally doctrinal, will not go away so easily, however. There are two central ways to try to resist the arguments just given, both appealing to the authority of Scripture. The first involves the obvious point that Scripture is full of claims that link faith and belief, and the second is that faith and doubt are contrastive states in Scripture, and what counts as a, or the, relevant contrast to a state tells us something important about that state. In order to sustain my complaint against doxastic conceptions of faith in the context of Christianity, we must examine those points of resistance to see why and how they are mistaken.

5.3 Some Methodological Reflections Concerning the Received View

In order to assess the defense of the received view by appeal to the language of belief in Scripture, we need to begin with a methodological account of the commitments involved in the received view. Philosophical accounts of various phenomena are given often in terms of necessary and sufficient conditions of varying strengths, corresponding with what kind of conditional is being used in the account. In the typical case, nothing short of metaphysical necessity would seem to be adequate for a philosophical account of this sort, so we can assume that those who give accounts of faith in terms of propositional belief take propositional belief to be metaphysically necessary for faith.[5] As we have seen, such an approach provides little hope of telling us what is fundamental to the thing in question, what is its basic nature. To answer that question, something more is needed, and one way to aim at doing so is to use the symbol '$=_{df}$' in place of 'iff', where the former is interpreted to involve identity by definition, i.e., an account of the meaning of the term used to pick out the phenomenon in question. Such accounts carry a heavy burden, however, since any interesting analysis of this sort will do more than provide obvious synonyms for the term to be analyzed. Once we move beyond obvious synonyms, one wonders how to defend the claim of meaning identity any more, a worry that crystallizes in the difficult

---

[5] I am mildly uncomfortable with the qualifier 'metaphysically' here, since it smacks of "philoso-speak." I would rather speak of necessity, full stop, contrasting it with relative necessities: logical (one for each system of such), scientific, physical, chemical, biological, anthropological, sociological, psychological, etc.). But explaining this picture of modality will take us too far afield for present purposes, so I'll stick with the more standard language of metaphysical necessity in the text.

paradox of analysis and is threatened by Quinean concerns about the presupposed analytic/synthetic distinction.[6]

As a result, philosophers may still use the connective '$=_{df}$.' without really intending to provide an analysis of the term in question, but when they use it in this weakened way, one wonders exactly what import they attach to it. One kind of response is to distinguish real from nominal definitions, noting that only the latter rely on some requirement of analyticity for the result. A real definition is not really anything linguistically defining at all: it is a decomposing of the phenomenon in question into its constituent parts, where the latter are more basic metaphysically, rather than semantically or conceptually.[7]

A related, though slightly different, approach replaces the language of definition with that of explanation. Instead of using '$=_{df}$.' or 'iff', this approach supplements the language with necessary and sufficient conditions with a 'because' clause: "X if and only if, and because, Y".

The slippage between 'iff', '$=_{df}$', and 'if and only if, and because' is fodder for philosophical abuse, however. Necessary conditions are easy to find, but constituents and explanatory bases much harder. So one can make the beginning of one's account much more palatable by using the language of necessary and sufficient conditions, even when the demands of one's project require something stronger. Suppose, for example, that one's project is to give a philosophical account of the property of being human. If one thinks in terms of constituents of this property, or explanatory bases of such, the project is daunting: where to start? Thinking in terms of necessary conditions, however, yields a harvest of possibilities: being a physical object, being an animal, being located in space-time, normally having hair in the actual world, not being born on Mars in the actual world, even being such that time exists or that 2+2=4.

Consider the latter disjunctive possibility. It is a plausible suggestion as a necessary condition for being human, but it is not a plausible suggestion about the constituents or explanatory bases of being human. If our goal is to understand what it is to be human, what is fundamental to that property, we will want something more by way of a beginning than a defense of the claim that a certain feature is necessary for being human. Claims of necessity are logically pristine, however, in comparison with claims about what is fundamental or explanatorily basic. As a result, a starting point in terms

---

[6] The paradox of analysis has roots in Plato, particularly in the *Meno* paradox concerning how learning anything not already known is possible, and can be found in both Frege's *Philosophie der Arithmetik* and G. E. Moore's *Principia Ethica* in the origins of analytic philosophy, though the phrase 'the paradox of analysis' is only first used in Langford (1942). The classic Quinean location for worries about the analytic/synthetic distinction is Quine (1951).

[7] Except, of course, for those who identify concepts with metaphysically basic entities such as properties. I think such an identification is a mistake: the property of being a quark is one thing, something that would have existed had there been (*per impossibile*, at least for theists) only quarks and no minds at all; whereas the concept of being a quark is mental in some way or other. For those who reject this way of distinguishing properties and concepts, the distinction between a real definition and a conceptual analysis might disappear.

of a necessary condition is attractive because tractable: the defense of it need only stave off counterexamples. The discerning, however, will detect the sleight of hand needed to get the account off the ground and insist that one begin more transparently and from a more useful starting point.

We can see this pattern in the received view about faith. We can see how by contrasting some resistance to the received view, articulated in different ways by Robert Bellah and Daniel McKaughan in passages quoted earlier, with a response by Alvin Plantinga, conceived as a defense of the received view. To set up the debate, we imagine a theorist begins by considering the relationship between faith and propositional belief, taking the latter to be necessary for the former. If such a theorist is methodologically unreflective, this might be thought of as the first principle for a full account of the nature of faith. To such a first principle, however, resistance comes: whatever one makes of the language of belief in various translations of Scripture into English, the kind of belief in question is hardly ever that of propositional belief. It is the language of *de re* belief (for example, Abraham believed the Lord and it was credited to him as righteousness) or "belief in" rather than "belief that" (for example, "You believe in God, believe also in me").

The passages quoted earlier, in which such a complaint about propositional belief construals of faith appears, are as follows. Bellah writes,

"Unbelief," like "theology" is a product of the Greek mind . . . . Where the word "belief" is used to translate the biblical Hebrew and Greek it means not the "belief that" of Plato, but "belief in," a matter not of cognitive assent but of faith, trust, and obedience . . . . Plato's "theology" is not in fact an accurate apprehension of traditional religion. It is the self-conscious intellectual's translation of that religion into terms that he can understand.   (Bellah 1991, p. 216)

McKaughan is similarly concerned that the received view distorts:

While belief now refers to a state of mind, a disposition to assent to a set of propositions, even within the early Christian intellectual tradition historically it had as much or more to do with love, loyalty, and commitments akin to pledging one's allegiance to a person as Lord or to a cause or to entering into a covenant such as marriage. The Latin word credo (apparently a compound of *cor, cordis* 'heart' and *-do, -dere,* 'to put' derived from the proto Indo-European root for placing one's heart upon something, **kred-dhē*) means 'I set my heart' upon the entity or doctrines in question. Even for scholastics such as Aquinas . . . credo meant to pledge allegiance to, to give one's self and one's loyalty. The Latin terms most closely expressing today's meaning of belief and opinion, *opinio* ('opinion, belief, supposition') and *opinor* (*opinari,* to be of the opinion, to believe) played an almost negligible role in Christian thought.

(McKaughan 2013, pp. 107–8)

The background for these complaints about the received view is that the language of belief in Scripture is linguistically related to the language of faith in a way that is absent in English. In English, there is no verb form of the noun 'faith,' whereas in Scripture, the noun *pistis* (in English, "faith") has verb forms which are translated in terms of believing, and when Scripture ties believing to faith and salvation, it uses these verb forms. So, the basic point that Bellah and McKaughan share is that the verb forms of *pistis* conveyed a more affective emphasis as opposed to the more purely cognitive tone involved in the current meaning of 'believe'.

To some, these points seem easy to resist, however, even if one grants that the language of belief in Scripture is more typically a matter of "belief in" rather than "belief that":

So believing in God is indeed more than accepting the proposition that God exists. But if it is more than that, it is also at least that. One cannot sensibly believe in God and thank him for the mountains without believing that there is such a person to be thanked and that he is in some way responsible for the mountains. Nor can one trust in God and commit oneself to him without believing that he exists; as the author of Hebrews says, "He who would come to God must believe that he is and that he is a rewarder of those who seek him." (Heb. 11:6).

(Plantinga 1983, p. 18)

The idea is clear: even if faith is a matter of belief-in rather than belief-that, the latter is necessary for the former, and so the latter can easily be defended as necessary for faith.

We will come back to the Hebrews passage that Plantinga relies on here, but it is also worth noting the way in which Plantinga identifies accepting a proposition with believing it. On the latter score, many philosophers think there is a distinction between believing and accepting, and the received view about faith is undermined if belief-in only requires acceptance-that rather than belief-that, if these philosophers are correct.[8] A defender of the received view can use the Plantinga quote to respond to Bellah and McKaughan, however, by treating Plantinga's appeal to acceptance as a slip of the tongue or as a commitment to the idea that there is no distinction between acceptance and belief, allowing a charitable reading of the above remarks that results if we replace the language of acceptance with the language of belief.

Returning to the main point, I want to insist that it takes a bit of methodological confusion to view this dialectic as a suitable defense of the received view. The received view is supposed to tell us what faith is, not just what co-varies with it, even if of necessity. In pursuit of this goal, the received view begins from the idea that propositional belief is necessary for Biblical faith. In response to the complaints of Bellah and McKaughan that the place of the language of belief in Scripture isn't that of propositional belief, the defender of the received view agrees, but insists that propositional belief is similarly necessary for the kind of belief-in that is central to the Scriptural language of belief. Such a dialectic would be suitable if all we wanted was a set of necessary and sufficient conditions for faith, but if we are explicit about

---

[8] Those who draw a distinction between belief and acceptance include van Fraassen (1980), Cohen (1992), Lehrer (1990), Bratman (1999), Velleman (2000), and Frankish (2004).

looking for constituents or explanatory bases of faith, the remarks about the priority of trust and obedience over and against propositional belief (or cognitive assent) are not so easily dismissed. For those remarks don't need to challenge the necessity of propositional belief for faith in order to undermine the received view. Moreover, the received view, conceived of as an account of the fundamental nature of faith, can't be defended against this objection by appeal to a purportedly necessary connection between faith and propositional belief.

So the first point to note is that the received view has to take more seriously the methodological requirements on giving an account of the fundamental nature of faith. It is not enough to defend the necessity of propositional belief for faith; if a defense of this starting point is going to be adequate, it must begin by taking the complaints voiced by Bellah and McKaughan much more seriously than can be done by relying only on the Plantinga point above.

Moreover, there is some theoretical discomfort in relying on the Plantinga point at all, for the claim that belief-that is necessary for belief-in is mistaken or strained in other contexts: does faith in democracy imply belief that democracy exists? That implication is clearly mistaken: one can have faith in democracy while also being certain that there aren't any democracies to be found. Consider a second example as well, the case of faith in or belief in equality of opportunity. Here the import of the language is readily understood: one is committed to such equality, one's life is arranged in service of this ideal. To suggest that such involves belief that something or other exists that is appropriately related to equality of opportunity is strained at best.

One might try to resist this concern in the following way: faith in democracy involves an awareness of what democracy is, and such awareness requires a belief that there is such a thing as democracy, even if it is only an abstract entity or possibility of some sort. This response is, however, strained: a believer in democracy or equality of opportunity doesn't seem to need to expend any mental energy making ontological commitments to abstract entities. Such a believer must know or be aware of what democracy or equality of opportunity is, and this knowledge or awareness will presumably involve some sorts of propositional doxastic commitments. But the point remains that there is no necessary connection between belief in X and believing that X exists.

A defender of Plantinga's remarks might note, however, that Plantinga doesn't claim that belief in X requires believing that X exists. Instead, he only says that belief in God requires believing that God exists. That claim can be true even if the more general principle is not. We should expect, however, that Plantinga's claim here derives from some sort of generalization, for it would be amazing to find him admitting that the requirement holds nowhere else except in the case of God. Perhaps it doesn't hold for any and every value of X, but even so, we should be able to ascertain some general category for which it does hold if it holds in the case of God. The Hebrews passage says (if we grant that the verb form of *pistis* is best translated as 'believe') it is true of God, and the most plausible reason for it holding in that case would seem to be because God is a person or a being: for such values of X, having faith in X requires believing that X exists.

We can often find evidence of a translation gone amiss by registering disagreements with what the translation says, and such is the case here with Hebrews 11:6. Upon reading the claim in question, one ought to be suspicious. One should wonder why such doxastic confidence in the existence of God and in his character as a rewarder are required in order to (try to) draw near to him. An extremely strong preference for nearness to God could prompt efforts to draw near to him in spite of significant uncertainty about whether he rewards those who seek him, for example. If the preference is strong enough, a mere hope that God would reward the search would seem to be strong enough to make drawing near possible.

Consider the following analogy. A young man from a remote village in colonial America can't decide whether to sign on to a seven-year apprenticeship to learn blacksmithing. He must make a decision soon, but doesn't know what to do. A traveling minstrel stops to chat and upon learning of the dilemma, reports that there are rumors of a very wise hermit living up in the hills who has provided sage advice to many young men about career choices. It is said that if he is willing to give advice, he'll spend a few days coming to understand the seeker, after which he'll make a recommendation. The rumor is that everyone who has heeded his advice has been happy with their decision, and that those who have not heeded his advice have generally rued their choice. The young man reflects, deciding to try to find the hermit and try to get his advice.

The question to ask is, in pursuing this plan, what our young man must believe. The answer is fairly obvious about what beliefs aren't required. He doesn't have to believe that the hermit will be a useful source of information, though he must take some positive attitude toward this possibility. He doesn't even have to believe that the hermit exists; it would be enough for him to have a strong hope that there is such a hermit.

Returning then to the Hebrews passage, the doxastic commitments required by the standard translation seem excessive. If you want to draw near to God, why would one need to believe that God will reward such an attempt? Just as in the case of the young man and the hermit, a strong hope would seem to be sufficient.

If one wants to preserve the full authority of Scripture in the face of such questioning, the obvious move to make is to consider whether the translation overreaches. Moreover, if we attend to the points in the McKaughan passage quoted earlier, noting the way in which a more ancient conception of belief had "more to do with love, loyalty, and commitments akin to pledging one's allegiance," one might gloss the verse in question as follows: if you want to draw near to God, you must be committed to, be loyal to, have your heart set on him and his interest in a relationship with you. Put in this way, the concerns about the requirement being too strong are no longer pressing. For, put in this way, the verse is counseling against half-hearted, casual efforts on the part of seekers. Failure to be fully committed in this way is an indication that one isn't really trying very hard to draw near to God.

The proper conclusion to draw, then, is that the Hebrews passage provides insufficient support for the view that belief in X requires belief that X exists, even when X is restricted to persons or beings. In light of the vignette of the young villager and the hermit, we should be suspicious of the requirement as well. For the villager sets out on a quest, showing a commitment to the project of seeking advice, but not needing to believe that the hermit exists in order to engage in the quest. He, we might correctly say, shows faith in and believes in the hermit (on the assumption that there is such a hermit) but doesn't yet believe that the hermit exists.

In addition, we can readily see why one might be tempted toward the requirement Plantinga endorses, in spite of its falsity. First, human history is the story of near unanimity on the question of the existence of God, and certainly in the Abrahamic traditions, the question wasn't one of the truth or falsity of theism, but rather one of allegiance toward the one true God. In such a context, where belief-in signals the kind of allegiance in question, such allegiance is built on top of a prior theism, and so it is appropriate to describe such allegiance in terms of going beyond mere theism (or mere Christian theism). Once we try to generalize beyond this context, however, faith in (belief in) a person or cause need not be built on top of a prior doxastic commitment and need not involve such, even if the fulfillment of that faith will result in such commitments in the future and even if those with such doxastic commitments will display greater psychological integration among conative, affective, and cognitive aspects of personhood.

Returning to a more general level of discussion, here is where we are. I have been emphasizing that we cannot make philosophical progress in thinking clearly about faith without being adequately reflective about what a good theory must answer to, and in particular without abandoning the idea that a good starting point is simply to latch onto some necessary condition or other and add qualifiers until one achieves a grand conjunction of conditions that are jointly sufficient for faith. Such an approach is methodologically unsound in the present context, in which we are attempting to determine whether faith-based religions such as Christianity appeal to faith of a sort that is axiologically fundamental.

A full defense of the received view thus requires more than what is contained in the Plantinga quote above. It is equally true, though, that the quotes from Bellah and McKaughan work better as a demand for further explanation by defenders of the received view than as conclusive objections to that view. It is thus incumbent on us in the current context to examine carefully what to make of the Scriptural language concerning the relationship between faith and belief to determine whether it is best explained by the received view.

I will thus turn to a more careful examination of the language of faith, doubt, and belief in Scriptural contexts, in order to loosen some of the grip that the cognitive account of faith has had on our understanding of Scripture. As we will see, several authors have noticed inadequacies of typical understandings of Scriptural passages that rely on a cognitive understanding of faith and the accompanying contrast between faith and doubt, but such reservations have not blossomed into a full rejection of the cognitive picture of faith. It is not surprising that no such rejection has resulted—we see the same phenomenon in scientific inquiry where a well-entrenched theoretical perspective remains in place in spite of a variety of known anomalies for the theory. Rejection of well-entrenched theories, whether in science or theology, depends not only on evidence that runs contrary to the theory, but also on the availability of alternative theories that predict the contrary evidence. My goal here will be to show that a functional account of faith is precisely such a theory: it explains well the variety of difficulties that arise when passages are understood against a backdrop of cognitive accounts of faith.

5.4 Faith and Belief in the Context of Scripture

We can begin such a discussion by first noting that the language of faith in the Bible has a complexity not found in English. This complexity arises from the fact that there is no verb form in English that is linguistically related to the noun 'faith', whereas the language of the New Testament translated using variants of the English verb 'believe' are verb forms of *pistis* (the noun translated "faith").[9] This relationship is present in the Hebrews passage to which Plantinga appeals. The pleasing of God is identified in the second part of the verse with coming to him or drawing near to him, and the language of *pistis* is used in both parts of the verse, the noun form first and verb form later. It would not be misleading, then, to translate as follows: "without faith it is impossible to please God, indeed anyone who comes to him must have faith that he exists and that he rewards those who earnestly seek him." The same point can be made of various other passages in the New Testament, such as those in the Gospel of John which are usually translated using the notion of belief. The Gospel reports Jesus as saying, "Whoever believes in him is not condemned, but whoever does not believe stands condemned already." Two points to note are these: here the language is that of believing in, not believing that something is the case; and several translations use the language of trust rather than that of belief. It would not be misleading, then, to understand such a claim as insisting that whoever has faith in Jesus is not condemned, and those lacking faith are condemned already. We should be cautious, then, in thinking that the language of

---

[9] Some details: the language of faith in the Bible derives from the Greek term *pistis*, the root form of which is *pieto*, with a primary meaning of "to persuade" but translated variously in the KJV, for example, as 'persuade' (22x), 'trust' (8x), 'obey' (7x), 'have confidence' (6x), 'believe' (3x), 'be confident' (2x). (See entry 4102 in Strong (2007 [1890]).) This verb has as root a term meaning "to bind", helping to explain the variation in translations of the term from 'believe' to 'obey', from something that seems to connote something purely mental to something that is most clearly behavioral. (It may also be worth noting the emotional and affective overtones of 'be confident', which is sometimes taken to be a purely cognitive notion, as in Bayesian epistemology and standard decision theory, but has a more primary connotation in ordinary language of a feeling of a certain sort.)

believing in or trusting is best understood in terms of a cognitive understanding of faith.

The significance of this point does not require that it is extended to every use of the language of *pistis* in the New Testament. That question can be left open, though I think we should be suspicious about all such translations. Considering one such example will be useful for the purposes of showing why such suspicion is warranted. One verse that seems to be a good candidate for translating in terms of the language of belief is James 2:19: "You believe that there is one God. Good! Even the demons believe that—and shudder." (NIV)

The context reveals, however, that a translation in terms of the language of belief is not necessary and misleads in a certain way. The author is aiming to show faith without deeds is a precarious possibility at best. Verse 18 issues a challenge: show me your faith without deeds. The imagined reply is in verse 19. If that reply is, "I believe that God is one," such a reply should perplex, since the question is one about faith, not belief. A reply that would be to the point would be, "I have faith that there is one God." To this reply, James has a relevant rebuttal: the demons have that kind of faith too! So, whatever that kind of faith is, it isn't saving faith—it is useless faith, in and of itself.

A translation using the language of belief cannot explain the dialectic appropriately, unless it is being assumed that belief is, all by itself, sufficient for faith. But nobody should think that, and no credible cognitive account of faith pretends that the cognitive dimension alone is sufficient for faith. In addition, some kind of pro-attitude toward the object of faith is also required. So when the linguistic connection in Greek is lost between *pistin* in verse 18, the noun translated "faith", and the verb forms *pisteueis* and *pisteuousin* in verse 19, we end up with an anomaly. James's interlocutor seems not to have grasped the challenge, which was to provide an example of faith without deeds, for an example of belief without deeds simply fails to be an example of such.

A further interpretive point is relevant here, once we correct the translation to restore the linguistic connection that is essential to the dialectic. If the interlocutor claims to have faith that there is one God, there is an argumentative flaw in James's rebuttal. For the demons don't have a relevant pro-attitude toward the claim that there is one God. To put it mildly, their heart simply isn't in it; more to the point, they take a decidedly anti-attitude toward the claim. So the imaginary interlocutor might reply to James's argument that the demons' reply doesn't undermine the claim that faith that there is one God is an example of faith without deeds.

Such a response would be to the point in one way, even though a mere diversion in a more important way. James's response to the possibility of faith without deeds may overreach in this way, but the general point is still well-taken: mere faith that God exists is far from enough for saving faith. For one can have such a limited faith without having faith in God, without making God and His Kingdom a focal element for one's life and behavior. In the language of the approach I favor, one can have faith that God exists but lack a disposition to respond in service of an ideal that involves God and His Kingdom. The point about the demons may not be as decisive as James makes it out to be, but it points to an underlying argument that is clearly correct.

We may also note that the author need not have been making a mistake in ascribing faith to the demons, for exaggerations and hyperboles may be at work in his rhetoric, and such figures of speech seem to be a family trait among James and his relatives: see, for example, Jesus's reported remarks about camels and eyes of needles. Such hyperbole about the attitudes of demons might be just the right rhetorical tool for getting an audience to appreciate the force of the argument presented in the last paragraph. Those of us inclined toward patient exposition of argumentation have direct experience of its rhetorical flaws: listeners have often lost interest or focus by the time we triumphantly draw the relevant conclusion!

This issue about the dialectic, moreover, is neutral on the question of whether to read the discussion in terms of a functional account of faith and a more cognitive one, as already noted. For a cognitive understanding won't fix the argument unless the cognitive account makes mere belief sufficient for faith. We have already seen, however, that no such account can be adequate. So the lacuna just noted in James's argument provides no fodder for those wishing to insist that the passage can only be properly translated using doxastic terms. The central point of the passage is one about faith: the only faith worth having is saving faith, and mere faith that God exists isn't such faith. Mere faith that God is One harks back to the opening passage of the Decalogue, but no adherent of the Jewish faith would allow such limited propositional faith alone to be sufficient for salvation, however the latter is conceived. So the challenge of the author is that he has located a kind of faith divorced from deeds, and though it is a kind of faith, it is a useless kind of faith.

Of course, it is compatible with this contrastive argument that faith worth having is something built on top of belief that something is the case. But it is equally compatible with the contrast that identifying what is fundamental to faith in terms of belief that something is the case is to have taken a wrong turn somewhere in the attempt to discern the nature of faith. Moreover, resorting to the language of belief takes the Jamesian argument on a conceptual detour that is unnecessary, so the passage on its own doesn't lend any credence to the claim that faith should be understood in doxastic terms in Scriptural contexts.

We gain additional evidence for understanding the passage in terms of functional faith by noting the natural reading such an understanding of faith gives to the remainder of the chapter. That paragraph argues that faith without deeds is dead, citing the examples of Abraham and Rahab. James does not deny a distinction between their faith and their deeds, but rather intends to point to the intimate relationship between the two: they are examples of faith and action working together, of faith being made complete by what they did. On a functional account, the discussion makes perfect sense: the disposition toward behavior in service of God and his Kingdom is one thing, and the triggering of that disposition in action that expresses it another. Moreover, if the disposition were present, but always and everywhere masked by competing factors, James's point is that such faith would be dead or useless faith. We measure the strength and value of functional faith in terms of the range of circumstances in which one's behavior expresses that faith, when the circumstances involve triggering conditions for the disposition in question. When the relevant triggering conditions never result in an expression of the disposition—never result in acts of faith—it is a metaphysical mystery how to maintain that the disposition is nonetheless present even though always masked.

For a piece of practical advice about life in The Way, the above explanation is all that is needed. For more theoretical purposes, however, we might want more. In particular, we might wonder whether, even if unexpressed faith is mysterious, it might not still be possible; and if possible, whether it would still count as saving faith and thus not completely useless. If so, James's argument leaves open a theoretical possibility that is a counterexample to his claims about faith. We needn't fault James's discussion to supplement it to address such a worry, since pastoral advice is sometimes best given with a modicum of impatience for theoretical possibilities that may be functioning as deflectors from more important issues.

The theoretical issue is nonetheless worth considering in its own right, and it deserves noting that there is more to be said on behalf of James's position here. To see why, consider the distinction between the masking of a disposition and the finking of it. A disposition is masked when interfering factors prevent its expression: a match is disposed to light when struck on an appropriate surface, but such a striking under water prevents the disposition from being realized. A disposition is finked when the obtaining of the characteristic triggering conditions for the realization of the disposition results in the loss of that very disposition, thereby explaining the failure for the disposition to be expressed because it no longer exists.

Consider then the possibility of unexpressed faith. While it is easy to imagine unfortunate cases where a faith is simply not very strong and circumstances are always unlucky enough to contain factors that keep the faith from being expressed, one option for defending James's position maintains that when we consider all possible circumstances, there is simply no disposition that can never be expressed in action. It would be like having a glass that one claimed is fragile, but which is incapable of shattering. Moreover, relevant evidence for the existence of a disposition is found in actualizing the relevant triggering conditions, so when every test situation is one where the expected outcome fails to occur, the best judgment to make is that no such disposition exists.

Such a position is attractive to those inclined toward verificationism and its celebrated motto that there is no difference that doesn't make a difference. Less empiricistic approaches, however, will resist, insisting that there can be differences that are simply undetectable. I plant my flag with the latter, so I'm not inclined to defend James's position by verificationist routes. But note that one doesn't need to appeal to verificationism to insist that there is no metaphysical possibility of a disposition whose triggering conditions are necessarily masked. In addition, even if one is not moved toward this conclusion by the example of a fragile but unshatterable glass, there is a further complication that a defender of James's position could appeal to: if you want to resist ruling out dispositions that can't be realized, why not think that the obtaining of relevant triggering conditions wouldn't fink the disposition rather than mask it? Going down this path, we thus are forced to grant the possibility of two different kinds of inexpressible faith: one that is necessarily masked and one that is necessarily finked. Moreover, the difference between the two is also a difference that is undetectable. One needn't have verificationist sympathies to think we now have at least one distinction too many.

Once we get to this point, we can see that the Jamesian attitude toward faith without deeds has fairly serious theoretical credentials, in addition to constituting sound pastoral advice. On the theoretical side, we start from the idea that there isn't a distinction between necessarily masked and necessarily finked dispositions, and we consider an explanation of this claim by the idea that there can't be any such thing as an inexpressible disposition. The challenge to those who want to argue for inexpressible dispositions is to explain the distinction between masked and finked inexpressibles, or try to find some other explanation for there to be no such distinction. The metaphysical contortions needed to take one of the latter routes suggests at least a preponderance of evidence in favor of the simpler hypothesis that inexpressible dispositions can't exist.

We then turn to the contingent circumstances of ordinary life and ordinary religious life, noting the evidential connection between universal masking and finking and the non-existence of the relevant disposition. We can grant the theoretical possibility of such universally masked or finked faith, but once we take into account the character of the one who ordains the circumstances of one's life, one who does not wish any to perish (see I Peter 3:9), we should expect that the testing of one's faith is designed to nurture whatever faith is present and thus for such faith to be realized in action. Taking these factors into account, we can argue that the possibility of dead faith—faith that is worth having because of its connection to salvation—simply will never show up in experience, or at least is so vanishingly improbable as to render the issue otiose. In every case in which we might suspect the presence of faith but notice that it is not expressed in deeds, the best explanation would be that no such disposition is present. For the theology in question makes participation in Kingdom-building part of the divine plan, thereby generating the obtaining of triggering conditions, with an attendant expectation that the building of faith is also part of the divine plan. So when the triggering conditions obtain and characteristic behavior doesn't occur, the conclusion best supported by the evidence is that the relevant disposition is absent.

These points are sufficient to sustain the Jamesian disdain for faith apart from deeds, for it allows us to grant the barest possibility of dead faith (which might still be a kind of faith) without being able to find any examples of faith worth having not expressed through deeds. It is also a conception of faith that is easily characterized in terms of the functional account defended here, and it generates none of the perplexity about the relationship between faith and works that results from the theological perspective of Luther that contrasts justification by faith with justification by works.

As a result, a passage that seemed initially to provide a strong reason for sometimes translating verb forms of *pistis* in terms of the language of belief rather than faith does not in fact provide such a reason. In fact, the tables are turned: the more carefully we inspect the passage and its context, the more reason we have for not using the language of belief to translate and the more reason we have for understanding the passage in terms of the notion of functional faith defended here.

Given these results, a natural question to ask is why do translations tend towards the language of belief when translating terms in the *pistis* group? A first point is simply one of efficiency: when translating a given term, it is cumbersome to use two terms in its place so translations in terms of having faith rather than in terms of believing are not as efficient. But there may be a deeper, more theoretical explanation as well: translating verb forms of *pistis* using the language of belief might simply show how impoverished our folk psychology is about cognition. Folk psychological explanations treat what we do as explicable in terms of various combinations of beliefs and desires. For example, those who have a headache take an analgesic, and we might wonder why they do so. Their behavior is easily explicable in standard folk-psychological categories: they want (desire) to be rid of the headache, and they believe that taking an analgesic will be effective in satisfying that desire. The same explanatory template may also be at work in the standard translations of, for example, the Hebrews passage about drawing near to God and having faith: if we find a person drawing near to God (or trying to), the folk psychological explanation will include wanting to draw near and believing that there is someone to draw near to who would reward attempts to do so. Anyone assuming such a folk psychology, then, would have no trouble replacing occurrences of the verb forms of *pistis* with the language of belief. This possibility of translation influenced by background theoretical assumptions cannot be ignored, and since we have no verb form in English to correspond to the noun 'faith', the search for an appropriate verb for the verb forms that correspond to *pistis* is especially susceptible to the influence of folk psychology.

What if one were convinced that the connections between the life of the mind and human behavior were more complex, however? What if one were convinced that not everything non-cognitive that motivates action can be reduced to (some degree of) desire, and what if one were convinced that not everything that guides action can be explained with reference to what is believed?[10] Then, it would seem, the verb

---

[10] It is worth noting in this context that our best understanding of human decision-making, encoded in standard decision theory, treats human behavior in terms of preference rankings and degrees of belief. There is some plausibility to the suggestion, then, that our best theories of human decision-making have already abandoned the folk-psychological conclusion that human behavior is explicable in terms of belief/desire complexes. What they haven't done, of course, is abandon the simplifying devices that I worry generate theories that are too simplistic.

forms of *pistis* must be translated more cautiously, reflecting that they are verb forms of a noun translated as "faith", and not relying on some background theory that all the cognitive work to be done in explaining behavior involves propositional belief. The best way to do so is to still use the language of faith in both cases, reflecting the obvious feature of the text which draws attention to the connection between the noun and the verb. We might even exploit the rhetorical device of turning a noun into a verb here (the device of antimeria), noting that the language of Scripture ties the faith of a person linguistically to what that person "faiths". We could begin to speak this way as well. We could say, for example, that we faith our positions in philosophy and politics, that Jesus faithed Peter in spite of predicting that Peter would deny him, that Caesar and his followers faithed each other in crossing the Rubicon, or that no matter how many times humanity lets us down, continuing to faith humanity is still to be recommended. Adopting this strategy, we could translate Hebrews 11:6, for example, as "And without faith it is impossible to please God, indeed anyone who comes to him must faith him and that he rewards those who earnestly seek him." The problem with such a translation, however, is that it is one thing to invent a new term and another to use terms already available, and relying on such rhetorical devices would thus be more likely to perplex rather than enlighten.

So a central point to note here is that translations can go wrong not only by erring about the internal features of the language to be translated, but also by relying on a mistaken background theory. We must note that there is no possibility of translation without such dependence, but it is one thing to take one's assumptions into account and acknowledge them and quite another thing to act on them unreflectively. This point and the noted relationship between the noun and verb forms of *pistis* in the Bible converge to show that the language of belief employed in English translations doesn't provide the evidence needed to endorse the received view. To the contrary, a functional understanding of faith provides a very clear understanding of passages in which doxastic language occurs, once we replace that language with the language of faith, understood as the kind of affective faith defended in this work.

Yet, even if the language of belief used in English translations of the Bible fails to justify the received view, the alternative explanations I've given of key passages should not be thought by themselves to compel us to reject the view. For in addition to the language of belief in Scripture, there is also the juxtaposition of faith with doubt, and the natural contrast between the two provides apparent confirmation that discussions of having faith are, at bottom, cognitive, in spite of some reasons to question the use of the language of belief in some of the passages. Moreover, it is a useful strategy to consider natural contrasts of a phenomenon when inquiring about it, for we often learn something important about the nature of a thing by noting its central contrasts. We learn something about humility by contrasting it with pride, something about modesty by contrasting it with vanity. So, in Scripture, what is the relevant contrast with faith? The answer, it would seem, is that faith contrasts with doubt. Once we endorse this claim, we generate an argument for the received view: lack of doubt requires full belief, and so if faith contrasts with doubt, it has a nature involving full belief. We turn, then, in the next section, to this defense of the received view.

5.4.1 Scriptural contrasts to faith

The language of doubt in English conveys the idea of a mental state involving uncertainty, and if we put this together with the idea that doubt is a contrast to faith, we end up with the view that faith requires, not merely belief, but (psychological, subjective) certainty. Such a conception of faith, though quite common in conservative Christianity, is certain to result in self-deception among those who wish to be people of faith, for uncertainty is hardly avoidable. Defenders of the requirement can take refuge in the thought that what is impossible for us is possible for God, with the presence of faith being as impossible as a rope fitting through the eye of a needle but miraculously happening nonetheless.[11]

We need not tread this path of defense, however. One of the hallmarks of Biblical studies of the twentieth century is the uncovering of differences between Hebrew and Greek frames of mind, and seeing the effects of the latter on interpretations of a document that is better understood in terms of the former. Caution is in order, of course, since by the time of New Testament writings, the influence of Greek culture on Jewish culture had been occurring for centuries. Even so, the writings in question are clearly best understood as products of the Abrahamic tradition, so when differences between Hebrew and Greek frames of mind are detected, it is worthy of note. In this regard, consider the remarks about doubt and certainty by Rabbi Akiva Tatz:

> A fascinating insight into the subject of doubt can be gained from examining the root words themselves, as always in Torah. The Hebrew word for doubt is "*safek*," and for certainty, "*vadai*." Amazingly, these commonly-used words are not to be found in the entire biblical writings! Nowhere does the Torah mention the Hebrew forms for doubt or certainty. Both these words are of Rabbinic origin.   (Tatz 1993, ch. 5)[12]

Given this fact and the consistent emphasis of the synoptic Gospels that Jesus was not a fan of oral traditions that added to the Torah, one can begin to wonder concerning those passages that employ the language of doubt to translate remarks by Jesus, what he might have been saying that would justify any Greek language that involves the current conception of doubt that contrasts with certainty. Or, more plausibly, one might begin to wonder whether the terms that are translated in this way might not be best understood in this way. The language of doubt in the New Testament typically involves one of two words translated as "doubt" (*diakrino, distazo*), so one

---

[11] For those preferring the actual Biblical metaphor, trade in the rope for a camel. I use the other metaphor because of an attraction for the plausible speculation that it is the metaphor Jesus used, having been miscopied because of the similarity of the (here transliterated) Greek words for camel and rope: *kamilon* and *kamiilon*. Here, though, the iota's difference isn't theologically significant!

[12] Rabbinic Judaism traces to the time of the *Mishnah*, the first written redaction of the Jewish oral traditions (around 200 CE).

might wonder whether these terms as used really do convey the current conception of doubt and uncertainty.

The most common of the two terms in the New Testament is *diakrino*, and it is used, for example, in James 1:6, where it is translated in the King James Version in terms of wavering: "But let him ask in faith, nothing wavering. For he that wavereth is like a wave of the sea driven with the wind and tossed." Other translations, however, favor using the language of doubt, so that the passage recommends asking in faith, nothing doubting. Regarding the possibility that we misunderstand this Greek term when we see it in terms of doubt and uncertainty, note that a meaning for *diakrino* involving the notion of uncertainty is simply unknown prior to or contemporaneous with the New Testament.[13] This fact provides evidence that the language of uncertainty is not a proper way to understand the use of this term:

> Similarly, in contrasting *diakrino* with words in the *pistis* group, it was not the NT authors' intention to invest *diakrino* with a previously unknown meaning, but rather to ensure that their readers understood *pistis* and [*pisteo*] as meaning "faithfulness" and "loyalty" rather than "certainty about a given proposition."   (De Graaf 2005, p. 739)

Notice that this conclusion about how to understand *diakrino* makes sense of it as a contrast to *pistis* as functionally characterized. If we understand *pistis* as a disposition to respond in service of an ideal, and we understand *diakrino* as a contrast to loyalty and commitment to a cause or person, the two form a natural contrastive pair, in much that same way as pride and humility do. Suffering from *diakrino* results in a weakened commitment to the ideal in question, and thus to a weakened disposition to respond in service of that ideal, and this understanding makes the KJV translation preferable, focusing as it does on wavering in one's commitments as opposed to experiencing some mental uncertainty.

Much the same can be said regarding the translation of *distazo*, the other term translated as "doubt". It is used, for example, in Jesus's remonstrance to Peter for sinking during his walk on the water during the storm: "Oh ye of little faith, why did you doubt (*distazo*)?" A similar conclusion to that above has been defended regarding this term as well, in connection with Matthew 28:17 (the only other place in which this term is used in the New Testament), where translations say of the disciplines, "Some worshiped and some doubted."[14]

A further preliminary is the famous difficulty of 'doubting' (*distazo*, v. 17b), which has brought forth numerous suggestions as to its possible significance here and is generally considered a puzzle. Much of the problem lies in a likely misconstrual of the Greek. The almost universal assumption is that 'doubting' is an alternative to reverent prostration, that is, that some reverently prostrated themselves while others doubted. But there is nothing either in the Greek

---

[13] As documented in Kittel et al. (1964).

[14] In the story in Matthew 28:16–20, where the disciples see Jesus on the shore of the sea of Galilee, and when they arrive on shore, it is reported that "some worshiped but some doubted."

or in the context to warrant this. . . . . All these problems are caused by the assumption that *hoi de edistasan* is meant to introduce a subgroup within the disciples, which then becomes puzzling precisely because of the lack of further reference to it. The problems are resolved by dispensing with the assumption. That is, the sense of the text is that *distazo* characterizes the response of all the disciples. . . .

Thus, one should translate: 'and when they saw him they reverently prostrated themselves. But they were hesitant, and Jesus came up and said to them . . . '

Why then the depiction of the disciples by *distazo*? The only other use of *distazo* in the New Testament is Matthew 14:31, where it is part of Jesus' rebuke to Peter for his failure to respond consistently in his walking on the water to Jesus. The rendering 'doubt' is probably due to its juxtaposition in 14:31 with 'little faith' (*oligopistos*) and the traditional Christian polarity of 'faith' and 'doubt'; but it is unhelpful in either 14:31 or 28:17 because it is likely to imply too much.   (Moberly 2000, p. 192)

There are two important aspects of Walter Moberly's argument here. The first point, and the less important one in our context, concerns the difference between grouping all the disciples together or separating them into subgroups when they are described in terms of worshiping and *distazo*. Moberly claims that no separating element is in the text, and so must be supplied by the translator as the best way to make sense of the passage. Moberly recommends against such supplementation, since the passage can be understood quite well without it. The second point is that the best understanding of *distazo* renders it in terms of 'hesitation' rather than 'doubt', and the translation that he proposes accommodates both of these points. In addition, Moberly suggests that a translation in terms of doubt is theoretically driven by a traditional understanding of the contrast between faith and doubt, and we have already seen how theoretical assumptions can cause problems for translations. Moberly says that the same happens here.

The passage also addresses the other New Testament occurrence of *distazo*, which occurs when Peter begins to sink. Regarding both passages, Moberly remarks that translations in terms of 'doubt' are "likely to imply too much." Though he does not elaborate, it is this argument that deserves careful scrutiny.

Central to the argument is that the term, used in the two places in which it occurs in the New Testament, can generate better understanding of what is being communicated by translating in terms of the language of hesitancy rather than doubt. While it is true that, unlike *diakrino*, there are well-attested uses prior to and outside the New Testament where *distazo* means "doubt," it is also true that this term can be used to refer to hesitating. Notice that the latter is overtly behavioral, while the former meaning refers to a cognitive state. Given our penchant for explaining overt behavior by attributing enduring character traits, it is natural to infer the presence of doubt when observing hesitancy, but the inference should be resisted.[15] Hesitancy can have

---

[15] I note that the very next sentence in the passage from which the Moberly quote above is taken confuses the two: "The sense of *distazo* in each text is that of hesitancy and uncertainty." My point is that even if the

many causes, one of which is uncertainty, but not always and not uniformly enough to make such an assumption when translating. This point is especially significant when it is noted, as Moberly does, that there is a traditional understanding of the polarity of faith and doubt that may play a role in inclining one towards the stronger translation. It is that tradition, however, that is being challenged here, so we should see what happens when we decline the assumption.

Once we so decline, we find evidence in favor of the behavioral notion of hesitancy rather than the mentalistic notion of doubt. The evidence here includes Moberly's discussion of the puzzle in Matthew 28 but also a similar puzzle about Matthew 14. Part of the puzzle in Matthew 28 is that a contrast between worshiping and doubting is not a natural contrast, whereas a contrast between worship and hesitancy is a quite natural contrast. (Of course, if Moberly is right that no groups are being contrasted, we get a natural contrast being used to communicate an informative and perhaps surprising conjunction about the disciples: they both worshiped and displayed hesitancy, a remarkable combination.)

A similar puzzle arises concerning the Matthew 14 narrative. The author of the gospel writes,

But when he saw the wind, he was afraid and, beginning to sink, cried out, "Lord, save me!" Immediately Jesus reached out his hand and caught him. "You of little faith," he said, "why did you doubt?"

Jesus's response here is mysterious. Our folk psychological categories would have us interpret behavior in terms of belief/desire complexes, and here the explanation offered by the author focuses on Peter's fear, which can easily be glossed in terms of an avoidance desire of some sort. So, the authorial explanation is affective in nature: he is afraid of drowning and doesn't want to drown. But then, the author attributes to Jesus a different explanation: you stopped and needed to call out because of uncertainty. The discord between Jesus's perspective and the author's is mysterious. If the first explanation is accurate, it is hard to see why we need the second; and if the second is accurate, it is hard to see why we need the first. Is there really a puzzle here that calls for resolution of some sort, or is the puzzle only apparent, arising because of inaccurate translation?

Let me be quick to point out that the two explanations can both be true, so it is not as if there is any inconsistency between the two explanations. Given the well-entrenched character of folk psychology, though, it would be natural for an author to indicate some awareness of competition between the two explanations. For they can't both be sufficient explanations of the behavior without overdetermining the result, and though such overdetermination is possible, such possibilities are unusual

---

two naturally go together, they need not. And that fact reveals the need for additional argumentation to move from a translation in terms of hesitancy to one in terms of doubt. As I will argue, there is no good reason to do so.

and remarkable. One can try to explain away the puzzling difference between Jesus's remark and the author's claim by pointing out that no matter how natural it would be to notice the puzzle and remark on it, at least indirectly, there is no requirement here, and so we don't need to question the translation simply in order to solve the puzzle. With that point I agree, but if we have independent reason to question the translation, and doing so makes the puzzle disappear, so much the better. And such is the case here.

If we adopt Moberly's recommendation about how to translate *distazo*, we can dissolve this puzzle, for we should then understand the passage in such a way that the contrast Jesus calls attention to is one between faith and hesitating. Peter hesitates, and that results in his need for help. This interpretation resolves any tension between Jesus's explanation of Peter's behavior and the authorial perspective. Jesus's explanation of Peter's call for help is overtly behavioral: "you sank because you hesitated, you wavered in your response to my invitation to walk to me on the water!" We can then consistently note both that Peter needed help because he hesitated, and that he hesitated because he was afraid of drowning. The tension disappears.

This interpretation of the language of doubt in the New Testament also fits naturally with the picture of functional faith involving a disposition to respond to the circumstances of life in service of an ideal. Where the ideal in question involves God and his kingdom, the appropriate contrast to faithful pursuit of this ideal is wavering, hesitating, and shrinking from the task when things become difficult. In such circumstances, the remark "Oh ye of little *pistis*, why did you *diakrino*?" is poignant indeed, whereas anything like "Oh ye of little faith, why were you uncertain?" sounds like a category mistake.

5.4.2 Dispositions to respond

There is a slightly different way to make this same point that also helps us appreciate what is involved in the kind of dispositional faith I am claiming is axiologically fundamental. Being disposed to respond in service of an ideal involves the integration of a wide variety of one's concerns and interests, and so a person of faith, in this sense, is a person with a mental, emotional, and psycho-social life that is integrated in terms of the ideal in question—integrated in a way that generates the disposition noted. But the organizational unity of a life is one thing, and the manifestations of it in thought, action, emotion, and will is another. This point is a straightforward implication of the general nature of dispositions and underlying structure of ordinary objects: a fragile glass is disposed to break when being struck hard with a hammer, but circumstances can be described coherently in which the glass is fragile but when struck hard by a hammer, it does not shatter. Possibilities of this sort, as we have already noted, arise out of the phenomena of masking and finking of dispositions. Masking occurs when there is conflict between dispositions: a match can be disposed to light upon striking, but it can also be disposed not to light when struck while wet. Finking occurs when the triggering circumstances for a given disposition are also triggering conditions for the loss of that disposition.[16] The examples of finking tend to be rather artificial—one might say they are the kinds of cases only a philosopher can love—but here's one.

A very fragile vase is so special to the king that he finds a wizard with special hexing abilities to watch over the vase. He charges him with leaving the vase precisely as it is unless threatened by breakage. The wizard is diligent in his duties (the king is known for rewarding the inept with beheading) and the vase remains undisturbed and thus fragile. Even so, any triggering condition for breakage will result in hexing by the wizard thus rendering the vase unbreakable. The vase is thus disposed to break upon being struck hard by a hammer but this disposition would be lost upon that very triggering condition.

Cases of this sort, those involving masking or finking, cause surprise in those who know of the dispositional character of the object in question. The same is true when the disposition involves persons: when someone known for being prompt is late for an appointment, we are surprised. When faced with such a set of circumstances, one is naturally puzzled: this isn't what we expected! This general phenomenon can occur as well with a disposition to respond in service of an ideal. The internal organization can be fully present, the integration of heart, soul, mind, and strength can be realized in such a way that the disposition is strong, and yet the expected outcomes fail to be realized in circumstances in which faith is tested.

In light of the possibility of the internal organization of a person becoming dissociated from expected and characteristic behavior, we should expect admonitions in favor of the preferred internal organization and cautions against failures of this preferred structure to be displayed. If faith is a disposition to respond in service of an ideal, hesitancy and wavering in particular circumstances will be the unexpected failure for the disposition in question to be realized on a given occasion. Because of such a possibility, the encouragement against wavering or hesitating is a non-redundant complement to encouragements to have faith.

The strength of one's faith, on this approach, is a measure of how resistant that faith is to being finked and masked by the circumstances of life. It is in precisely this sense that the test of Abraham's faith in the Akedah passage is to be understood. The circumstances involved are at the extreme of the kinds of circumstances likely to generate finking and masking of his disposition to respond in service of God, and yet he does so. On more cognitive pictures of faith, such as that of the received view, one searches the Scriptural record in vain for signs of some strength of conviction or belief that God exists, that God is good, that God is to be trusted.[17] To the contrary,

---

[16] The language of finkish dispositions is due to Martin (1994), though the date is misleading—the possibility of such was noted by Martin in the 1970s (on that issue, see Lewis (1997)).

[17] Defenders of this perspective on faith will turn to Hebrews for comfort: "He considered that God is able to raise people even from the dead . . . " (11:19). A few points are in order here. The first is that the passage doesn't say that Abraham's faith consisted in having this attitude, so the passage offers some hope for cognitive portrayals of faith but falls far short of confirming them. Second, even if Abraham agreed

a proper understanding of axiologically fundamental faith can note that the story contains all the details necessary for seeing it as a supreme test of faith: his behavior is an expression of a disposition, and the strength of the disposition is a function of its manifestation in the most dire of circumstances. So understood, it confirms the strength of Abraham's faith in the most direct way possible.

The dispositional character of fundamental faith helps us see why it is a mistake to try to identify particular beliefs and other attitudes that are required for such faith. For Abraham's faithfulness in action to count as a realization of his disposition to respond in service of an ideal, the pattern of response has to be an instance of a certain pattern. It is important to note, though, that the pattern is multiply realizable by a wide variety of underlying intentional states and attitudes. We are familiar with this phenomenon from our understanding of human behavior. The underlying cognitive, affective, and conative states that can generate the same overt behavior are quite indeterminate. The taking of an analgesic when experiencing a headache can occur whether or not a person believes that taking an analgesic will get rid of the headache; it can also occur whether or not one wants to get rid of a headache. We might expect the behavior to result from believing or desiring in this way, but if we adjust the other mental components sufficiently, we can still see why a person might take the pill in spite of not believing it will be effective. For example, consider a young army recruit so indoctrinated by basic training that he'll do whatever he's told (unless moral scruples intrude). He might believe the pill won't help and still take it. Or think of someone who likes headaches of a mild sort, but doesn't want other people to know of this weirdness. The variety of ways that a given action can be associated with various prompting conditions is open-ended and wide indeed.

Just so with the disposition to respond in service of an ideal. This disposition is multiply realizable. What matters is that the responses fall into a pattern of the sort that counts as an instance of that disposition. Once we begin to see faith in this way, we no longer need to pretend that only those experiencing no cognitive uncertainty can be people of faith, any more than we need to pretend that only very specific kinds of intentions and feelings are compatible with faith. Even in the most impressive displays of faith in God, as in the Akedah passage, we don't need to go beyond the text and impute to Abraham some conclusive conviction that God exists and can be trusted, nor do we need to attribute to Abraham some total trust in God. What matters is that whatever level of trust he had and whatever he was thinking, his behavior constitutes a display of a disposition to respond in service of an ideal, a specific combination that

that God's power extends to raising the dead, that belief doesn't really help with the moral horror of the experience of receiving a divine command to sacrifice Isaac. One still has to plunge the knife and take a life, and the horror of that remains even if the son is brought back from the dead afterwards. Finally, the belief about the power of God doesn't actually get us to the cognitivists' favored cognitive attitude, to the claim that God is good and to be trusted. A belief about God's power is not yet a belief about God's goodness. (I hasten to add that I don't wish to deny that Abraham had the beliefs in question; I'm only arguing that attempts to defend a cognitive picture of faith have to read more into the Scriptural record than is actually there, unlike the approach I am taking in terms of axiologically fundamental faith.)

falls within a range of possible combinations, all of which are specific realizations of the general disposition.

A further complication which I will note but not pursue at length concerns the individuation conditions for patterns and dispositions. We individuate dispositions in terms of patterns of response, but doing so requires some way of individuating combinations of responses as being of the same type. It is clear that pattern sameness doesn't require identity of actions that are part of the pattern. For example, baseball players follow a preparatory pattern before entering the batter's box, but not every detail of the preparation needs to be identical for two occasions of preparation to instance the same pattern. Instead, what we look for is some high degree of overall similarity. This point holds when we move to the response patterns by which we individuate dispositions. Two pieces of glassware can both be fragile, even though the response patterns upon being struck by a hammer are not identical. So when we identify the presence of functional faith in two different individuals, we must leave room for the faith to be the same even in the face of different response patterns, including the precise combinations of affective, cognitive, and conative components. Exactly how wide the variations can be isn't a topic we need to explore in depth at this point, but it is important to notice that sameness at the functional level involves some account of pattern individuation that falls short of strict identity of components in the pattern.

Returning to the main point being pursued here, we can thus see that there is little cause to think of religious faith and Christian faith in particular as requiring a kind of faith that cannot be defended as axiologically fundamental. Just as with more mundane faith, one can embrace an account of axiologically fundamental faith that meshes nicely with a defense of faith as a virtue.

Once we see the attraction of such a functionalist account, we can anticipate counterexamples to every attempt to cite particular features of a person—cognitive, affective, or conative—that must be present in order for a person to count as a person of faith, even axiologically fundamental faith of the sort a religion might say is saving faith. Once we adopt such a frame of mind, we can see where to look for such counterexamples, but perhaps more importantly, we have a theoretical stance from which to correct the practice of listing pieces of doctrine that one must affirm in order to count as a person of (Christian) faith.

Moreover, thinking of faith in these terms has an additional advantage of changing the focus of the long and (to my mind) unproductive discussion of the relationship between faith and reason. I take up this issue in the next section.

5.5 Faith and Reason

The typical, cognitive approach to faith leads directly into classic discussions of the problem of faith and reason, where the issue is whether items of faith can survive epistemic scrutiny. The path to this question arises directly from a prior identification of faith with a kind of belief that has doctrinal commitments as content. The discussion then focuses around arguments for and against the existence of God, since that claim would seem to be a common presupposition for at least a vast majority of the doctrinal claims in question, as well as around the prior question "what hath reason to do with argument?".

Things look quite different when it is functional faith that is under consideration. First, religious faith is but one small part of a much wider and more general phenomenon, and second, the more general phenomenon is not to be identified with nor requires any particular propositional beliefs, no matter how generic a specification is given to the propositional component. Any particular example of such faith will have some underlying substrate that will typically involve an assortment of cognitive, affective, and cognitive states, but as with functional items in general, changes in one underlying component can be compensated for by changes in other components. The same points hold true even when discussing specifically propositional faith even of a religious sort: we will need to find the propositional element in some of the underlying states, but the functional state itself is still capable of multiple realizability.

Given this different perspective, the problem of faith and reason, conceived of as a problem about the epistemic standing of various religious beliefs, devolves into a question about the epistemic standing of certain beliefs held by some or most people of religious faith, but that problem is not a problem of faith and reason, any more than there is a concern about some inherent conflict between European ethnicity and reason. There are beliefs common among many people from this geographic region and many of them may have difficulty surviving epistemic scrutiny. But such a fact, if it is one, would reveal no inherent conflict of any interesting sort between reason and some specific ethnicity. All it would show is that there are lots of people with irrational beliefs, not exactly a shocking revelation and certainly not a situation in which one might expect some analogue of the New Atheists[18] to arise, counseling everyone to do whatever they can to rid the world of European ethnicity.

Think again of our young Little Leaguer, despondent after giving up a game-winning home run and resolving never to let that happen to him again. In the days, weeks, months, and years to come, we find him practicing diligently, focusing his routine—exercise, sleep, diet, etc.—around the project of being a better pitcher, and in the process expresses the kind of faith that involves a disposition to act in service of an ideal. One thing leaps out about such faith: it is obvious that such mundane faith is often a good thing, and anyone who begrudges our young Little Leaguer such faith and its effects deserves remonstrance. We owe people our full support in their pursuits of such hopes and dreams, or at least the hands-off stance of not working

---

[18] I am thinking of critics of religion such as Christopher Hitchens, Sam Harris, Daniel Dennett, and Richard Dawkins. Representative works include Dawkins (2006), Dennett (2006), Harris (2004), and Hitchens (2007).

to undermine their efforts. Of course, if we change the example sufficiently, we get different assessments: if the goal is to become the greatest dragon-killer of all time, the unrealistic character of the goal calls for intervention of some sort. But such is not the case in our Little Leaguer example. Nor are the values implicit in trying to be a great pitcher sufficiently problematic to warrant concern, even for those dismissive of a culture that places inordinate value on athletic accomplishments. Even relatively unimportant projects, such as amassing the largest stamp collection in history, or surfing the largest wave on record, or growing the largest pumpkin, can involve mundane faith to which opposition is generally inappropriate.

The point of this discussion, then, is to point to the tolerance and respect that such expressions of faith deserve. We should acknowledge the indefinite variety of forms of the good life, granting the usefulness and need of such mundane faith, and refraining from chastisement except in extreme cases. The mere fact that you place no value whatsoever on being a great pitcher is irrelevant. Of course, if you are convinced that the goals are repulsive and disgusting, then perhaps something must be done. Most likely, though, it is something that must be done about you, not the young pitching prospect.

My point is not simply to insult, but to call attention to the extreme difficulty of life without such mundane faith. One might even say, though I will not defend it here, that there is no such thing as a good life without it. But whether or not there can be a good life without such affective faith, it would be deeply mistaken to suggest that faith of this type is morally, practically, or epistemically deficient. So, if the epistemic complaints of the New Atheists—the belittlers of religious faith—are to be defensible at all, they must be on the basis of crucial and important contrasts between such mundane faith and religious faith. I turn, then, to the question of the relationship between the two and whether there is something about the distinction that generates some conflict with reason.

5.5.1 Mundane faith and religious faith

We can move from mundane faith to religious faith by first enlarging the scope of the projects, plans, and purposes that might be adopted. For mundane faith can be exhibited about the most trivial of interests, and a person might clutter a life with a wide variety of such projects and plans. Such a person might do so with a metaplan in mind as well: that a life full of a variety of interests is what makes for a full and flourishing life.

Even so, neither the presence of mundane faith, nor the presence of mundane faith attached to a metaplan is to be counted as religious faith. I will make no attempt here to give a full and complete characterization of religious faith, one that separates it from every other kind of faith, but it is important, in assessing the complaints of those who wish to criticize religious faith in particular, to move as close as we can toward what religious faith involves. The first step is the one noted, that religious faith has a kind of all-encompassing character to it. This feature is one it shares with purely moral faith, as well as the philosophical faith found in the Stoics and Epicureans, and the utopian faith of certain forms of Marxism.

So, let us ask what kinds of questions and complaints might be lodged against such persons, without impropriety. Well, not quite, since human beings have a nearly infinite capacity for generating new kinds of criticisms; we are, as Ernest Sosa has pointed out, "zestfully judgmental."[19] So let's distinguish between central and important criticisms of a way of life, and all the rest (never mind that there will be no agreement on which category a given criticism falls into—I'll simply appeal to the reader's good judgment on this score). So we might criticize the Stoic for lacking a proper interest in pizza, and the Marxist for lacking a proper respect for scuba diving. And both criticisms might be exactly right. They are nonetheless irrelevant. Instead, the proper response on hearing such a criticism is an eyebrow raised toward the one bringing the criticism, or at least a soft chuckle at the distortion of values required to view such a lack as important.

We thus need to focus on criticisms that focus on what truly matters, and here it is worth noting the impropriety of criticism of the affective source in question and the values involved in the faith that results. Ameliorating the amount of suffering in the world is noble and admirable, and working toward happiness and fulfillment by lessening the amount of distress caused by the proliferation of desires we are all subject to is also a good thing. Moreover, devoting one's life to the pursuit of such goals is, from an affective point of view at least, hard to criticize. Such devotion to important things is itself a thing of beauty and inspiration.

Of course, there are other commitments to a way of life, prompted by the affections, that may produce a bit more consternation. One might aim at becoming the consummate Parisian upon being overwhelmed by the beauty of the place; one might, in more ancient times, become attached to Rome because of the ideals it embodies. One might also find the beauty of nature strong enough that one devotes one's life to its preservation, or one might find science itself to be such an astounding human accomplishment that allegiances are formed with the enterprise of such strength and fervor that the life that results can only be properly characterized by the language of fidelity and faith. For each of us, some of these expressions of faith that involve the full integration of a personality with teleological purposes, both first-order and higher-order, will strike us as unseemly, perplexing, and difficult to understand. But at the same time, it is a smallness of spirit to insist that the desires of the heart have to match or overlap significantly with one's own to make any sense, a failure with respect to magnanimity, and it is a failure of imagination to be unable to appreciate the vast variety of forms of the good life.

My point here is not meant to render free from criticism every way of life involving morally neutral passional elements. We may point out, for example, that some such lives are incomplete; that they are missing out on important goods, even if organized

---

[19] Sosa (2007, p. 70).

around desires of the heart that are either neutral or good in themselves; that the ideal human life involves aspects that are being ignored in lives of such truncated dimensionality.

Note, however, the category into which these critiques fall. They are not about the cognitive dimensions of such expressions of faith, but rather about the affective dimensions involved. As such, there is little room here for talk of epistemic impropriety or defect, for such talk is only appropriate when focusing on the cognitive dimensions of a way of life. So, if we are looking for ways in which epistemic impropriety or defect might be an appropriate charge to raise against certain types of faith, we will have to identify first which cognitive commitments are involved in a life of faith of the sort being described.

Returning to the cases of utopians and Stoics, let us ask how to go about identifying the cognitive elements involved in such a life of faith, in order to determine whether any such elements are epistemically inappropriate or defective. What exactly are those cognitive aspects? What cognitive dimensions are required of our Marxist or Stoic?

A natural answer here is this: you have to believe some version of Marxism or Stoicism. So tell us which version you believe and we'll go from there.

But this response is inadequate in the context of assessing general charges about the unacceptability of religious faith. The goal here is to raise the possibility that the cognitive dimensions of a way of life and the faith it embodies might involve epistemic difficulties. For that purpose, it is not enough to find some expressions of such a way of life to be problematic. Instead, one must identify certain cognitive features as essential to that way of life, and then find these essential features to be epistemically troubling.

My hope is that the examples of pursuing *ataraxia* through *apatheia*, and pursuing the alleviation of human misery through a utopian construction make clear how difficult it is to say precisely which cognitive commitments such ways of life require. And to that extent, it is equally difficult to find generic epistemic criticisms of such ways of life that are appropriate. That is not to say that there are not appropriate criticisms of specific individuals who have embarked on such a way of life, but the issue here is the way of life itself and not particular embodiments of it. Shall we say that a utopian must believe that the achievement of the utopian ideal would usher in an era in which all misery has been eliminated? That would be a silly position: why would a utopian have to be so oblivious as to think that natural disasters such as tornados, forest fires, hurricanes, and the like would either disappear or have no negative consequences for human beings were the utopian ideal achieved? Must a Stoic believe that it is possible to have no desires whatsoever? Surely not. The way of life is a path toward greater fulfillment, and the path involves the pursuit of *apatheia*, a pursuit that can lead to increasing levels of fulfillment even if it is impossible to achieve the absence of all desires of any sort (as well as any other affective states that might lead to the loss of tranquility).

Perhaps the criticism should be that the goals in question will not or cannot be achieved. Well, the modal claim is surely unsustainable, and the charge of the ways of life being unrealistic does not penetrate deeply. For no way of life needs to hang its respectability on likelihood of success: to insist otherwise is to miss the fundamental role that hopes and dreams play in the expressions of faith involved. Such hopes and dreams may be dashed in the end, but such is life, and it is a particular way of giving in to despair to insist on pursuing no goal that one is not likely to achieve.

5.5.2 The cognitive dimensions of religious faith

Are things relevantly different when we limit our gaze to the religious landscape itself? Here I will focus discussion on Christian faith, even though much of what I say here will have wider application to most if not all religious faith. Given the understanding of faith and what we have learned by considering non-religious expressions of it, we can insist that religious faith can be of the kind I am describing, a kind of faith that arises from the affections, as described above. Perhaps it arises from the sublime and terrible experience of being thrown from a horse on the road to Damascus; it may arise from the apparent majesty and greatness of spirit found in a prophet or shaman or holy man of a particular religious tradition; it could arise from experiencing the beauty of creation and the moments of pure joy at its wonders; or it might be the darker experiences of misery and despair and injustice that cry out for a ray of hope and somehow receive it. Such affective sources are surely as immune from criticism as any similar source that gives rise to secular ways of life and the kind of faith they embody.

My point here is to insist that it is a shallow understanding of faith that does not recognize the possibility of such fundamentally affective faith, both in terms of source and sustenance. So, we must consider, given that criticism of a life of faith that is fundamentally affective in source and sustenance can gain no decent foothold within the passional dimensions themselves, whether there are certain unavoidable cognitive accoutrements to such an affective faith that are worthy of criticism.

By now, I'm sure many belittlers will be impatient: "Isn't it obvious that to be a Christian, and thus to display Christian faith, one has to believe that God exists,[20] must believe that Jesus is God's Son,[21] must believe a host of other things in order for the faith in question to be *saving faith*; so even if there is an affective faith of the sort described, it is not the faith that is essential to being a Christian." And not only belittlers will say such things—such language is ubiquitous among Christians themselves. So, it would seem, if the target of the belittlers is the particular doctrinal commitments that are standard fare here, the targets would seem to be fair game: they are precisely the sorts of things that even Christians themselves treat as essential.

As we have seen, however, there are good reasons to be hesitant to endorse the doxastic requirement in the impatient reply above, in spite of the fact that it is a

---

[20] "And without faith it is impossible to please God, because anyone who comes to him must believe that he exists and that he rewards those who earnestly seek him." (Heb. 11:6, New International Version)

[21] "Whoever believes in him is not condemned, but whoever does not believe stands condemned already because he has not believed in the name of God's one and only Son." (John 3:18, New International Version)

quite common presupposition about what Christian faith involves. It is a theoretically inelegant story to focus on *belief* in its modern sense when describing Christian faith and the life of the believer. Central to the message of Jesus is that true life is found in moving away from a central concern for self and following him. Though there is much more to the story of Christianity than the paradoxes of the Kingdom,[22] these paradoxes cut to the heart of a central and basic point in the message of Jesus, and this ideal of selflessness simply isn't about belief in the modern sense. If we begin with the idea that the central essential feature of being a follower of Jesus has to do with losing one's life rather than seeking it and in terms of servanthood rather than a pursuit of power, fame, fortune, or even honor and glory, it is hard to see how to fit talk of belief in the modern sense into this picture. For the topic of discussion isn't cognitive; instead, it is about one's cares and concerns, desires and motivations. With respect to this feature of being among the faithful, even entrenched atheists can be included. For here we find, not concepts such as truth and falsity, evidence and its lack, but what we find attractive, what is beautiful, what we adore, and that for which we wish, hope, and long.

Moreover, such a description fits nicely and is the natural offspring of a fundamentally affective faith of the sort being described here. Whether the motivational source is in a sense of guilt and shame, or in an experience of overwhelming beauty and goodness in a person, the natural expression of such an experience is a commitment to the good and the right and the just, together with a sense of urgency both for oneself and other people that we all not miss out on something of great importance. It is a life directed toward certain moral and religious ideals, and involves a turning away from a life directed toward the self in pursuit of fame, fortune, and the goods of this world.

The critic will be impatient again, however, this time with the failure to address the central question of the content of various cognitive states, whether or not accurately characterized in terms of our modern notion of belief. The complaint still is that there are various cognitive commitments that cannot be avoided, if one is to be among the Christian redeemed. Among those contents are those listed above: that God exists, that Jesus is God's Son, that he lived and died to secure our redemption, etc.

Recall, however, that the issue is more generic than the question of who self-identifies as a follower of Jesus. The question is rather, from the Christian point of view, when is saving faith present and when isn't it, and it is clear that one can possess saving faith and never have heard about Jesus. That is precisely the point of giving the saints of old—Abraham, Isaac, Jacob, and all the rest—their due. To avoid misunderstanding, let me point out that affective faith and the way of life embodying it will always involve cognitive commitments of one sort or another—how could it not? The point, however, is that the precise nature of those cognitive commitments is quite indeterminate. There

---

[22] Included are claims such as these: the last shall be first and the first last, he who wishes to be great must be the servant of all, it is in dying that we live, those who find their life will lose it and those who lose their lives for Jesus's sake will find it, etc.

is no ready answer, in general, for the question, "What precise propositional contents must a person believe or cognitively endorse in order to be saved?"

My point here is not, nor does it rely on, the banal point that the range of adherents of the Christian religion runs from the most conservative fundamentalism to the most liberal theologies, or even atheologies. Even from the point of view of the most right-wing, inerrantist Evangelicalism, the case can be made that there is no ready answer here.

Part of the attraction of this affective picture is that it can make sense of such indeterminacy. For even if it is in some sense required that one come at some point to believe certain things and to adopt a particular cognitive perspective on all there is and one's place in it, it would be a strange gospel to impose this requirement in the backtracking fashion that insists that what must be true in the end in order to be saved must be true now in order to be being saved. It is, in a phrase, a confusion between process and product, between the path and the destination.

Furthermore, it is a more fitting picture of the Christian life to think of cognitive commitments as arising through the process of being saved, rather than being imposed by religious authority from the outset. At the heart of Jesus's message about following him is an emphasis on motivation and intention rather than on product, and his initial followers had no good idea what a commitment to him would involve, either in terms of practical consequences or cognitive commitments. Why initial commitments and faithful follow-through should have changed so dramatically since then is beyond me to fathom. In particular, the idea that one must believe a certain set of doctrines, independent of coming to see them as true from a love of truth, is baffling.

Even the most theologically conservative must grant this point regarding the cognitive development that occurred with Jesus's disciples during his lifetime and with the early church as it sought to sort out orthodox positions on central doctrines of the Christian faith. It shows a smallness of spirit to think that Nestorians, for example, are damned because of their beliefs. The most that could plausibly be claimed here is that there will be no Nestorians in heaven—by the time they get there, they will have seen the light. A simple version of such a point might appeal to a spiritual analogue of the slogan that ontogeny recapitulates phylogeny: one should expect the possibility of the individual maturation process to take the form of whatever process of doctrinal maturation occurred in the course of salvation history. But a more general point can be made, mirroring the failure of the slogan in question in the scientific context: the variability of individual maturation has no particular doctrinal or cognitive boundaries, whether or not tested in the course of religious history.

Seen in this way, the process in question may involve the affective faith I am focusing on, and the cognitive aspects of such ways of life may vary considerably.[23] Is

[23] Perhaps something stronger can be affirmed, though I won't defend it here. Perhaps religious faith, or the only religious faith worth respecting, is that which arises in the contrast between the faithful pursuit of the self, through seeking honor, or glory, or fame, or riches, and the faithful pursuit of the good. In

there anything within this variability that is suitable as a target for the attacks of the belittlers? I turn to this question in the next section.

5.5.3 An alternative story about the role of cognition in a life of affective faith

Begin with a central example of truly admirable faith. Consider Abram, who is told to leave Haran and go to a foreign land. He does so in commitment to a certain way of life, and it counts as an expression of saving faith. What propositional contents must he have believed in order for this story to make sense? Did he have to believe that God exists? I expect he did so believe, but the same story could have been true if he had only been disposed to believe such, or disposed not to believe the denial, or if he had merely mentally assented to the claim and was determined to behave in accord with the assumption or presupposition that God exists. So I assume Abram was a theist, both before and after leaving Ur, but it is hard to see why that is required for the story. After all, the story is about being faithful to a perceived directive from God, and the credit that ensues is a function of this faithfulness. The contrast to faith of this type is not doubt or disbelief, but change of direction, loss of heart, and weariness of spirit, a failing to follow through on what one sees in terms of what is worth pursuing or, even stronger, what is required of one. And it is obviously possible for a person to commit to a certain way of life, fully and wholeheartedly, while finding belief beyond them—all they have is hopes and dreams and possibilities.

We must grant, of course, that such lives of faith are not the norm. The human drive of curiosity aims at systems of understanding of what there is and our place in it,[24] and the ordinary human experience is to satisfy that drive by drinking deeply from one's current culture and those who have come before. So when one fully embraces an ideal, such as becoming a follower of a certain person, and there is a long history of other people who have taken the same path, the ordinary human experience will involve adopting the traditional system of understanding developed by one's forefathers in the faith, and the human predilection for fixation of belief typically results in an adoption that takes the form of belief rather than mere assent or some lesser state of intellectual commitment. Furthermore, the historical development of

ages and places where theism can be assumed, this distinction is that between faithful pursuit of a theism as talisman, hoping for more rain and better hunting, and the ethical monotheism characteristic of, but not limited to, the Abrahamic tradition. When theism is no longer assumed, an adequate philosophical soteriology ought to begin from the fundamental distinction between seeking a talisman and seeking the good, often involving a commitment to ideals connected in some way with the feelings of being forgiven and accepted and belonging or of being one with or in accord with something unspecifiable, and being thankful (when no particular object can be cognitively identified as intentional object of such emotions). It is for that reason that one can think of nontheists as falling under the rubric I choose: affective theism. (But this point should not be confused with a closely related point, that religious faith worth respecting is nothing more than a purely moral faith: to draw that conclusion would confuse process and state just as much as what I've accused cognitive pictures of faith of doing.)

[24] For defense and explanation of this view of curiosity and the fundamental role in cognition of the goal of understanding, see Kvanvig (2013b).

Judaeo-Christian theology makes the experience of injustice and the responses of faithfulness in standing against it central to the development of the central platitudes of the Christian religion concerning the fallenness of the natural order, the possibility of redemption, and the hope of a life to come. It is in the crucible of reprehensible moral monstrosities of human history that the pursuit of religious ideals comes to be tested and fallenness experienced. The development of theological perspectives emphasizing the possibility of redemption and hope of a life to come can be seen as natural cognitive responses that express the continued disposition toward a way of life that involves the affective faith in question, in opposition to the despair and despondency and loss of such faith displayed in cognitive responses that conclude that we are on our own. In the process of making sense of the totality of experience presented to us, optionality reigns in the range of experimental attitudes a person might take in the all-things-considered rational pursuit of understanding the world and our place in it.

But belief in such a system of understanding is never to be confused with what is essential for a way of life expressing the kind of affective faith under discussion here. Such is the nature of the human experience: to approach life experimentally, sorting when to defer to one's culture and associates and when to demur. In this grand experiment to make sense of the world and our place in it, we adjust across time on what weight to give to which sources of information, and at every moment of decision regarding such, the options are wide and broad—that is the lesson of the Quine–Duhem thesis.[25] This fundamentally pragmatic process results in various changes to total cognitive state, some of which involve belief formation and change, and others of which involve intellectual commitments that need not be doxastic in character. One might, in a thoroughly experimental fashion, engage in mental assents of a strong form, perhaps with the expectation that such engagement will likely result in doxastic commitments of some form in the future. One may think such non-doxastic commitments are rare among, say, conservative Christians, but I suspect that a nuanced psychology here will find this experience rather widespread. There is the Shakespearean suspicion here that protesting too much is a useful indication that we don't have the whole story, and too much adamant bluster about various doctrinal points may be an indication of a commitment to a point of view that one doesn't quite (or fully) believe.

Moreover, the standard narrative on faith creates cognitive dissonance in those for whom the life of faith is a life of affective faith of the sort I'm focusing on here. For the standard, doxastic narrative is presupposed to such an extent that it is hardly noticed how it fails to cohere with the more natural narrative of affective faith and a story of cognitive commitments arising out of it. As a result, self-deception becomes highly likely among people of affective faith, with reaction formations against the

---

[25] See Quine (1951); I discuss and defend this Epistemic Optionalism in Kvanvig (2011c, 2013d,c).

very idea of apostasy forcing one to endorse with greater and greater vehemence the standard doctrines required on the standard narrative. And perhaps that narrative, presupposed deeply enough, can have the desired effect, the effect of getting people standardly to believe what they have been told they must believe to be saved.

Regardless of how common it is for beliefs of a particular kind to be present or absent, epistemic criticism of the cognitive dimension here cannot make any blanket assumptions about what the essential cognitive elements are concerning expressions of affective faith. In the process of finding ways of life compelling or attractive, it may be true that we express affective faith at least initially in ways that exemplify whatever systems of understanding are ready to hand, and it would be strange fruit of the tree of epistemology to find that such reliance on testimony and community always and everywhere, or even typically, is irrational.

It is worth noting the essentially pragmatic role played by the drive for understanding as well as the interest in full integration of cognition with affection. We should expect a fundamentally affective origin to yield cognitive fruit and efforts at systematic understanding that cohere with such affective features. In the process, it can be fully rational to adopt points of view that fail to pass epistemic scrutiny, much as we might find among scientists committed to a certain research program, whether a dying one or one that merely shows some promise. And all of this, without mentioning the ways in which our typical philosophical views, and especially our epistemic views on what it takes to survive suitable epistemic scrutiny, fail to measure up to the standards of knowledge in more mundane contexts.

Given this background, it becomes easy to see what kinds of opposition by belittlers would be appropriate and what kinds would not. The moral offense taken by the belittlers at much of the historical behavior of Christians[26] is an offense all should share, religious or not, and the strongest expression of contempt for such behavior is appropriate. If affective religious faith led inexorably to such, no further criticism would be needed.

In addition, even some forms of belligerence are appropriate for the standard cognitive accouterments of typical expressions of faith, especially in the context of Christianity in America. Bobby Jindal has claimed that Republicans must cease being "the stupid party,"[27] and similar advice is sorely needed among conservative Christians. The belittlers are not alone in experiencing consternation at the current state of religion in America, but it is equally true that it is not a criticism of the life of faith as such to point out the indefensibility of certain beliefs held by vast swaths of contemporary Christians.

My rebuke of the belittlers is thus not one that focuses on questions of truth or falsity when it comes to the beliefs and other cognitive attitudes of Christians or of any examples of faith. What is distinctive about the attacks of the belittlers is that

---

[26] See in particular Hitchens (2007).
[27] 26 January 2013 at the Republican National Committee retreat in Charlotte, North Carolina.

there is something lacking from a normative perspective in such examples. Charges of irrationality and the like form the core of the criticisms. It is this core that I am opposing, not the related but distinct issue concerning alethic matters. On the latter issues of truth and falsity, the discussion is and should remain open. What I resist is the idea there is some additional normative and distinctively epistemic criticism of lives of religious faith *in general* that can be sustained. If the criticisms were only concerning what is true and what is false, no rebuke of any sort would be appropriate.

The central point, then, is this. The critiques raised by the belittlers are orthogonal to the way of life at which they are directed. It is a fundamental misunderstanding of the life of faith, at least when involving the affective faith I'm focusing on here, to draw conclusions about the propriety or rationality or justification of religion as such or Christianity in particular on the typical grounds given by critics such as Dawkins, Dennett, Harris, and Hitchens. Written in the tradition of concern over the clash of faith and reason, all such approaches think of faith as something belief-like or at least requiring quite specific cognitive commitments, so that the central question about religious faith is whether the beliefs involved can be held rationally. And then the question of whether religious faith makes any kind of sense turns into the question of whether adequate grounds can be found for these beliefs. By contrast, if my description of a life of faith is where we start the discussion, there will be no specific cognitive contents that can be identified as the ones that are both epistemically problematic and essential to affective faith as such. On the picture of faith developed here, people of this kind of (religious) faith might include various kinds of skeptics and agnostics regarding the existence of God and any or all of the central claims of the major world religions. That is, one can commit to a certain ideal, even to being an unconditional follower of Jesus or Mohammed or whatever, without any of the standard cognitive attitudes of ordinary folk on such paths, and still be a person of faith—on the straight and narrow—in spite of one's cognitive uncertainties and confusions. The faith in question is a function of the depth of commitment to the chosen path and the disposition or orientation that leads to following through on such an unconditional commitment. As such, epistemic criticisms that attempt universal destruction of the rationality of people of faith cannot succeed. There will, instead, only be piecemeal criticisms to be raised about particular cognitive and affective combinations, and no such criticisms could possibly sustain such blanket judgments as that religion poisons everything.

5.6 Conclusion

The view I have been characterizing and defending allows for a quite wide variety of cognitive stances compatible with Christian faith. One can almost say that the account here resists the cognitive picture by accusing it of a scope fallacy. The affective picture allows that for every instance of Christian faith, there will be, or come to be, beliefs or other cognitive commitments of some type and intensity present; but that it is false that there are some types of belief of some intensity which are present in every instance of Christian faith. Once this new picture of faith is in place, the belligerence of the belittlers is hard to fathom, and the standard discussions of the problem of faith and reason become otiose. Against particular lives of faith and the particular beliefs held, criticism, including epistemic criticism, is certainly warranted. Here I'm on the side of the belittlers. But in any kind of sweeping, general way, there could be no epistemic grounds for rejecting the very idea of religious faith, any more than there could be for rejecting the very idea of mundane faith.

We are thus in a position to conclude that functional faith is widespread, deserving of tolerance and praise, and not the sort of thing that calls for a robust body of literature contrasting faith and reason. This kind of faith has another benefit, however, for it plays an essential, interactive role with other virtues that are central to the good life, in spite of a capacity to distort a life when present in isolation. I have in mind, specifically, the virtue of humility, which I want to defend as a virtue, and in a way that requires the balancing virtue of faith for it to be an asset to the pursuit of the good life. To that topic we turn in the next chapter.

6

Faith, Humility, and Virtues in Isolation

6.1 Introduction

Faith worth having is a virtue, and as developed over the course of this work, it is a character trait under the guidance of the executive function of the will to contribute to a good life. This executive function balances the role of each of the virtues to contribute to such a life, and though this process is holistic, there are generalities regarding different virtues that this holistic process encodes. Some pairs of virtues are complementary—for example, justice and mercy, or honesty and tact. When we find such pairs, each of them protects against the drawbacks of the other, where the expression of a virtue in excess leads to a more disvaluable state than not having that virtue at all. Tact in excess, for example, leads to lying and deception, and mercy unqualified leads to never holding anyone responsible for anything.

These facts lead some to question whether there are any character traits that are valuable in themselves. Strong versions of such a concern lead to a strong Platonic thesis about the unity of the virtues: that there simply is no such thing as having a given virtue in isolation from having every virtue. Others qualify the virtues so that the virtue of tact, for example, isn't a matter of finding ways to say things without hurting others' feelings, but rather a matter of doing things in this way when it is the right thing, or a good thing, to do.

A better approach, however, acknowledges that being virtuous is intrinsically and instrumentally valuable even though in some cases, the virtues expressed lead to bad consequences and wrong behavior. So even though the thesis about the unity of the virtues is false, there is pressure toward the idea that what makes the virtues matter is a holistic fact about the virtues in combination being under the control of the executive function of the will, or to use a more ancient term, to be under the direction of *phronesis*, or wisdom.[1]

Here I endorse such a holism about the connection between the virtues and the good life, acknowledging that the virtues in isolation can easily undermine human flourishing. This fact leads directly to a need for a non-holistic component in our

---

[1] This role for theoretical wisdom is articulated and developed in Linda Zagzebski (1996).

theory of the virtues to supplement the holistic point above. Virtues have an upside and a downside, and the downside calls for a compensating virtue to neutralize the possible negative effects of the virtue unchecked. As I will explain, virtues have an intrinsic but defeasible value, and the possibility of defeat requires a kind of holism that can include the entire range of virtues but can also involve a kind of atomistic selectivity so that the proper balance needed is primarily a function of individual virtues that complement each other.

In this chapter, I will argue that affective faith and humility stand in this balancing relation to each other, so that these virtues in equilibrium are crucial for the intrinsic value of each to contribute to a life that is, all things considered, a good life. A defense of this point requires two aspects. The most obvious one is a defense of the value of both faith and humility, and though we have seen a defense of the former, we also need a defense of the latter. On that score, the history of discussion has been significantly mixed, for many have doubted the idea that humility is a virtue (apart from some quite specific religious contexts—as Hume puts it, it is a "monkish" virtue at best (Hume 1777 [1748], Section 219)). Part of the skepticism here is that there is a significant downside to humility, so I will begin our discussion of the virtue of humility with this argument to the contrary, the argument from the disadvantages of humility.

Central to the argument I will develop for maintaining that humility is a virtue is an appeal to the holism noted above involving also a more atomistic element that finds in faith worth having an appropriate complement to humility. This combination can look theoretically perplexing, however, and even impossible: you can have holism or you can have atomism, but you can't have both. So the second aspect of my defense of this complementarity thesis is an explanation of how the holism and atomism can co-exist. I begin, though, with the question of whether humility is in fact a virtue.

6.2 Is Humility Bad for You?

There is significant empirical literature on the practical value of arrogance. Arrogant people, full of self-confidence and *hubris*, believing in their own capacities to make the world conform to their desires, succeed in getting what they want at a significantly higher rate than the less arrogant. Many of these same people, once having achieved high status, extol the value of humility when speaking of what they value in co-workers, and it is easy to be cynical in response: part of the story of how the arrogant get to be so highly successful is that they can take advantage of the meek, the humble, the lowly in spirit; so *of course* they value this feature in others!

These points raise an important concern about the value of humility. If humility is a good character trait, how could it be so in the face of of the compelling literature that arrogance is more valuable from a practical point of view?

A first point to note is that many vices contribute to practical advantage, and there should be no surprise at the fact that the arrogant join skilled liars at securing advantages that elude the less detestable. Even given the point that the wicked often prosper, however, one might grant the point about lying, cheating, and stealing, and still wonder whether our priorities are not askew. Why not think, for example, that humility and arrogance are merely characteristics of alternative psychological profiles, leaving them among the variety of differences between persons that are morally neutral? Think, for example, of the spectrum of personality styles ranging from being strongly introverted to being amazingly extroverted. Each personality style has some mixture of advantages and disadvantages, and it should not surprise us if the more extroverted tended to achieve higher levels of prominence during their earthly lives. No moral negativity need accompany this recognition, for such success is simply not of the same sort as that achieved by lying, stealing, and cheating. We, perhaps, have some greater inclination to resist the proud than to resist the extroverted, but the aversion is not quite of the same sort as our inclination to complain about thieves, cheats, and liars. In the latter case, we know, prior to the considering settled features of character, that lying, cheating, and stealing is wrong. In the case of pride and arrogance, there is no specific action whose moral status underlies our character assessments, and this fact may incline us to a bit more openmindedness to the possibility that our evaluation of character traits is harder to defend in the case of pride and arrogance. Perhaps, that is, our evaluations are simply the result of a cultural setting that involves the influence of Christianity with its elevation of humility as a virtue (largely because the humility of Christ in becoming human is a non-negotiable, central feature of it[2] and because of Christ's teachings, especially the Sermon on the Mount), so that if we ask about the evaluations that are proper to make from the moral point of view alone, there is no explanation available for a negative assessment of arrogance and a positive assessment of humility. Such a point of view is reinforced by noting that humility is thought of negatively in other important cultural settings, most notably in ancient Greek culture at the time of the rise of Western philosophy in the life and works of Socrates, Plato, and Aristotle. Aristotle's magnanimous man is most decidedly not humble, and the Greek mindset underlying this perspective insists that humility is a vice rather than a virtue.

My goal here is not primarily to defend the value and virtue of humility, but rather to reveal how to think about the role of pride and arrogance in human accomplishment and the natural way in which the opposite character trait of humility can debilitate. This point, by itself, serves as fodder for those who seek to undermine a positive appraisal of humility, but once we appreciate the defeasible nature of the value of character traits, there will be no straightforward argument from the downside of a character trait to the conclusion that it isn't a virtue. When humans are deeply racist, courage leads to spiteful and abusive behavior; when Bernie Madoffs abound, faith

---

[2] Note especially Philippians 2:5–8: "[H]ave the same mindset as Christ Jesus: who, being in very nature God, did not consider equality with God something to be used to his own advantage; rather, he made himself nothing by taking the very nature of a servant, being made in human likeness. And being found in appearance as a man, he humbled himself by becoming obedient to death—even death on a cross!" (NIV)

in humanity leads to loss of fortune. These points do not show that the character traits mentioned are not good character traits. What they show, instead, is that virtues in isolation are not the ideal. Instead, what we need is virtues in abundance, and especially virtues that tend to compensate for the downside of other virtues, both socially and individually. And, of course, we need a non-hostile environment as well, for nothing internal to a person or society can secure well-being without the face of nature itself smiling down on us a bit.

One way to secure this result is to pursue the holy grail of an ancient approach to the virtues: a full defense of the doctrine of the unity of the virtues, the doctrine that you can't have any virtue without having them all. What a miraculous achievement that would be! Even for those who believe in miracles, some miracle reports are simply beyond belief, and this is surely one of them. I say that as a form of confession, though, and not to indicate what I intend to argue for here. Instead, I will assume that no such miracle can be performed, and attempt to explain how compensating virtues can accommodate both the fact that humility, by itself, has deleterious effects and the fact that humility is nonetheless of central importance in the pursuit of the (or a) good life.

A better approach begins by noting the essential role of wisdom, *phronesis*, in the good life, where wisdom is an executive virtue that arranges the character traits of a person so as to achieve a flourishing life (see Zagzebski (1996)). Such an approach succeeds in showing the importance of an *orchestration* of the virtues, while granting that it is futile to hope for a defense of the unity of the virtues.

The central question, then, becomes this: what balancing character traits need to be present and available for wisdom to exercise its executive function in a way that can yield a flourishing life? If we can identify the appropriate balancing or compensating virtues, one or some that will serve the function of blocking the downside that is surely present when humility alone dominates, we will have an answer to our initial concern that arrogance is more useful than humility.

A natural, perhaps the most natural, suggestion for the relevant balancing trait for humility is self-confidence, self-assuredness, and a positive self-image. No doubt each of these attributes is important in a well-functioning human being, and a quick browsing of recent epistemology shows a significant amount of discussion of the role of self-trust in a properly arranged intellectual life (see, for example, Lehrer (1997) and Foley (2007)). But it is a mistake of a very deep sort to view these traits as the proper antidote to the downside of humility.

This proposed antidote is problematic for at least two reasons. First, a person of wisdom will want the counterbalance to be selective rather than pervasive: just being confident about everything everywhere is surely no mark of a person of wisdom. Second, a person of wisdom will want a counterbalance that highlights what is important, what matters, and in this respect, the results achieved to this point in understanding affective faith are especially promising for providing the appropriate counterbalance to intellectual humility for a person of *phronesis*.

The answer I propose, then, is that the distinctive antidote to the downside of humility is faith of a certain sort. The kind of faith is the faith worth having of the previous chapters, a faith involving a disposition to organize one's life around the pursuit of a course of behavior involving an ideal of some sort. This kind of faith is first a disposition toward responses of various sorts, and the kind of responses are those involving a *telos* toward which the agent in question takes a pro-attitude. These ideals can be relatively fleeting or permanent, highly significant or of personal interest alone. One can be disposed toward behavior aimed at making it possible to run the Boston Marathon, or toward making a nice cheesecake. The initial relevant feature here is that of moving away from a merely Humean sort of existence, where the entirety of life is just one damn thing after another, with no connections or links between the various moments of that life. Perhaps it is not possible to live a life with absolutely no connections between momentary instances of time, but it is possible to live a life involving no significant intention or plan to achieve goals beyond the immediate concerns imposed on a life by survival and reproductive interests alone. Faith lifts a life out of the mere biological drive for survival and reproduction toward something more significant, engaging the will in terms of what is (responded to as) good and beautiful. In this arena are found our dreams and aspirations, our fears and hopes, all that is holy and admirable, what we sacrifice short-term interests for the sake of, and that which may be worth dying for.

This affective reaching beyond mere biological imperatives can itself be more or less fleeting as well as more or less fragmentary. Some people bounce from one attraction to another, and build a life out of a collage of these little things. It is epitomized by Gus McCrae in Larry McMurtry's epic novel *Lonesome Dove*:

Lorie darlin', life in San Francisco, you see, is still just life. If you want any one thing too badly, it's likely to turn out to be a disappointment. The only healthy way to live life is to learn to like all the little everyday things, like a sip of good whiskey in the evening, a soft bed, a glass of buttermilk, or a feisty gentleman like myself.

Such a life is the life of the aesthete, one that cherishes variety in the small pleasures of life. The list of such things can, of course, change in the process of enjoyment: the fragmentary elements of such a life can easily be replaced, bit by bit, by other fragmentary elements.

At the other end of the spectrum is a life lived with single-minded devotion to a single cause or purpose (beyond the biological imperatives already noted[3]). Such lives

---

[3] A digression to note but not pursue here is the way in which such devotion can actually compete with the biological imperatives in question. Honoring vows of celibacy can do so, especially when coupled with a monastic existence that severs all ties with surrounding culture, thereby undermining even the indirect ways in which a genetic profile can be propagated by, for example, caretaking for the offspring of siblings. As interesting as these possibilities are, they take us away from the line of thought being pursued here, which involves tabling the role of the biological imperatives in order to focus on the way in which non-biological interests structure a life.

are unusual at best and perhaps described only in the kind of historical biography in service of an ideology. Even if no such single-minded purposive existence has ever existed, however, we can imaginatively abstract from the actual lives of our heroes—both their other admirable pursuits and their defects, in order to focus on the aspect that interests us—to envision a life of such single-minded devotion. Such possibilities include the one who gives all for God or country, the hero who lives only for the salvation of others, the philosopher guided only by the pursuit of understanding and wisdom. Such a life is one in which all that is done (beyond, again, what is involved in satisfying biological imperatives) is organized by an over-arching purpose or plan, in service of which all other motivating elements play their distinctive roles. One's desires, for example, can be controlled in service of such an overall plan, and even one's fears can be overcome in order to fulfill a larger purpose.

The kind of faith that involves a disposition toward behavior in service of an ideal encompasses all these ways of moving from a life that involves nothing more than satisfying biological imperatives to a life involving larger purposes, plans, goals, and ideals. It is this kind of faith that counteracts the tendency of humility in isolation from other virtues to lead to a life of no accomplishment. Combining faith with humility is the proper antidote to such, providing something worth pursuing, from the perspective of the agent in question, generating an attraction of sufficient strength that effort and activity follow naturally from the strength of the resulting disposition. It is an effort and activity that comes tinged with the traces of a humble acknowledgment of the risk or probability of failure and perhaps also the recognition of being a vessel not suited to, or not worthy of, the pursuit of such a noble project. The result is an attitude toward self that is not self-stultifying and an endeavor that can be more beautiful and compelling for the tincture.

This last point must be accompanied by a qualification, for it is important to recall that such faith can be perverse, focused on completely egocentric goals, as one finds in devotees of Ayn Rand, or on reprehensible goals, as one finds in various forms of fascism. The idea is thus not that faith always turns a humble existence into something more accomplished and admirable, but rather that faith is a necessary addition to a humble life if it is going to be a life of accomplishment and admiration. The alternative view maintains that the disposition to act in service of something perverse is not, in fact, faith, but some poor simulation of it. Such a view of virtues, articulated well by Philippa Foot (see Foot (1978), see also Foot (2001) and Foot (2002)), is not sustainable: Nazi and Stalinist courage is still courage, however perverse.

Such a view appeals to holism about the virtues in order to provide the needed link between the virtues and the good life. Such a view, however, threatens the possibility of an atomistic relationship between individual virtues, and a full response to the perspective that Foot articulates requires an explanation of how holism and atomism can both be affirmed in this way. To this issue I turn in the next section.

6.3 Holism, Atomism, and Complementarity

The concern about the threat of incompatibility between the holistic and atomistic components involved in the complementarity thesis concerning the relationship between faith and humility is hazy enough at this point that clarity is needed before proceeding. We can gain greater clarity by considering a context in which the charge of incompatibility has been leveled with some plausibility. In the theory of justification, the champions of holistic conceptions have been coherentists, and one of the central attacks on holistic coherentism over the past fifty years or so has concerned a difficulty it faces concerning the idea of what it is to base a belief on the reasons one has for it.

The concern here is that the theory of reasons and reasoning is an atomistic affair, relating individual propositions or beliefs in terms of a relation of epistemic support, with the accompanying worry that if justification or rationality of belief is a holistic matter involving a relation of coherence over an entire system of information, we will not be able to link properly the theory of justification with the theory of reasons and reasoning. That link is required in order to distinguish mere propositional justification from doxastic justification. A classic example of this distinction involves Sherlock Holmes and Dr. Watson, who both share the same information about a crime they are attempting to solve. Sherlock reflects on the evidence, and reasons his way to the conclusion that the butler committed the crime. Dr. Watson is more emotional when he reflects on the same evidence, and such reflection causes him to lose his balance and fall down the stairs, hitting his head so as to render him momentarily unconscious, and upon waking, firmly believing that the butler committed the crime. Both Holmes and Watson have propositional justification that the butler did it, but only Holmes bases his belief on the evidence in a way that generates doxastic justification for the belief. (The significance of the distinction for the theory of knowledge is that, as a result, only Holmes can know that the butler committed the crime: proper basing on evidence is essential to any knowledge that depends on such evidence.)

The attack on holistic coherentism thus proceeds as follows. Holistic coherentism maintains that what justifies a given belief is some relation with an entire system of information. But proper basing requires that one hold the belief in question because of that which justifies it, and so one could only properly base a belief if the entire system of information were causally involved in the production or sustenance of that belief.[4] That requirement makes a shambles of the theory of reasons and reasoning, which is a much more atomistic affair than coherentism can allow, so holistic coherentism must be abandoned.

The significance of this issue for our discussion is what lies beneath the objection. The difficulty raised suggests that if there is a good that is characterized in holistic

---

[4] This objection is raised most directly by John Pollock, though the assumptions that generate Pollock's formulation are also present in Alvin Plantinga's characterization of coherentism as the view that all justified beliefs are foundationally justified. See Pollock (1986a), Plantinga (1993) and my discussions of these issues in Kvanvig (1995a,b) and Kvanvig (1997).

terms, then no good-making characteristics will be able to be found among the ingredients in the holistically-determined good in question. That is, the holism eliminates the possibility of atomistic relationships related to the good in question. So, if justification is characterized holistically, there can't be justification-conferring atomistic connections available to use to explain the notion of proper basing. Just so, if the connection between the virtues and the good life is holistic in character, there will be no relationships available between individual virtues that are themselves good-making. Instead, all we'll be able to say is that the system of virtues as a whole has to involve the right kind of balance for such goodness to be present.

This challenge is therefore serious, but, I will argue, capable of being answered in a way that allows both an epistemology and a theory of virtue to involve both holistic and atomistic characteristics. In the epistemic arena, the key to avoiding conflict is to note that the connection between the theory of justification and the theory of reasons and reasoning need not endorse the idea that good reasons and good reasoning have to impart some degree of justification to what they support epistemically. The link between the two theories need not be of that sort. For example, a coherentist might claim that good reasons are connected to justification in a weaker way, but being integral and non-redundant elements of an overall system of information that is itself not needed in order for the claim in question to be justified but nonetheless sufficient for such justification.[5] Such a claim implies a relationship between the theory of justification and the theory of reasons and reasoning without endorsing the claim that good reasons impart some degree of justification.

A similar point can be made in the context of the theory of virtue. Two individual virtues can provide an appropriate balance for the weaknesses of each, taken in isolation, without this relationship functioning so as to generate a closer approximation to the good life. Such approximations are always, on the holistic picture presented here, a matter of arranging all of the virtues in proper measure by the executive function of the will. That point, however, is compatible with individual relationships among the virtues that are integral and non-redundant elements of an overall holistic arrangement that is itself not the only way to achieve the good life but nonetheless sufficient for it.

The central point here should not surprise, for it is well-known that the defeasibility required in any adequate theory of reasons and reasoning shows that holism of some sort is going to be required in the theory of justification, since there is no way to predict where and when defeaters might arise within a system of information. This holistic fact about justification leaves in place the *pro tanto* defeasible relation between

---

[5] Those familiar with J. L. Mackie's work on causation will see a connection between the claims here and his INUS condition theory of causation. (An INUS condition is one that is an insufficient condition for an effect, while yet a non-redundant part of a larger condition that is both sufficient but unnecessary for that effect.) See Mackie (1974) for details. I should note, however, that the value of the use here of these ideas doesn't depend on the adequacy of Mackie's account of causation.

various bits of information, so that a given claim can constitute defeasible evidence for another claim, in spite of the fact that the latter claim cannot be justified, all-epistemic-factors-considered, without taking into account an entire system of information. One way to characterize this *pro tanto* defeasible relation is in terms of one item generating some degree of justification or warrant or rationality for another claim, but that explanation is not the only one available. So if such a characterization conflicts in some way with the appropriate type of holism generated by defeasibility, some other option will be needed. So long as the holism engendered by the defeasibility of reasons leaves intact the distinction between *conferrers* of justification and *enablers* of it, no theoretical conflict needs to arise between the holistic theory of justification and the more atomistic theory of reasons and reasoning.[6]

This conclusion allows us to retain the earlier position on which the value of the virtues doesn't require that they cannot be put to odious service. What is true is that the real value of the virtues is not typically realized except in combination, under the control of the executive virtue of wisdom. Such is unity enough in the virtues, and no stronger unity can be found for rejecting the obvious point that a good trait on its own isn't enough to overcome the depravity of bad people. Such holism can be embraced while at the same time noting that individual virtues bear special compensating relationships to each other, so that faith in isolation calls for the presence of humility while humility alone demands faith. Such relationships provide no guarantee of the good life, nor do they even sustain the promise of an enhanced likelihood of achieving the good life. But the special, balancing relationships are important nonetheless, and important precisely on the basis of a connection to the good life.

We can benefit in our understanding of this special relationship by considering an example that puts flesh to the bones of abstract description. For such a purpose, I turn to the example of Moses.

6.4 A Case Study: Moses

Moses, as an adult, is a man of courage. He comes to the aid of a Hebrew slave being beaten by an Egyptian, and he drives away a bunch of shepherds harassing the daughters of Reuel, a Midianite priest, shepherds preventing the daughters from drawing water from a well for Reuel's flock. He is also generous toward these daughters, not only securing their access to the well, but watering the flock for them.

So when we get to the remarkable story of the burning bush, it is important to notice that we are not considering a person who has never undertaken risks in service of the good. We might notice that Moses' prior displays of courage were not premeditated, but rather arose on the spur of the moment. And we might thus wonder whether he is capable of more than hotheaded courage. This possibility must be taken seriously, but

---

[6] For further discussion of this point and the distinction in question, see Kvanvig (2011c, 2013d) and Kvanvig (2014).

we cannot reasonably suppose that he has a settled disposition against undertaking risks in service of justice. To the contrary, he is easily moved by perceived injustice, even at risk to his own well-being.

It is not fear or lack of courage, then, that underlies Moses' hesitancy when God tells him from the burning bush, "Go . . . I am sending you . . . " (Exodus 3:10). Moses' response, "Who am I?", is rooted, rather, in a sense of his own insignificance. He knows that he has no political power, that he has no army or authority to tell Pharaoh what to do. His indecisiveness is met with divine reassurance: "I will be with you."

Moses' reluctance does not dissipate. He expresses skepticism when considering the Israelites' response should he inform them that the God of their fathers has sent Moses to them. His skepticism is again met with reassurance, including the giving of the tetragrammaton to identify who the God of the fathers is.

Moses is not finished, however, and pursues a path of further diffidence: "what if they don't believe me or won't listen?" In response, Moses is given miraculous signs, the sign of the staff turning into a serpent and that of healthy skin turning leprous. In addition, he is told that water from the Nile, if poured on the ground, will turn to blood.

Moses' hesitance is unremitting, however, and he points out that he has never been eloquent, but is instead "slow of speech and tongue." Once again, God provides reassurance: "I will help you speak and teach you what to say." Moses still resists: "please send someone else."

This response angers God, but he does not give up on Moses. In response, he promises to send alongside Aaron, one known to speak well.

Thus begins the saga of the exodus, and it is a remarkable story about the faith and humility of Moses. Moses does not lack courage, but he knows his limitations. He is focused on his inability to articulate to the Israelites who has sent him and on his inability to convince Pharaoh of the wisdom of releasing his slaves. He is convinced enough of his limitations that he concludes, initially, that trying isn't prudent. He thus employs a bevy of stalling tactics, voicing one excuse after another in the face of God's directive.

These stalling tactics inform us of Moses' attitudes. He doesn't reject God's command outright, but rather attempts to deflect it. He doesn't say, "No, I won't go," but becomes evasive instead. Such behavior reveals hesitance, of course, but more importantly in the present context, it shows an underlying attraction for doing the will of God. Without that underlying attraction, the expected response would be, simply, "No, I won't go."

One might resist this assessment, noting the experience of awe in the presence of a burning bush that isn't consumed. The experience of a divine being, whatever one's theology, can be awful. Perhaps Moses isn't disposed to act in service of the divine, conceived as an ideal of some sort, but is rather behaving simply out of self-interest. His evasive behavior, rather than being motivated by some underlying faith, might be motivated by fear instead.

This assessment is too negative to be sustained. Moses ultimately relents, not because of some overt threat, but as a result of continual divine reassurance and the final offer to send Aaron to help. He does not do so while in the process showing any sign of resentment at being told to do something that is not really worth doing. The best understanding of his behavior, then, is that he responds, finally, to something he finds positive and worth doing, even while at the same time deeply experiencing his own inadequacy for the task. He is, to put it simply, deeply humble and also deeply attracted to the goal in question and toward the idea of obeying God's commands and securing the release of the Hebrew captives. He desires the task to be given to others but he doesn't reject the task and finally acquiesces, without any sign of irritability or exasperation at having to go. Viewing all of this as merely arising from fear or self-interest distorts the narrative.

Moses thus displays a kind of intellectual humility concerning his suitability to the task, but also displays the kind of affective faith that embraces these self-assessments while still being faithful to the divine commands he has received. He is not unaware of his limitations, and he is disposed to be attentive to these limitations when assessing various possible plans about what to do. Moreover, he acts on this attentiveness, resisting any rash decision to avoid warning signs of possible disaster. But he also feels the pull of the cause of justice, as well as the ideal of fulfilling the call of God when it occurs. His humility, alone, does not incline him toward greatness. If anything, it inclines him not to try. But he is not simply a humble man, but also a man of faith, in the sense of being disposed to act in service of compelling ideals. He thus ultimately abandons the evasions rooted in accurate self-appraisal, in favor of the ideals that lead him to greatness as a deliverer.

6.5 Reversing the Scales

Not only does affective faith provide a useful balance to the potential downside of humility, it is equally true that humility, especially intellectual humility, provides a useful counterbalance to the havoc that affective faith can wreak. We are all familiar with the excesses of affective faith, whether in the form of religious zealotry or in service of ignoble political and social goals or even in the form of illegitimate means directed at achieving laudatory ends, and the disasters that result should give us the same kind of pause about whether faith is a virtue that we experienced when noting the downside of humility.

So, what goes wrong when faith yields disastrous consequences? First, the ideal pursued might be defective, and second, poor judgment is shown about appropriate means for pursuing the ideal. The second defect is primarily intellectual, but the first is both intellectual and affective. People can find themselves caring intensely about things that are unsavory, and in a way that is subject to legitimate criticism on the basis of its interference with the health and well-being of humans, animals, and even the planet itself. Even though there are no guarantees that the ideals we pursue will not be comparably objectionable, a healthy sense of our own fallibility—of the sort that is an integral component of humility—provides a useful counterbalance to the zeal that is part of affective faith. A person of faith has to have their cares and concerns always subject to an awareness of our capacity for a specious sense of what is good and right, in a way secured by a balancing of faith with humility.

This result also makes sense of the role of faith and humility in the context of religious faith, especially Christian faith. As noted above, the humility of Christ is an essential feature of the Divine love that reaches down to the human predicament as described in the doctrine of the Incarnation. Moreover, it is through allegiance to the cause of Christ by which one becomes and remains a member of the Kingdom in question. It is thus especially fitting in the context of Christian faith to note the balancing relationship between faith and humility. We shall have occasion in a future chapter to see if this picture of Christ can be sustained by an adequate account of humility, but for present purposes it is easy to see how the divine activity in the Incarnation is clearly an expression of a disposition to act in service of an ideal. We are told as well that it is motivated by humility (Philippians 2:8), so if this claim can be sustained, we have as well another example of the interaction between faith and humility in religious contexts, this time a specifically Christian one.

6.6 Conclusion

The central contrast between faith as the appropriate balancing virtue for humility and and the natural alternative viewpoint, according to which the appropriate balancing virtue against the self-deprecation involved in humility is self-trust, is this: faith looks outward, toward what is good and beautiful, as a source of motivation for future endeavors, whereas self-trust looks inward. That description alone ought to incline us toward the former trait over the latter as the appropriate balance for an excessive humility that debilitates, that leads to self-abnegation, and to a life of little consequence.

The needed balancing act runs in the other direction as well. Faith unchecked by humility has no guards against the kind of intellectual arrogance that generates zealots of the most despicable sort. Though there are no magic pills against demagoguery and villainous behavior in service of objectionable ideals, humility provides a useful counterbalance for inclinations to zealotry by continually sending cautionary signals about our capacity for errors of both heart and mind. To understate: not always does what we care about align with what is good and beautiful and not always does what we think align with what is true. The measure of caution introduced by true humility is just what is needed as a deterrent to faith in the despicable and quixotic.

We have seen as well how to embrace these atomistic connections between faith and humility while at the same time endorsing a kind of holism about the connection between the virtues and the good life. Such a holism falls short of the Platonic requirement that one can't have any of the virtues without having them all, but that unity thesis is subject to such serious criticisms that falling short of endorsing it is probably a good thing. There is one advantage we might obtain if we could endorse the stronger thesis, for the holism endorsed here fails to show that the pursuit of the good life will end in disappointment unless it involves the presence of faith and humility.[7] In the end, while I think such a claim is true and wish to find a way to sustain it, I don't think any considerations in favor of such a claim can be decisive, so the failure of the holistic theory endorsed here to imply a need for faith and humility is not problematic even if disappointing.

It is not that there is nothing to say on behalf of this claim of necessity. For one thing, a life devoid of faith would either be one that involved no endorsed ideals or no dispositions to respond in service of such. Perhaps no life can flourish in the absence of such, but I don't see how to show that no such possibility exists. Moreover, the absence of humility may always and everywhere be lamentable, but as the Psalmist noted, the rain falls on the just and the unjust, a nice metaphor for things going well for some people in spite of, rather than because of, their character traits. Such moral luck irks us immensely, though of course only when experienced by others whom we don't care for very much!

In any case, in spite of there being some things to say on behalf of the centrality of faith and humility to the good life, the holistic link between the theory of virtue and the good life is not strong enough to sustain any claimed need for these virtues. Perhaps the best that can be said is that the reasons just noted make it a failure of prudence to aim at the good life while scoffing at faith and humility, maybe even enough of a failure to make one a fool. Even in the absence of a defense of the necessity of faith and humility for the good life, the complementary nature of these virtues remains.

This result requires an understanding of humility that can support this implication, which we will pursue in succeeding chapters. As motivation for this effort, note the way in which the above discussion has lumped together ordinary human humility, involving a propensity for self-abnegation and discouragement at prospects for success, with the humility of Christ, which is a seemingly more ontological feature and not one involving the propensities in question. Is there a common understanding of humility that can cover both cases? This question is addressed in the following chapters.

Before turning to the logical space and nature of humility, however, there is a prior issue concerning proper expressions of humility, especially intellectual humility, and

---

[7] Thanks to Tasia Scrutton for raising this issue in discussion at the conference on Faithful Attitudes at the University of Manchester, 17–18 May 2017.

the danger of paradox that results from such expressions. Moreover, it isn't just the verbal, outward expressions found in human speech that threaten paradox, but also the internal encoding of such expressions in the form of belief. If so, however, there is the danger that intellectual humility of the sort needed as a counterbalance for zealous faith cannot coherently exist, and thus that the promise of humility to provide the needed offsetting is empty. To that issue we turn in the next chapter.

7

Expressions of Humility and Epistemological Psychology

As when with downcast eyes we muse and brood,
And ebb into a former life, or seem
To lapse far back in some confused dream
To states of mystical similitude;
If one but speaks or hems or stirs his chair,
Ever the wonder waxeth more and more . . .

Lord Alfred Tennyson

7.1 Introduction

Intellectual humility can be merely implicit, but can also be articulated. One context in which it is expressed gives rise to the preface paradox, which, when applied to the belief system of an individual (rather than the contents of a book), is often called "the fallibility paradox". The paradox involves holding a number of beliefs combined with a preface belief that at least some of one's beliefs are false. In the original formulation, the paradox involves a book in which the author is justified in believing every claim in the book, but then writes a preface expressing conviction that errors remain. This judgment also appears to be justified, but appears inconsistent with the conjunction of the total collection of claims made in the book. In the fallibility version of this paradox, the book is assumed to be the set of beliefs of a given individual, and the preface remark is such a person's expression of awareness of fallibility. It can thus be seen as an expression of intellectual humility, but just as with the original paradox, it appears inconsistent with the totality of other beliefs.[1]

Some responses to the inconsistency of belief involved in the paradox deny that such combinations of beliefs can all be justified. John Pollock (1986b) holds that

---

[1] To get an actual inconsistency, the person must also hold a belief about what is included in the totality of the belief system in question. This requirement is typically not satisfied for ordinary humans, but any solution to the paradox should apply both to ordinary humans as well as the idealized sort who do know what they believe and what they don't. In what follows, I'll elide this distinction, claiming inconsistency when it is actually only present in the idealized examples. Doing so will make the discussion less cumbersome, and is justified by the need for a solution to the paradox that doesn't trade simply on how far short of the ideal some reasoners are.

lottery and preface paradoxes need to be treated differently,[2] with lottery solved by noting that each claim regarding the losing status of a particular ticket is negatively relevant to every other such claim, resulting in what he terms "collective defeat" of each particular claim that a given ticket will lose. The preface paradox is handled on his view differently. Pollock holds that every claim in the book can be justified, as well as the claim that the book is of a type that generally contains errors. What is not allowed is inferring from this latter claim that this very book contains errors, or is highly likely to contain errors, since the argument here is defeated by the claim that all the claims in the book are true. More generally, coherentists have a strong motivation to deny that the preface claim can be justified, since the hallmark of that view is that coherence is something over and above logical consistency, but at least requires such consistency.[3]

So one response to the paradox is to counsel against the preface belief. It is this line of thought that poses a problem for any view that places a high value on intellectual humility. If we become suspicious of preface beliefs, it will be a challenge to explain how expressions of fallibility and intellectual humility are appropriate, whether voiced verbally or encoded mentally.

One might go further than the authors above and simply deny that any expression of humility in such a context is important or legitimate. One might hold such a view, insisting that it would be perfectly proper to express the arrogant attitude that one's book contains no errors at all, since each claim in it has the mark of truth. More plausible is the quietist position, according to which neither expressions of arrogance or humility are appropriate: simply let the book stand on its own, without prefatory commentary.

Such positions engender discomfort. It is natural to reflect on any accomplishment, and artisans of any sort typically view what they've done as less than perfect. A woodworker, for example, might make very fine furniture, but it would be surprising to find a woodworker who either thought the piece was perfect or took no attitude toward the idea that perfection had been achieved. The idea here isn't that taking such an attitude is required, but if there is such an attitude, it is hard to see how it could be inappropriate to express. So the quietist position that bans any expressions of intellectual humility, or humility about accomplishments more generally, makes silence contrived and should be rejected for that reason. Moreover, banning expressions of intellectual humility is especially disturbing in our context, for such a preface claim is just the sort of

---

[2] The lottery paradox is due to Henry Kyburg (1961). The preface paradox is from D. C. Makinson (1965). Both paradoxes threaten the possibility of justified contradictory beliefs, the former by deducing that no ticket will win from one's justification for believing that each individual ticket will not win, even though one knows that some ticket will win; and the latter by deducing that everything in one's book is true by conjoining all of one's justified beliefs about the content of the book, even while adducing in the preface that errors remain.

[3] Foley (1979) presents this standard view and argues that the epistemic paradoxes thus show that coherentism is false. I defend coherentism from this charge in Kvanvig (2011a), denying that the possibility of justified inconsistent beliefs undermines coherentism.

expression of intellectual humility that is supposed to provide a barrier to the costly damage that can be done by zealous faith found in various forms of fundamentalism. If intellectual humility leads to paradox, its promise as a balancing virtue for affective faith is threatened.

Even so, there is still a faint glimmer of hope for this quietist approach to the paradox, for it might be that appropriate expressions of intellectual humility do not involve belief reports of the unqualified sort that threaten paradox. One might try to avoid the paradox by weakening the content of the belief report, or by changing the type of mental state being reported. I will consider each option in turn.

7.2 Weakening the Content of Belief

Perhaps the simplest idea is to insist that the stark claim "errors remain" is too strong. Instead, we should be more circumspect, and we typically are. We don't write, simply, "errors remain" (wouldn't that prompt the reader to think, "why don't you fix them?") but something a bit more complex, such as "in spite of my best efforts, I am sure errors remain," or "I remain convinced that the reader will be able to see the mistakes I have not seen as yet." The complexity here raises the possibility that the preface claim isn't really equivalent to the claim that errors remain, but is a bit more guarded than that. And if it is more guarded, it is fairly easy to see how we might use that fact to escape the paradox. If the author says only that he or she is sure that mistakes were made in the process of writing the book, that claim doesn't imply that errors remain. Or if the author writes that it is highly likely that errors remain, or that fallible authors typically make mistakes somewhere in the process of producing original work, these claims don't imply that errors remain either. So changing the content of the preface claim reveals many roads one can take that do not lead to paradox, even if the bald assertion that errors remain does so lead.

There is an even simpler approach. Instead of writing about the content of the book, if the point of the preface remark is to note one's fallibility and express one's intellectual humility, one can do that by simply noting in the preface that one is fallible, and one's fallibility is on display in the present work as much as it is everywhere else. That modal claim does not imply that there are errors in the work in question, but only that the work is *liable* to contain them. Moreover, noting such pervasive fallibility clearly expresses humility, so such a prefatory remark accomplishes everything one could legitimately ask.

So it would seem, but things are not that simple. The term 'fallible' is a modal one, and so the simple belief that I am fallible involves a possibility claim of some sort. Perhaps the idea is that it is possible that I am in error about some of my beliefs, or that I am prone to error here as elsewhere. I believe that claim is true, but upon writing it in a preface, I would hear an undesirable tone of understatement. I could equally write about each statement in the book, "I am fallible and so prone to error, but I'm not wrong about this claim." After all, it is perfectly consistent to note a possibility while pointing out that it is unrealized. We do that when explaining what contingent truths are to students: they are truths which might have been false. But it is no proper expression of epistemic humility to point out that even though it is possible that I hold a false belief, I really don't. Moreover, if I conjoin the admission of fallibility to each of the claims of the book, I have thereby written a book that contains no expression of intellectual humility at all, but rather one of repeated expressions of hubris.

Perhaps there is a modality that prohibits such concessions, so that it is contradictory to say, in that modality, "I might be wrong but I'm not."[4] If there were such a modality, one might then insist that epistemic humility is best expressed using that modality, since it couldn't be conjoined to a denial of being wrong. If there is such a modality in ordinary language, it will be in the ordinary notion of epistemic possibility, for it is that notion that ties modal terms to what we know or don't know. When we aren't sure or don't know, we note that things might go either of two ways (for example, the claim might be true or it might be false), and one might argue that it is a distinctive feature of such a notion that it is contradictory to say that I might be wrong but I'm not.

Though an attractive initial position to take, we must ultimately reject the idea that the ordinary notion of epistemic possibility generates such a contradiction. Remarks to the effect that it is possible that one is mistaken but that one isn't, are generally infelicitous, but to claim that the explanation of the infelicity is semantic is more than can be defended. For even if, in a given context, it would be infelicitous to conjoin "but I'm not" to the claim "I might be wrong," one might say only the latter while still coherently thinking the conjunction. The result for our context is that the fallibility assertion itself would not, in that case, count as an expression of humility but rather as a self-serving attempt to mask hubris.

So something more than noting a liability to error is needed in order for a preface claim to be an unambiguous expression of intellectual humility. To be such, preface claims must be forceful enough to avoid the conjunction problem just noted, and it is worth pointing out the rather obvious fact that substituting probability claims for possibility ones won't go far enough to avoid the conjunction problem. So, for example, it won't help to endorse or express the idea that I'm likely to err, since I can coherently claim that, for example, I'm likely to make careless mistakes filling out the answer key on a logic test while at the same time insisting that I didn't make such mistakes on this one. I can even coherently note that all my past selves have felt the same way, and that they were mistaken more often than not, while still insisting that I, now, am not like them in that regard.

---

[4] For a defense of this claim, see Lewis (1996). For discussion of needed qualifications, see Stanley (2005) and Dougherty and Rysiew (2009). The needed feature of such a modality is one of the axioms of the epistemic logic of Jaakko Hintikka (1962), to wit, that epistemic possibility is to be understood in terms of the denial of knowledge of the opposite: i.e., $\Diamond_e p =_{df.} \sim K \sim p$. For discussion of the relationship between this logical notion and the ordinary notion of epistemic possibility, see, among others, DeRose (1991) and Huemer (2007).

It is no better if we try to locate our humility in some claim about the fragility of true belief among human beings, more generally. The arrogant recognize this point, and revel in it, thanking the powers that be that they are not like others in this regard.

These attempts are specific instances of the general strategy of trying to express our sense of fallibility in terms of a claim that gives good but non-entailing evidence that some of my present beliefs are false. The problem is that each such attempt is subject to the conjunction possibility, where we cite the evidential claim and conjoin it to a denial of what it is evidence for. This possibility is sufficient to show that citing the evidential claim alone is not adequate to the context of the preface. What we seek in the preface remark is an unambiguous expression of fallibility and intellectual humility, not some claim that might instead be a deceptive expression of arrogance by being conjoined to an attitude of contingent inerrancy.

One might worry that I am setting the bar too high here, that there is nothing we can legitimately require to rule out the possibility of a true preface claim being misleading in this way. To demand that a legitimate expression of humility rule out being used by the arrogant to obfuscate is, it might be claimed, to impose a demand that no linguistic construction could ever satisfy.

This complaint is not legitimate, however. What we seek is a claim that is actually believed and wholeheartedly endorsed by the person in question. Of course it is always possible to use language to deceive, but that is not the standard being used here. Note that the stark remark, "Errors remain," is not subject to the conjunction problem, nor is the claim that one is lamentably certain of that fact. So there are ways to express intellectual humility that do not succumb to the conjunction problem. The approaches to the paradox we are considering wish to avoid such stark admissions in hope of avoiding the paradox, and so are attempting to substitute something less stark that can nonetheless serve the same purpose as the stark admissions. To succeed in that task, I've been arguing, their proposals must avoid the conjunction problem, and because they don't, it is better to try a different tack.

So the question in our context is whether weakenings of the preface claim (in service of avoiding the paradox) are an adequate expression of the intellectual humility that we are presuming the author to intend to convey. Relative to this desideratum, these weakening proposals look suspect. The arguments given above lend credence to the concern raised at the beginning of this section—that weakening the preface claim leaves things too understated. Given that result, and the still-intact assumption that the baldly-put preface claim must be avoided in order to prevent paradox, two options remain. The first option is the quietist attitude that we should simply resist the urge to express intellectual humility, and the second is to look for attitudes other than full belief for expressing such humility.

I haven't argued extensively against the quietist position, but a couple of further remarks might be useful to dislodge any remaining gravitational attraction toward that position. Whatever a full account of humility involves, it will have to take account of the fact that this virtue concerns, not merely some set of beliefs or attitudes toward oneself, but patterns regarding what one attends to, what one focuses on, what stances one takes and reinforces toward one's abilities and accomplishments and significance. Given these points it will be hard to sustain the view that intellectual humility should not be expressed in prefaces to one's works or in meta-beliefs about one's own success in getting to the truth and avoiding error. One can't recommend refusing to take the attitude of humility, consistent with its importance and value, and there is no solace in the face of the paradox by letting the author believe everything in the book, believe the preface claim, and simply refuse to testify to the latter through inattention to this detail. For such a position generalized would undermine the virtue in question, since it counsels not attending to some of the central, lamentable aspects of the human cognitive condition. Given this conclusion, we are left only with the option of finding an attitude other than full belief for identifying as an expression of intellectual humility and which can be the source of an unqualified preface claim that implies that even our best efforts end up tainted with error.

7.3 Changing the Mental State Reported

What options do we have for such a role, short of belief? The history of epistemology in the twentieth century suggests an obvious route. Instead of thinking of full belief, we could focus on partial belief or level of confidence. Instead of believing the preface claim, perhaps it is enough to have a high degree of confidence or partial belief that errors remain.

By way of background, partial belief involves some measure on the degree to which one is cognitively committed to a given claim. The key idea here is that we are more sure of some things than other things, and that this fact shows that, beneath the phenomenon of belief itself, there is an underlying reality that is more fine-grained. Probabilism is the epistemology theory that results from attempting to develop a theory of rationality that assesses this underlying reality rather than the more coarse-grained phenomenon of belief itself, and Probabilism involves two central claims: there are such things as degrees of belief, or credences, as I will call them; and credences must satisfy the probability calculus in order to be rational.[5]

The usual strategy for identifying the degree in question is in terms of betting behavior, deriving from the operationalist account of the notion first articulated by Bruno de Finetti.[6] His definition is:

The probability P(E) that you attribute to an event E is therefore the certain gain p which you judge equivalent to a unit gain conditional on the occurrence of E: in order to express it in a

---

[5] These two conditions can sometimes be thought to reduce to one, since degree of belief is sometimes offered as an interpretation of the notion of probability that characterizes the probability calculus (opposing, for example, frequentist, logical, and propensity accounts of it). Since this probabilistic constraint on degrees of belief is not in focus here, we need not pursue this issue.

[6] "In order to give an effective meaning to a notion—and not merely an appearance of such in a metaphysical-verbalistic sense—an operational definition is required. By this we mean a definition based on a criterion which allows us to measure it." (de Finetti 1974, p. 76)

dimensionally correct way, it is preferable to take pS equivalent to S conditional on E, where S is any amount whatsoever, one Lira or one million, $20 or £75.   (de Finetti 1974, p. 75)[7]

Let the unit gain we are assuming be $1, and the event in question be the result of the flipping of a particular coin (assumed to be heads). What degree of belief do I have regarding the event of the coin landing heads? The answer is: whatever amount of certain gain I "judge equivalent to [$1] conditional on [the coin landing heads]." The idea is simple: you offer me a given amount of money and I get to choose that or the result of flipping the coin (where I get $1 if the coin comes up heads and nothing otherwise). If I judge that the certain gain of $.50 is equivalent to getting $1 if the coin comes up heads and nothing otherwise, then my degree of belief that the coin will come up heads is .5.

The difficulties with such approaches, and with every approach,[8] to the nature of degrees of belief, should not blind us to the theoretical usefulness of the notion. Even if such accounts fail to specify the nature of this feature of cognition, they might still be useful as evidential cues for what degrees of belief are. (At least, they can be such to the extent that degrees of belief, like belief *simpliciter*, are guides to action.) Degrees of

---

[7] It is worth noting, for those hoping for an account of degrees of belief that makes them fundamental, with belief itself defined in terms of degrees of belief, this definition causes problems. It relies on the notion of judgment itself, which is typically thought of as a form of belief. That is, to judge that p is to believe that p, and hence the de Finetti definition requires the priority of the notion of belief over that of degree of belief.

One might try to avoid this result by replacing the notion of judgment in de Finetti's account with that of preference. Instead of judging equivalence, one might talk instead of neutrality on preferences, in this way avoiding characterizing degrees of belief in terms of belief itself. In the context of behavioristic/operationalistic assumptions, this change is of little help in attempting to understand a mental state without appeal to other mental states (for this objection to Behaviorism, see Chisholm (1957)), but the change gives at least a glimmer of hope to those who have no affinity for Behaviorism but merely want an account of degrees of belief that allows a definition of belief *simpliciter* in terms of the degree'd notion. (Actually, to be more precise, this new account defines degree of belief in terms of a relation between conditional and unconditional preferences.)

One should be suspicious of such a move, however. Preferences are affective states while beliefs, whether degree'd or not, are cognitive states. The direction of fit for each is different—beliefs aim to mirror the world while preferences aim to change it—making it at least initially suspect that we can understand the former in terms of the latter. This point becomes more pressing when we consider philosophies and religions that counsel minimizing or eliminating preferences: Buddhism and Stoicism, for example. Such counsel doesn't require minimizing or eliminating cognitive states, and that point should be enough to make us suspicious about understanding degrees of belief in terms of preferences.

This worry afflicts views that attempt to derive a credence function from a representation theorem (originating from Ramsey (1990, 2010 [1926])) that begins with axioms for preferences, showing that if a set of preferences satisfies those axioms, they can be represented as resulting from a utility function and a set of probabilistically coherent degrees of belief so that the preferences maximize expected utility relative to the utility function and degrees of belief. The idea of deriving a credence function from such theorems is fraught with difficulties beyond what I note here (see e.g. Christensen (2001) and Hájek (2008)). Even apart from other concerns, however, there is still the problem of minimized or eliminated preferences, holding cognitive states constant, as one should expect from successful applications of Buddhist and Stoic thought (to say nothing at all of the results of deep and unremitting depression that involves chronic and complete apathy). The lesson should be that there is an important difference between what is really inside the head of a person and how we might be able to represent what is there.

[8] For an excellent summary of the faults of the major attempts to clarify the nature of degrees of belief, see Erikkson and Hájek (2007).

belief might be theoretical entities that, like other theoretical entities, are connected only evidentially to the realm of experience and definable if at all only in terms of some more general theory of which they are a part. So definitional difficulties of the sort that appear in the literature on subjective probability need not make us skeptical of the notion of degrees of belief, but instead might come to be seen as expected in light of the theoretical status of the entities in question. Thought of in this way, degrees of belief might be a useful notion in our context in spite of these definitional difficulties. Let us consider, then, the plausibility of using this resource in our context concerning the preface paradox and appropriate expressions of humility.

It is noteworthy that usual expressions of the preface claim are not the flat assertion "errors remain," but rather something in the form of a self-reporting avowal: "I am sure this isn't perfect," "I am certain that errors remain that are my fault, not the fault of those who provides extensive comments on previous drafts." A flat assertion rather than a self-report would be an awkward claim indeed. What would we make of it? Such an assertion ("There are errors in this book") would naturally lead the audience to think, "Well, fix them!" As such, the flat assertion may not be an expression of intellectual humility or an acknowledgment of fallibility at all. To get such an expression or acknowledgment, (something like) a self-report is much better.[9]

If the self-report is of a certainty, degree of belief acknowledged is so strong that resorting to degrees of belief will have no advantage in the context of the paradox over belief *simpliciter*. For, whatever the precise relationship between belief and degrees of belief, a maximal degree of belief is clearly an instance of belief *simpliciter*. Moreover, the Lockean thesis that understands belief itself in terms of some contextually determined threshold in degrees of belief, as defended in, for example, Foley (1992, 1993), Hawthorne and Bovens (1999), Sturgeon (2008), and Hawthorne (2009), threatens to imply full belief for expressions of confidence that are high. So if the paradox of the preface is viewed as avoidable only when the preface claim is restricted to something weaker than belief, it is not obvious that standard expressions of degree of belief can do any better than expressions of full belief.

One might then opt for expressions of levels of confidence that fall below the threshold needed for full belief. In such a case, however, the expression would be equivalent to the claim, "I am an agnostic about whether errors remain, though at the high end of range of levels of confidence that fall within that category." Such a remark is not so much an expression of fallibility or humility, but rather a disavowal of extreme forms of arrogance. In short, pointing out that one is not very arrogant, or not arrogant at all, is not an expression of humility.

---

[9] The parenthetical qualification "something like" is aimed at possibilities such as this: "I am a human being; human beings write books that always or nearly always still contain errors since humans are fallible; I leave it to the reader to infer the obvious." Such a remark contains a self-report "I am human," but no self-reporting avowal of fallibility. So I include the parenthetical remark to avoid unneeded precisifying in the text.

The equivalence claim made could be resisted by claiming that a level of confidence in errors remaining might not count as full belief nor in the range of levels of confidence that involve agnosticism by falling in the vague territory where it is unclear or indeterminate whether such an expression counts as full belief. In such a case, no deduction of a contradiction from contents of belief would be available, and perhaps in this way the paradox could be avoided.

It is important to notice, however, that this solution to the paradox is threatened by the possibility that epistemicism is the right approach to vagueness. Epistemicism is the view that, for every vagueness with respect to any feature F, there is a precise boundary between the presence of F and its absence, but that we are never in a position to be able to know what that precise boundary is.[10] In such a case, the vague territory in question will involve either an expression of full belief or it will not. If it does involve an expression of full belief, then the inconsistency at the heart of the paradox remains. And if it does not, then the avowal is not yet an expression of humility rather than one of lacking arrogance.

Whether or not epistemicism is the best approach to vagueness, appeal to an unclear boundary between full belief and agnosticism for the degree of confidence being expressed leaves us in the uncomfortable position where the claim in question amounts to an avowal that it is unclear whether to be agnostic or committed about whether errors remain. If we are looking for an appropriate expression of fallibility and humility, such a remark underwhelms. In order to express intellectual humility, a full commitment of some sort, even if not that of belief, appears to be required.

One might opt for other cognitive attitudes other than belief in hopes of avoiding the teeth of the paradox. One might hope, for example, that the recent work in epistemology distinguishing acceptance from belief might help. Perhaps a person might accept that errors remain, and voice this acceptance, even if the attitude of full belief is not present and is not appropriate.

The central issue here is the nature of acceptance and the explanation of how it differs from belief.[11] One might use this distinction to help in our context by claiming that there is no paradox if one believes (and does not accept) each claim in the book, while accepting (but not believing) the preface claim; or if one accepts (but does not believe) each claim of the book (as well as their conjunction), while believing (but not accepting) the preface claim.

In order to sustain such a response, one will have to defend these contrastive conjunctions, and on many of the accounts of acceptance, the needed contrasts won't be available. On L. Jonathan Cohen's account of acceptance, for example, to accept is to have or adopt a policy of positing, postulating, or deeming that the claim is true,

---

[10]   For a defense of epistemicism, see Williamson (1996).
[11]   Important discussion of the distinction begins with van Fraassen (1980) and includes Harman (1986), Cohen (1989, 1992), Lehrer (1990), Bratman (1992), Velleman (2000), Frankish (2004), and a good survey article is Weirich (2004).

to use the claim in question in reasoning and deliberation (Cohen 1992, p. 4). Given this understanding of acceptance, it is fairly clear that one can both rationally believe and rationally accept the individual claims of the book, and thus if the resolution of the paradox hinges on introducing acceptance into the story of the paradox, it would seem that it is the preface claim that must be resisted. If so, however, resorting to acceptance, in this sense of the term, requires demurring from the preface claim, and that response is surely no expression of fallibility or humility.

The second response above is that taken by Mark Kaplan (1983) and Patrick Maher (1993), extending the earlier work of Bas van Fraassen (1980) to the effect that a more responsible approach to science will countenance accepting theories but not believing them. These accounts try to balance the goals of comprehensiveness and accuracy in such a way that accepting the improbable is often rational (even though believing the improbable, understood in terms of believing something for which one's level of confidence is below .5, is incoherent). Preface claims can then be understood in terms of belief itself, without compromising one's acceptance of the contents of the book.

Such approaches to the paradox do a good job of retaining the intuitive attractiveness of the preface belief as a legitimate expression of fallibility and humility, but they have more difficulty explaining why belief in the contents of the book is to be avoided. Equally relevant is that this approach depends on a too-narrow conception of the goals of cognition. Typical accounts of the goals of cognition include comprehensiveness and accuracy (Kaplan 1983, Lehrer 2000), getting to the truth and avoiding error (Chisholm 1957), not being deceived but also not missing out on what's important (James 1897), or maximizing expected cognitive utility, understood in terms of closeness to the truth and informativeness (Maher 1993), but none of these explicitly addresses the importance of understanding in the aims of cognition. Intellectual curiosity is sated by understanding, involving the "aha" experience that comes from it (see Kvanvig (2013b)), and once the focus is on understanding, the problem is that the preface claim itself is central to a proper understanding of the world and one's place in it. So, to the extent that understanding is the goal in question, there is reason to think that whatever cognitive attitude is involved in understanding, it will appear *ad hoc* to carve off part of the system of understanding as appropriate for belief and save part of it as appropriate for acceptance. Hence, it would seem, a different approach is called for.

Perhaps some progress can be made by further pursuing the idea that there are other cognitive states to consider other than outright belief, outright acceptance, and degrees of either acceptance or belief. Here, the model of work in moral psychology might be fruitfully followed in epistemology, pursuing the idea of epistemological psychology. The temptations of reductionism incline us to want to treat all of epistemological psychology in terms of the notion of beliefs or degree of belief, taking one of these two notions as fundamental and explaining the other in terms of it (see, for example, Foley (1991), Sturgeon (2008)). Regardless of the success of such positions, we still theorize with an impoverished epistemological psychology, for in addition to the notions of belief and degrees of belief, there are also the notions of acceptance, supposition, presupposition, assumption, opinion, affirmation, (propositional) faith, confidences, and mental assents, along with stranger breeds of cognitive states such as suspicions and speculations. And there are the more generic attitudes involved in taking a stance on an issue or cause, making a commitment to an ideal, a person, an idea, a thought, etc., and the notion of judgment itself. Even in conscious cognitive states, such as we find in theory-laden experience with its attendant content, we need to separate awareness from attention. So there can be two awarenesses that are the same, even though what is attended to in each is different.

We should not assume that there are easy reductions to the notion of belief to be found here, but more importantly, we should take seriously the idea that an expanded epistemological psychology also renders problematic the notion of belief itself. Regarding that notion, there are two main guiding platitudes: belief is that which guides action, and belief is that which is reported in sincere assertion. These guiding platitudes, however, cannot both be true, when understood as exceptionless and necessary features of belief, unless one introduces notions of unconscious and tacit beliefs introduced solely to salvage the platitudes. Think, for example, of finding out in therapy that you haven't really believed what you've been sincerely asserting, perhaps because you were mistaken about what you thought you believed. Or examine the implications of high stakes cases where you have to choose to bet large sums either with or against experts with whom you disagree, or the same kinds of cases where you disagree with a strong majority of your peers. In such cases, it is plausible to think that what one sincerely avows can come apart from what guides action, both in terms of speech and other behavior.[12] And yet, sincerity of avowal would seem to need to track some cognitive state or other, even if it doesn't always track belief. Once we allow cognitive states other than belief into our epistemological psychology, we allow for exploration of whether some of these notions might provide a suitable cognitive expression for intellectual humility without generating paradox.

This idea of questioning the standard assumptions concerning epistemological psychology is thus an idea present, at least obliquely, in recent literature. It is thus

---

[12] For a taste of the literature on this conflict, see Gendler (2008a,b), Zimmerman (2007) for defense of the view that is pro-judgment regarding what is believed (i.e., that you really do believe what you sincerely avow even though you don't act on that belief), Hunter (2011) for defense of the view that is anti-judgment regarding what is believed (i.e., you really don't believe what you sincerely avow, since you refuse to act on the claim in the question), Rowbottom (2007) for defense of the view that what is believed shifts from context to context, and Gertler (2011), Sommers (2009) for defense of the view that there are contradictory beliefs in such cases. Schwitzgebel (2010) defends a vagueness account of such cases, according to which it is neither correct to attribute belief nor to deny it. Especially interesting in this regard is the work of David Henderson and Terry Horgan on implicit content in a cognitive system that is not representational at all (see Henderson and Horgan (2011) and Henderson and Horgan (2014)); see also Horgan and Potrč (2010, 2011).

worth considering whether other cognitive states can be put to service for appropriate expressions of intellectual humility in both thought and talk.[13]

7.4 Acts and States

We can begin by noting that some of the variety noted earlier can be categorized in terms of the distinction between mental acts and mental states. For example, when attempting a proof in logic, we often make assumptions. When we make an assumption in the context of attempting a proof, we have performed a mental act of a certain sort. But it is not the kind of thing we should be focusing on when we ask whether assuming p can be explained in terms of believing p. This latter issue must be thought of in terms of states of a person rather than a state and an act (since the reduction is meant to apply to mental states only).

The same is true for other items on the above list. The nature of judgment is vexingly related to the nature of belief, but not if we are asking about the act of judging itself: the act is certainly not something required by the state of belief. In general, then, when we are asking about items within our epistemological psychology, we will begin with those items that fall within the category of states, rather than acts.

What then is a state? In a good ontology, states differ from objects (they often have objects as constituents or participants) and events (states do not involve the notion of change, whereas events do). For the kinds of states involved in our investigation, it is types of states that are relevant. The types in question are elicited by abstraction from given concrete realities—for example, a specific believing by a cognizer with a specific content. Such a concrete reality may be momentary or extended in time, but once it ceases to exist, it is over and done with, never to appear again. Even if at a later time and place that very same person comes to believe that very same specific content, it will be a different believing. Call such unrepeatable concrete realities 'token believings'. From such tokens, we may abstract to the type level, which is repeatable. If we abstract from the specific content, we get one abstract type; if we abstract from the person, we get another. So, for example, from the token believing of p by S, we can abstract to a believing of p itself. It is such abstract state types that we investigate here. A belief in p is a state that more than one person can share, and can be multiply realized over time in the life of a given cognizer (one can be in that state at one time, cease to be in it at a later time, and come to be in that very same state at a later time).

---

[13] Some of the literature relevant to our discussion includes that concerning the relationship between beliefs and credences, including Sturgeon (2008), Audi (1982), Foley (1992, 1993), Kaplan (1998, 2010, 2013), Jeffrey (1992), and Hazlett (2012). I should note as well that much of what I discuss here has been influenced by conversations with Keith DeRose, who hasn't published his ideas on this matter, except in the unusual forum of Facebook posts. The notes on Facebook include "Do We Believe the Philosophical Positions We Accept?", "The Philosophical Positions We Take: Belief, Acceptance, Alston, and the Problem of Mercenary Acceptance", and "Stringent vs. Easy Construals of Belief: What to Make of Wishy-Washy Verbal Affirmations?".

7.5 The Economy of Belief

The extant literature on cognitive states attends carefully to the relationship between belief and degrees of belief. This literature is orthogonal to our interests here, but it is helpful nonetheless. If our initial target is to ascertain whether the territory of belief deserves the fundamental place it has in our theorizing about the epistemology of cognition, we should consider whether reduction is possible using both belief and degrees of belief as weapons. For the target is not the Lockean thesis that belief can be explained in terms of degrees of belief (plus a perhaps contextually determined threshold), but rather that the doxastic phenomena themselves are but a small part of the cognitive realm.

We can make progress on this issue by inducing some perplexity first. Start with our attitudes toward controversial matters: religion, politics, ethics, and philosophy more generally. In these areas, disputes abound. Even if there are other areas where we find widespread agreement among cognizers (simple arithmetic, for example), these areas are not like that.

One explanation here is that, in highly contentious arenas, knowledge is simply not possible. I do not think that position is correct, but I do think it is correct in certain cases. For example, we can divide philosophical positions into positive and negative ones. If your position is that, for example, knowledge is not justified true belief, that is a negative philosophical position; if your position is that Foundationalism is the proper solution to the regress argument for skepticism, that is a positive philosophical position.

I do not pretend that this distinction is precise. For example, if Internalism and Externalism exhaust one's options regarding theories of justification, the position that Internalism is false is, in some sense, the same position as the position that Externalism is true. But the first looks like a negative position and the second like a positive one. For present purposes, we need not chase this rabbit. The rough, intuitive distinction is all we need. That is, all we need are some clear cases of the two.

We only need some such clear cases to appreciate the point that even if knowledge of negative positions is possible, we shouldn't conclude that knowledge of positive positions is possible. It is (now) fairly easy to know, for example, that knowledge isn't justified true belief. But it seems an exaggeration to maintain that we know that Foundationalism is true (even assuming that this claim is true). I would think the wiser view is that we don't know such things, even when we have really good arguments for our (positive) positions. For purposes of discussion, let's assume that I'm correct, since all we need here is for such a metaphilosophical position to be held firmly in view.

So suppose you are both a Foundationalist and agree with me that you don't know that Foundationalism is true. Do you believe that Foundationalism is true? In favor of a positive answer is this: it is your position! What could be more obvious than that your position, when sincerely asserted and defended, is what you believe?

It is important here to notice the platitude about belief at work in this ascription of belief:

Sincerity Platitude: Belief is what gets reported in sincere assertion.

We've already seen reasons to doubt that this principle is true. It is simply not that difficult to make honest mistakes about one's own mental states, including beliefs. One of the more interesting features of psychological counseling is coming to discover that what one took oneself to believe is not in fact what one actually believes. Skilled counselors are good at detecting patterns of behavior that, when noticed, make it difficult to maintain that one actually believes what one has been sincerely claiming. It must be admitted that this phenomenon, where one learns that one doesn't believe what one sincerely avows, is easy to confuse with the phenomenon of masking, where what one believes doesn't show up in behavior because it is masked by other factors, leading a person to doubt that the belief is present at all, when it really is. Yet, the experience itself is enough to see the possibilities here: sometimes, the pattern of behavior shows a masking phenomenon, sometimes it shows that the Sincerity Platitude is not an exceptionless regularity, much less some kind of psychological law governing the relation between sincere speech and the doxastic realm.

Moreover, the phenomenology of adopting and defending a philosophical position is quite a conceptual distance from ordinary belief of the sort acquired in the process of mundane experience. I believe my neighbor just got a new white truck, having seen him driving it this past week, parking it in his driveway, asking him about it, etc. Belief arrived at deliberatively, in the process of developing or maintaining a philosophical position, is a quite different phenomenon. It is an experience with a feeling of optionality throughout: what should I make of that point, why might one resist this argument, etc.? It has the feel, that is, of being in the domain of agency, whereas the ordinary experience of belief formation about the observable world around us does not have that feel (except to the extent that is controlled by what we attend to).

These points are sufficient to prevent the simple inference above from the Sincerity Platitude to the conclusion that one's positive philosophical position is what one believes. There are two other lines of argument to this same conclusion. The first arises from consideration of norms for assertion and belief, and the second arises from a second platitude about belief: to wit, that belief is what guides action.

Since this second consideration inclines, as does the Sincerity Platitude, toward the conclusion one's position on an issue is what one believes about that issue, I take it up first. Since it is also a platitude, let's name it:

Action-Guidance Platitude: Belief is what guides action.

If belief guides action, the natural conclusion to draw is that the action of asserting and defending a philosophical position is one guided by what one believes, and the obvious candidate for playing this role is belief in the truth of that position.

It is here that modern decision theory presents an enormous advance over folk theory, one aspect of which is this Action-Guidance Platitude. We should expect, according to modern decision theory, that the rational behavior of rational people is a function, not of what they believe and desire, but rather a function of credences and preference rankings. From this perspective, the Action-Guidance Platitude is less like a necessary law of human psychology and more like the rules of thumb for proper conduct learned at mother's knee: an excellent rough-and-ready guide, but insufficient for advanced theoretical purposes.

I make no commitment to the idea that it is degree of belief, rather than belief itself, that guides action, but only that such a position is a theoretical improvement over the blunt position encoded in the Action-Guidance Platitude. By making progress in epistemological psychology, we will better be able to assess whether the resources of decision theory need to be supplemented or whether the current approach in terms of degrees of belief and orderings on preferences is adequate.

There is also a third consideration against identifying one's position with what one believes. We can approach the issue a bit indirectly by first considering the relationship between belief and assertion together with a plausible explanation of a norm for assertion. It has been argued recently that the fundamental norm governing assertion is the knowledge norm: don't say what you don't know to be true.[14] While there is no consensus that this norm is exceptionless and necessary, it is plausible as at least a rough-and-ready guide to appropriate speech.[15]

It is also true that there is an interesting inner/outer connection between belief and speech. We should expect (again, at, at least, the rough-and-ready stage) that belief is to assertion as inner is to outer, so that if the outer is subject to a knowledge norm, so is the inner.[16] We thus have a reason to think that there is a knowledge norm for belief: don't believe what you don't know to be true. Again, to be clear, none of this reasoning presumes that the norms in question are exceptionless, only that there is some plausibility to the idea that, to the extent that one feels bound to say only what one knows to be true, to that same extent one should feel bound to believe only what one knows to be true.

I am not persuaded by this line of argument, but that is not relevant for the use I want to make of it. What is relevant is that many people, especially philosophers, will find this line of reasoning persuasive, and they often live out (or at least we can imagine them living out) their convictions so that they refrain from believing anything they don't know to be true. And yet, we find even those philosophers most inclined toward this kind of argument aggressively defending and articulating their (positive)

---

[14] See e.g. Williamson (2000), DeRose (2002), Hawthorne and Stanley (2008).

[15] For contrary viewpoints, Lackey (2008) defends the idea of saying only what one has good reasons to believe, Weiner (2005) argues for saying only what is true, Bach and Harnish (1979) endorse a sincerity norm, saying only what one believes to be true, and in several places I develop the view that one should only say what one rationally believes (in Kvanvig (2009a, 2011b,c, 2013d) and most fully in Kvanvig (2014)).

[16] As suggested in Williamson (2000).

positions on various philosophical matters quite regularly. If such articulation and defense counts as assertion, normative consistency is threatened. One explanation would be that there is no inconsistency here, since such philosophers may take themselves to know that their positive positions are correct. That is possible, but hard to swallow. The hubris it would take to be like that is enormous. That's not an argument that it isn't the case, of course. But I want to use it as a reason to consider what it would be like for the less optimistic among us to act the way philosophers do when defending and articulating their positive views.

We are assuming, still, that these less optimistic models embrace the inner/outer relationship between belief and assertion, and nonetheless defend and articulate their views in unqualified ways. Two options present themselves here. The first is to insist that the notion of an assertion is a technical one, so that what they are doing doesn't really count as assertion after all. (Leave it to a philosopher to always have at the ready the distinction-drawing card to avoid inconsistency.) The idea would be that all such public claims on behalf of one's position really count as having an implicit qualifier: "By the standards appropriate to the domain of inquiry, p is true," and that claim is something one could reasonably take oneself to know even while granting that knowledge of p itself is too much to expect.

What is clear, however, is that the distinction-drawing ploy doesn't save a view from disconfirmation by a counterexample. It can save a view from inconsistency, but plausibility requires much more than consistency. And here, the ploy is especially inadequate, since the distinction is motivated by nothing more than the need to save the collage of viewpoints from the difficulty posed by the behavior in question. There is no general approach to the contextuality of utterances that would allow one to say that in certain contexts, declarative utterances count as assertions and in others they don't, which when applied to utterances of philosophical dogma, yields the conclusion that such utterances don't count as straightforward assertions. Instead, all we have is the *ad hoc* use of the general possibility that some utterances don't count as assertions to save embarrassment for speaking so directly and forcefully.

A better approach here would be to grant that philosophers are asserting, but insist on the defeasible character of the knowledge norm of assertion, noting that it can be overridden by the value of speculative thought, perhaps in service of the goal of getting to the truth in the long run (or, for those inclined toward attitudinalist construals of normative language, in service of the kind of cooperation that makes for individual and societal flourishing). Restoring consistency here could be achieved by simply endorsing and publicly affirming a Socratic meta-norm: in certain matters, including philosophy, religion, and politics, we hardly ever know, and when we speak, we do so in a way that doesn't violate the knowledge norm, or if it does, its normative force is overridden by conflicting factors.[17] Such a viewpoint is much better than the *ad hoc*

---

[17] I call the norm "Socratic" because it endorses the Socratic dictum that philosophers, including Socrates himself, have little or no knowledge of which they speak.

maneuver above, so let's adopt this interpretation of the scope of the knowledge norm of assertion for the present.

Once we've reached this point, the question to ask is one about belief: what exactly is the relationship, in the practice as envisioned, between a philosopher's position on a given issue and what is believed by that philosopher about that issue? Pretty clearly, it is a mistake to identify the two. The rubric in question (the knowledge norm plus the inner/outer symmetry) puts a kind of generalized pressure on a person not to believe things not known to be true, in the same way that rules-of-thumb in morality put generalized pressure on a person to tell the truth, for example, even when it isn't required. So it should not surprise us to discover that philosophers, when reflecting on whether they believe the views they espouse, often deny that they believe them. The views in question are ones that they defend, articulate, develop, and champion, but this combination of attitudes and behaviors is compatible with lack of belief, and many take themselves to be doing all of these in spite of not really believing the claims espoused. So, once again, we see reason to doubt any simple identification of one's position on an issue with what one believes about that issue. If we grant that philosophers (are aware that they) do not know their positive positions to be true, many of them will also not believe them to be true, even when they aggressively defend those positions.

Notice as well that the defenses and articulations of a philosophical position need not involve overt behavior of any sort. The stance involved in taking and defending a position can be purely mental. In the usual case, expressing such a stance involves public behavior such as saying out loud what the stance involves or writing down what the commitments come to. But such stances and commitments can be as purely mental as paradigmatically mental entities such as beliefs, hopes, wishes, and fears. Moreover, adopting such a stance or making such a commitment is explanatorily central to overt behavior. We want to know why people are so adamant in defense of a certain claim, and the answer is that they are committed to that claim; and this explanation is correct even if the commitment is not a belief.

It is not only in philosophy that such commitments and stances occur. Commitments to a cause, whether by religious zealots or campaigners against various forms of injustice around the world, explain the behavior of those involved in the cause. In many, perhaps most, such cases, there is little reason to suspect that those so committed do not have the relevant beliefs, beliefs that the religion in question is true, that the cause is just, that injustices have occurred that must be righted, etc. Equally so, however, there is no reason to suppose that commitments to a cause require these beliefs. Just as Pyrrhonian skeptics needed patterns of reinforcement to keep themselves on the path of avoiding belief formation, it is easy to see why many of those who participated in, say, the Crusades had to remind themselves often of the reasons for the campaign. Rulers trying to mobilize subjects to take on such a commitment are well-served by citing reasons for the cause that the subjects already believe, so it is not surprising that the mobilizing rationales often appeal to religion.

But notice that such mobilization would work just as well if the appeal were not to *beliefs* but to *commitments already in place*. So the fact that mobilization can succeed by a certain set of proffered reasons does not decisively show that these reasons appeal to beliefs already in place.

Note as well that if one thinks carefully about how Pyrrhonian skepticism can provide a model for such commitments, the connection between belief and commitment can more easily be seen to be tenuous not only inside philosophy but outside it as well. For Pyrrhonian communities are more like religious communities than they are like current, professional philosophical communities (whether local to a particular university or located only in cyberspace). Commitment to the ideals of the community involved daily practices to reinforce such commitments, and it is a regular aspect of religious communities to engage in public affirmations of the stance one has adopted (where the stance itself is an internal, mental feature of some sort). Such practices could be engaged in by those who lacked the beliefs that one would normally expect to be present in such individuals.[18] Such commitments may well involve cognitive features such as making a judgment on the matter, accepting or embracing a position, or (in the preferred language of the Pyrrhonians) affirming or acquiescing to appearances of one sort or another.

In the face of such alternative vocabularies, our reductive tendencies in philosophy lead toward a conclusion that multiplicity is illusory and that they are all forms of belief: to judge that *p* is true is to believe that *p* is true, as is to affirm or accept that *p* is true. Religious zealots are "true believers," etc. Yet, the ways in which philosophers embrace their positions is more like the way the faithful relate to their religions: they are believers in the sense of believing *in*, and believing in is more a matter of what one's commitments are and what stand one is taking than is propositional belief. And as we've seen above, there are multiple reasons for thinking that one can be a believer in this sense without actually propositionally believing the claims in question.

By attending to this gap between one's commitments and one's beliefs, we can come to see why we might want to use terms such as 'assent' or 'affirmation' to indicate the relationship one has to one's commitments. Philosophers may be said to affirm certain positions and assent to them. We might even describe them in terms of having certain opinions on these issues, provided we are careful to note that we are using 'opinion' in a way that is not a synonym for belief.[19]

---

[18] It is a further and more difficult question whether these practices could be engaged in by those who held absolutely no beliefs of any sort at all, as would be required for consistent Pyrrhonians (on one interpretation of their opposition to belief). All that is needed for present purposes is the limited possibility of taking a stance, adopting a position, making an intellectual commitment, and reinforcing all of that through public activities, rituals of various sorts, devotional practices (using perhaps Sacred Writ or even the Ten Modes of Skepticism—see Annas and Barnes (1985)), and other activities, all the while not actually believing the claims in question.

[19] There is precedent for a non-synomymous use of the term in the ill-conceived distinction between fact and opinion taught to our children in elementary school. In such exercises, the actual target is a fact/value

Central to what one affirms or assents to, in the sense just indicated, is a matter of focus and feel. For example, there is a different kind of feel that can be present when considering positions one adopted many years ago. In some cases, the positions are a matter of continued focus over the course of one's life, but in other cases, one's focus has moved on to other matters and the previous positions are no longer in view as part of one's present projects. When one is then asked about such prior positions several years or decades later, the positions previously adopted have a strange feel to them, a different feel than beliefs adopted that remain below the level of consciousness for decades. I never think much about the fact that Hettinger is southeast of New England, but I've believed it since my youth. When I mention this claim, it has a familiarity to it, it is a part of me. But when asked about the positions I defended two decades ago and haven't thought about since, the feeling is one of either needing to reaffirm the positions or refusing to do so. Those positions are part of a former self, but not clearly a part of me now until and unless reaffirmed.

Of course, many of one's positions come to be things believed as well as affirmed, and such positions, after long periods below the level of consciousness, will not have this alien feel to them. Moreover, the road from commitment and affirmation to full belief is an easy one, wide and well-traveled. For many people, there may never be a difference between what they affirm and what they believe. Whether or not one's own psychology leaves room for such differences, the distinction between them can be appreciated through the grounds for the distinction given above.

7.6 Commitments as Expressions of Humility

This notion of a commitment, stance, or affirmation that is centrally a matter of focus, feel, and attention (or dispositions toward such) dovetails nicely with an approach to intellectual humility that treats it as a virtue of attention. Note first, from Nicolas Bommarito's work on the virtue of modesty, the general category of virtues of attention:

The virtues of attention are virtues that are rooted in how we direct our attention. These virtues are sometimes moral but not always. It is an academic virtue of attention to be able to focus one's attention on a long and technical lecture. It is an aesthetic virtue of attention for one to pay attention to the relationship between the narrative and shot composition in a film. Gratitude is a moral virtue of attention because it involves directing one's attention to the value of what someone else has done for us. (Bommarito 2013, p. 100)

Bommarito's account of modesty then proceeds as follows:

[I]t is necessary to have a good quality to be modest about. Contrary to most contemporary views, it is not necessary to underestimate the good quality nor is it necessary to have an

distinction, but the linguistic practice in question is widespread enough that dictionaries have an entry for one meaning of the word in terms of "a personal view, attitude, or appraisal."

accurate assessment. Instead, what is necessary is to direct one's conscious attention in certain ways—away from the trait or its value or toward the outside causes and conditions that played a role in developing it.

Attending in these ways, however, is not sufficient for modesty; it must happen for the right reasons. (Bommarito 2013, p. 103)

Bommarito explicitly uses the term 'modesty' as a synonym for 'humility', so the idea is thus to view humility as a virtue involving a commitment or stance of a certain sort. Bommarito's suggestions are a good start toward an account of this sort, though we will want to work on the details a bit. We turn to this project in the next two chapters, first exploring the logical space of humility, including its relationship to modesty, and then investigating the topic of the nature of humility itself and whether an attentional approach to that topic can survive scrutiny.

7.7 Conclusion

We can note, however, that we have achieved resolution of the worry that expressions of humility engender paradox, provided the account of humility hinted at above can be defended. The idea is to treat the preface claim as an affirmation of, an endorsement of, a way of maintaining focus on, one's fallibility and thus an appropriate expression of humility. Such an affirmation or endorsement, in order to be sincere, cannot stand in opposition to what one truly thinks of one's grasp of the truth, but it can be undergirded by nothing more than a generic belief or acceptance of the claim that one is fallible or liable to error. To remark that one is sure that errors remain in even one's best work is to strip the modal dimension of what one accepts or believes to make vivid to the reader what one is attending to or focusing on in remarking on one's own fallibility. It is thus an affirmation of the claim that errors remain, and is sincere even if or when it is not accompanied by full belief or acceptance of the claim that errors remain.

This particular speech act and its internal correlate thus serve the purpose of keeping the eyes downcast as one stands before the bar of Reason and Truth: one could just have appropriately remarked that not only do errors remain but so do flawed arguments that do not serve to make rational all the opinions expressed. Central to the phenomenon in question is the downcasting itself, accomplished through the vehicle of speech with a particular content. Remarking on general liabilities to error or common human foibles, on specific liabilities to such in one's past, present, or future selves will strike most authors as too oblique to serve the function in question. The downcasting sought calls for the bluntness involved in modal stripping: fallibility turns into error personified, in order to serve as the sought-for expression of intellectual humility. In all of this, there is no insincerity or confabulation involved even if the remarks in question do not constitute a report of full belief. For the function in question is about focus and attention, constituting a different type of context than that of the book itself, where the more standard context of assertion governs.

This viewpoint dovetails nicely with an account of humility itself as a virtue of attention, in much the same way as gratitude is a virtue of attention. Pursuing that line of thought will occupy us in the next two chapters, but what we have here is what was desired, to be able to explain how unqualified preface remarks can be exactly the right way to express intellectual humility, in a way that need not generate fodder for those looking to create paradox from them.

We are thus in a position to move beyond concerns that might lead one to doubt that humility is a virtue or that its expression threatens paradox. What remains is a more careful locating of humility within logical space and a focused attempt to say exactly what humility involves. We take up these two topics in turn in the next two chapters.

8

The Logical Space of Humility

8.1 Introduction

The goal of this chapter is to pin down as well as we can the logical space of humility by distinguishing it from closely related concepts such as modesty, arrogance, pride, and vanity, as well as addressing the vexed issue of how and whether intellectual humility requires abandoning one's autonomy. Doing so will put us in a position to explain the nature of humility in the next chapter by preventing some confusions between humility and closely related notions. It will also aid in defending more fully the claim that it is a virtue and thereby has value in the pursuit of the good life.

Consider first the relationship between humility and modesty, two closely related character traits. In the literature, one sometimes finds an identification of the two: "I take the terms to be interchangeable but will use the term 'modest' in my discussion" (Bommarito 2013, p. 93, n. 1). Others, however, see a distinction between the two, with humility being the more exaggerated of the two. One version of this idea is voiced by Fritz Allhoff:

Humility differs from modesty in that the former is a Christian virtue that would not have been endorsed by the Ancients, whereas modesty is one that I take to be more time-honored and less culturally emergent. Nevertheless, it is interesting to ask what the relation is between modesty and humility. I think they are clearly similar, but, different in an important way. Humility entails having a low opinion of oneself whereas modesty entails having a moderate opinion of oneself. ('Modest' comes from the Latin 'modestus' which can be translated as 'moderate.' 'Humility' is derived from Old French 'humilité' which in turn came from Latin 'humilis' which translates as 'low.') Thus, it seems to me that the two could come apart if someone had an excessively low opinion of oneself; in this case, he could be humble but not modest.   (Allhoff 2010, p. 184)

Allhoff claims that humility requires a low opinion of self, while modesty requires a moderate opinion. Others have voiced the same idea: A. T. Nuyen (1998) and Aaron Ben-Ze'ev (1993) claim that humility requires underestimating one's capacities (echoing a point first made by Julia Driver (1989) and argued more extensively in Driver (2001)) while modesty does not.

All these views see modesty and humility on the same continuum. They do so by either identifying the two or seeing humility as a more exaggerated form of a basic orientation of a person toward their capacities or abilities.

I will argue that both of these perspectives are mistaken. I will argue, that is, that this continuum hypothesis regarding the relationship between humility and modesty is false. The argument I will develop aims at showing that humility and modesty, though closely related, are not to be thought of on a continuum involving opinions toward oneself.

It is worth noting the particular continuum that is involved here. The continuum involves cognitive self-assessment, with Driver's original idea being that these virtues require a mistakenly low assessment.[1] Others, including Ben-Ze'ev (1993), Nuyen (1998), Flanagan (1990), Richards (1988), and Statman (1992), have argued in favor of an explanation of the value of such traits in a way that involves accurate self-assessment, but it is worth noting that none of these defenses challenge the continuum hypothesis itself. To the extent that the two traits can be identified, their value involves accurate self-assessment, these authors maintain; to the extent that they are distinct in such a way that humility has an exaggeratedly low assessment of self, only the value of modesty is defended.

I want to focus first on the continuum hypothesis itself, leaving to one side the question of the value of these traits. I assume they are valuable, but nothing I say here about the continuum hypothesis depends on the value issue at all. The argument I will develop arises out of consideration of the relevant contrasts for these two character traits, and to this issue I turn in the next section.

8.2 Contrasts to Humility and Modesty

We can begin to see what is mistaken about the continuum hypothesis by first noticing the relevant contrasts for humility and modesty. The contrasts to humility that leap to mind are pride and arrogance as well as conceit. We see this contrast in quotes commonly attributed to St. Augustine and Frank Lloyd Wright, respectively:

It was pride that changed angels into devils; it is humility that makes men as angels.

(St. Augustine)

Early in life I had to choose between honest arrogance and hypocritical humility. I chose the former and have seen no reason to change.

(Frank Lloyd Wright)

Nor must we forget the adage dear to the heart of all true Tarheels:

North Carolina, a valley of humility between two mountains of conceit.

(Mary Oates Spratt Van Landingham)

---

[1] This view she shares with Hume, who held that humility was a "monkish" virtue which is really a vice (Hume 1777 [1748], Section 219) involving known underestimation of one's accomplishments or abilities. He claimed that it was understandably valued, since there is a "much greater propensity to overvalue than undervalue" ourselves, and hence that we tend "to regard, with a peculiar indulgence, all tendency to modesty and self-diffidence" (Hume 1777 [1748], Section 213). The difference between the two is that Driver insists that the low self-assessments involve ignorance, and thinks that the value of these assessments can be defended in this way and contrary to Hume's negative assessment.

When it comes to modesty, however, the contrast is quite different. When we think of those lacking this virtue, we think of those who suffer from vanity and those who engage in ostentatious displays. This contrast between modesty and vanity, showiness, ostentation, and gaudiness is a common theme:

Nothing so soothes our vanity as a display of greater vanity in others; it make us vain, in fact, of our modesty.   (Louis Kronenberger)

Every author, however modest, keeps a most outrageous vanity chained like a madman in the padded cell of his breast.   (Logan Pearsall Smith)

What is the vanity of the vainest man compared with the vanity which the most modest possesses when, in the midst of nature and the world, he feels himself to be "man"!
(Friedrich Nietzsche)

A vain man finds it wise to speak good or ill of himself; a modest man does not talk of himself.
(Jean de la Bruyère)

Style is the dress of thought; a modest dress, Neat, but not gaudy, will true critics please.
(Samuel Wesley)

This, then, is held to be the duty of the man of wealth: First, to set an example of modest, unostentatious living, shunning display or extravagance ...   (Andrew Carnegie)

I had rather be shut up in a very modest cottage with my books, my family and a few old friends, dining on simple bacon, and letting the world roll on as it liked, than to occupy the most splendid post, which any human power can give.   (Thomas Jefferson)

These remarks about humility and modesty, and their contrasts, are instructive in our context. They should make us suspicious of the idea that humility and modesty are the same thing, and suspicious of the idea that one is an exaggerated form of the other, unless we are willing to say the same thing about the primary contrasts of each. I'm not claiming that these quotations constitute a decisive argument here, but only that they should raise our suspicions, leading us to investigate the continuum hypothesis more directly and more carefully. We can begin to do so by comparing vanity and pride.

8.3 Vanity and Pride

We may note, first, that vanity, conceived as a excessive attitude toward how one's abilities or attractiveness appear to others, is often thought of as a form of pride. Perhaps closer to the truth is that both fall under a more general category, one concerning self-regarding attitudes. In both cases, the attitudes are excessive in some way, and often, perhaps most often, both types of attitudes are found together. Not always, however, for when we think of instances of vanity that involve a predilection for ostentation and pretentiousness ("you had one eye in the mirror as you watched yourself gavotte"), we can appreciate how pride can be present without vanity. Vanity is more centrally about how one takes oneself to appear to others, placing great stress on the significance of this appearance. Pride does not require acknowledging the significance of the perspective of the other, since one can be so proud as to cherish the negative appraisals of others, taking it as further confirmation of their inferiority.

So pride without vanity is possible, but so is vanity without pride. Solomon, adorned in all his glory in service of the image it presents to his subjects, might still view the spectacle as a chasing after the wind relative to how he views himself, but it could still be a display of vanity. It could be, that is, a self-conscious display of vanity for political purposes by a person who recognizes his own impermanence and insignificance in the grand scheme of things—a person who thus displays vanity while at the same time not being proud and not engaging in prideful behavior.

The instrumental role of the ostentation might lead some to resist the Solomon example. The idea would be that what we should be looking for is an example in which vanity is involved for its own sake, just as it is when we find examples of pride without vanity. The claim would then be that if we control for this distinction between what is valued for its own sake and what is valued only instrumentally, we won't find any examples of vanity without pride, thus threatening the idea that neither of these is a special case of the other.

This attempt to defend the subclass relation between vanity and pride does not withstand scrutiny. If vanity entails pride, then it does so whether or not in service of an instrumental good. One might wonder whether there are examples where vanity is not present in service of an instrumental good and yet pride is not also present, but no answer to that query will threaten the general point that the examples above reveal: vanity can be present without pride, and pride without vanity.

The basic point to make here is that vanity is more other-oriented than pride needs to be. A vain person places quite a bit of stock in the opinions and attitudes of others, relishing a capacity to generate admiration and perhaps even envy; whereas a proud person need not attach such significance to the opinions and attitudes of others, perhaps to the point of not caring at all what others think. As Mary Bennet observes in Jane Austen's *Pride and Prejudice*, "Vanity and pride are different things, though the words are often used synonymously. A person may be proud without being vain. Pride relates more to our opinion of ourselves, vanity to what we would have others think of us."

The usefulness of this difference between pride and vanity is that it tells us something important about the difference between humility and modesty. To the extent that these character traits have different paradigmatic contrasts, to that extent we should distinguish the two. Since pride and vanity can each appear without the other, we should expect that humility and modesty can come apart in the same way. If the continuum hypothesis were true, one would expect these paradigmatic contrasts to also fall on a continuum, where one type of contrast is a more exaggerated form of the other. But they need not. Vanity is not a more exaggerated form of pride, nor is pride a more exaggerated form of vanity. Moreover, they are obviously not the same vice either, and these points remain even after noticing that particular forms of one tend to appear as forms of the other.

Given the continuum hypothesis, we should have expected that if there is a difference between humility and modesty, it would be the difference between very low self-
assessment and low self-assessment. Whatever that difference amounts to, however,
it is not a difference answering to the difference between humility and modesty. The
continuum hypothesis is false. So humility is neither the same as modesty nor a more
exaggerated form of negative self-assessment, even if there is a strong correlation or
even a causal relationship of a probabilistic sort between the two.

To sum up, the continuum hypothesis is false. Humility and modesty are different
virtues, if virtues they be. The second is more other-responsive than the first, and the
result of this point is that each can be present without the other. This point should
be supplemented by noting how and why they are likely to be thought to be related,
perhaps even synonymous, for those who display the distinctive contrasts to these
virtues tend to display both contrasts together: if they are proud, they tend to be vain;
and if vain, proud. Even so there is an important distinction to be made here, and
confusion results from trying to understand humility by thinking about vanity or by
using pride to help one understand modesty.

8.4 A Threat to Autonomy?

In considering the logical space of humility, we should not only consider its relationship to modesty, pride, and vanity, but we should also consider its compatibility
with autonomy. Whereas confusion about the former leads to mistakes in isolat-
ing the nature of humility, assumptions about the relationship between humility
and autonomy leads not only to mistakes about the nature of humility but also
to difficulties in defending the virtue and value of humility. The difficulty arises
because of the central role that autonomy plays in human life, but also because
of its central (and to my mind, indispensable) role in the theory of rationality,
both practical and epistemic. Along with several others,[2] I have argued (in Kvanvig
(2014)) for such a role for autonomy. Such a role, I argue, is required in order to
find a middle way between two extremes in theorizing about rationality. On one
extreme are views that overemphasize what we have in common with the beasts,
identifying human rationality in the same kinds of terms that are used for identifying
the rationality of the beasts (reliability, skills and excellences at getting to the truth,
proper functioning in terms of a design plan, etc.). At the other extreme are views
that focus so much on our capacity for self-consciousness and reflective awareness
of our epistemic practices and patterns that they identify rationality only with that
which is displayed in reflective, self-aware moments of our intellectual lives (such as
is displayed by Descartes when he takes a seat in front of the fire to sort his beliefs
into those to keep and those to discard). An intermediate position acknowledges

---

[2] See e.g. Lehrer (1997), Foley (2007), and Zagzebski (2012).

the epistemic significance of reflection in the life of the mind without sacrificing the idea that such reflective dimensions to rationality are only a part of its story. Once the epistemic significance of reflective ascent is acknowledged, however, the central question is one concerning the mechanisms by which the standards for rational opinion change in light of such reflection. The appropriate answer, I argue, involves an appeal to intellectual autonomy, in the Kantian sense—an answer adverting to rules one gives oneself as an intellectual being, one whose only concerns are the classic concerns of epistemology, concerns such as truth, knowledge, understanding, and theoretical wisdom.[3] But if rationality involves autonomy in this way, we have some difficulty explaining how humility can be an intellectual virtue. For autonomy and humility seem in tension: to be autonomous appears to involve a high degree of self-trust and self-direction, whereas humility involves a disposition toward at least a modicum of self-deprecation. In the context of the theory of rationality thus articulated, it would seem, then, that intellectual humility makes it difficult to be rational.

If this tension can be resolved, we will have a better understanding of the logical space of humility and we will be in a better position to reach a conclusion about whether humility is a virtue and is valuable because of it. One way to try to explain the tension views it as arising out of a failure to recognize the possibility of conflict between different domains of normativity. I consider this possibility in the following section, arguing that it doesn't provide an adequate solution to the problem in question. I then turn to my preferred solution, arguing that a proper understanding of both humility and autonomy involves no conflict at all.

8.5 Conflicting Domains

A first possibility tries to account for the tension by claiming that it arises from different domains of normativity. Just as something can be both morally required and politically damaging, or practically valuable and yet morally forbidden, so can a particular mental attitude or characteristic be both morally admirable and epistemically inadequate. On this approach, one maintains that humility might be an intellectual virtue, in the sense that it is a moral virtue of the functioning of the mind, claiming at the same that it is nonetheless an epistemic vice.

In favor of such a position is the commonplace possibility of conflict between epistemic and moral normativity. One can be morally required not to hold certain beliefs even if one has good evidence for them, and one can also perhaps be morally required to hold certain beliefs even in the absence of adequate evidence for them. On this latter point, recall the claims of Simon Keller (2004b) and Sarah Stroud (2006) about what is involved in friendship noted earlier in Chapter 5. Keller writes:

---

[3] See also Zagzebski (1996) for a similar approach.

It can sometimes *feel* as though loyalty to a friend pulls you in an opposite direction from your better epistemic judgment. Suppose that your friend is denying an accusation, and that the evidence against her is strong but not conclusive. You might find yourself believing your friend's story, while having the nagging realization that, did she not happen to be your friend, you wouldn't. . . .

The thesis that the norms of friendship can clash with epistemic norms offers one explanation of these observations.   (Keller 2004b, p. 331)

One might resist Keller's conclusion, pointing out that the story as told might involve an epistemically unjustified belief that results from friendship while denying that the belief in question is morally required or even appropriate. In response to such a viewpoint, however, consider Stroud's claims about the central role of commitment in the moral life:

Similarly, our friendships function as commitments. To be someone's friend is to have cast your lot in with his and, indeed, with his good character; and this properly affects how you respond to new situations and new data. . . . A commitment to your friend's merits is more something you bring to the various situations which confront you than something you take away from the information you receive. This is reflected in our epistemic partiality toward our friends.

(Stroud 2006, p. 512)

If this picture of the moral life is correct, then it is possible to have morally appropriate and perhaps required beliefs even in the absence of adequate evidence for them. In one sense, the possibility of such conflict should be expected for those already convinced of the possibility of beliefs that are justified all-things-considered but unjustified from a purely epistemic point of view, cases of the sort emphasized by Blaise Pascal and William James in defense of religious belief.[4] Even those who reject the particular conclusions such defenses aim at often grant the possibility in question, rejecting the kind of Epistemic Fetishism requiring that epistemic factors must of necessity overrule all others.[5] The proper conclusion to draw, then, is that the possibility of such conflict should be granted.

To resolve the tension between humility and autonomy, however, more is involved than merely embracing the possibility of conflict between the epistemic and the moral. For using this possibility to resolve the tension requires denying that intellectual humility is a virtue that falls within the domain of the epistemic. Instead, it is a moral virtue while also failing to be an epistemic one, since the explanation given traces the moral significance of the trait to its role in intellectual life and not to its epistemic significance.

It is worth noting that such a position fits nicely with approaches to the preface paradox of the sort defended by John Pollock (1986b) discussed in the last chapter. One specific example of the preface paradox is the paradox of fallibility, where the

---

[4] See Pascal (1966 [1669]) and James (1897).
[5] Exceptions exist, of course, most notably W. K. Clifford (1877 [1999]).

preface statement is the fallibilist's motto that some of my (other) present beliefs are false and the contents of the book are all these other beliefs. Given the above account of the Preface Paradox, Pollock's strategy tells me I can't have this metabelief, but only some weaker claim.

As we saw, the fundamental problem with both Pollock's approach to the paradox and the general idea that intellectual humility is an epistemic vice is that preface statements seem entirely appropriate and a sincere expression of intellectual humility. Moreover, they seem not only appropriate from a moral or all-things-considered point of view, but also from the epistemic point of view understood in terms of the goals of getting to the truth and avoiding error and of securing the great epistemic goods of knowledge, understanding, and theoretical wisdom.

So something more than an appeal to conflicting domains of normativity is needed in order to characterize properly the relationship between humility and autonomy. Such an approach recommends embracing the idea that from a purely theoretical point of view there is no basis to be found for recommending intellectual humility. It is only when other dimensions are considered, especially the moral dimension, that such a quality can be recommended. This position, however, is mistaken: when the only considerations taken into account are purely intellectual or theoretical ones concerning successful connections between mind and world, intellectual humility has much to recommend it. It would appear to be sober and sound judgment at its best to see our limitations for what they are. It may also be a moral virtue, but we should not (at this point in our investigation) settle for the pessimistic view that it is not a virtue falling within the domain of epistemology, understood in terms of inquiry into adequate, successful connections between mind and world from a purely cognitive, intellectual, theoretical point of view. Perhaps we will have to embrace such pessimism, if the best account of the nature of humility requires it. But we should land ourselves on that shore only when driven by the winds of material to be considered in the next chapter. At this point, we should see whether there is a way to characterize the relationship between humility and autonomy that doesn't require such pessimism. We thus seek an account of these matters that resolves any apparent tension between humility and the role of autonomy in epistemology, for only such an account can leave open the possibility that intellectual humility is both an intellectual virtue (conceived of as a kind of moral virtue) and an epistemic virtue.

8.6 Two Conceptions of Autonomy

One central idea about autonomy in the life of the mind involves independence or self-sufficiency. As Benjamin McMyler frames it, "fully rational cognitive agents are always solely epistemically responsible for the justification of their own beliefs" (McMyler 2011, p. 30) and Elizabeth Fricker says the autonomous knower "relies on no one else for any of her knowledge" (Fricker 2006, p. 225).

If we think of autonomy in these ways, autonomy is not a promising aspect of a good epistemological theory. The Fricker account is easy to refute simply by pointing out the possibility of testimonial knowledge.[6] Under whatever theory one wishes to endorse about such knowledge, it involves relying on someone else. The belief one forms is a causal result of what is said by another person, and this causal relation is sufficient to show reliance of the knowledge gained on the testifier.

What of the McMyler quote, however? That quote mixes three different epistemic notions, that of justification of belief, that of the rationality of an agent, and that of epistemic responsibility for something (either a state or an activity, depending on whether the phrase 'justification of belief' refers to the state of being justified or the activity of justifying).

We need not pursue the nature of and relationships between this smorgasbord of epistemic delights, however, since my complaint about the kind of autonomy on display in these quotes bypasses such concerns. My complaint here is not that there are not interesting notions of autonomy of the sort described by McMyler and Fricker, but rather that a discussion of intellectual autonomy needs to go in a different direction. Instead of characterizing autonomy and then seeing whether the item so characterized has epistemic value, we can proceed best by looking for ways in which it is permissible or required to be autonomous and ways in which it is not.

Our question, then, concerns the role of humility and whether it compromises the kind of autonomy that can be defended with respect to the sphere of the epistemic. The arrogant and haughty have no need to be taught by anybody, and thus display a high degree of (indefensible) autonomy. The humble are not so, and thus display a lesser degree of autonomy. So the mere fact that humility conflicts with autonomy is not a concern. What would be a matter of concern is if the only kind of autonomy that is valuable is one that conflicts with humility in epistemic contexts.

We can see why this is not the case by contrasting the self-sufficiency model of autonomy with a different, Kantian notion of autonomy. On this notion, autonomy is a function of following rules that one gives to oneself as a rational agent. Autonomy plays a role not in the sense that one is too confident of one's own ability to get to the truth and avoid error, but rather in the sense of having nowhere else to go except to use one's best judgment about how to go about figuring things out. Autonomy doesn't demand that one never acquiesces to the opinions or recommendations of others, for it often is obvious to us, from our own perspective on things, that others' expertise is to be acknowledged and honored. It is rather the more modest claim that one has no choice but to make the best judgments one can about when to acquiesce and when not to. This kind of autonomy in the theory of rationality is the Kantian one, thinking of it in terms of following the dictates of one's own best judgment about how to conduct one's intellectual life.

It is worth noting that there are constraints on such autonomy for it to play the legitimate role it needs to play in the life of the mind. I address these issues in

---

[6] I hasten to note that the quote doesn't represent Fricker's view, and calling it her account should be understood as a reference to the content of the quote, not to her own view, which rejects the claim in the quote.

the penultimate chapter of Kvanvig (2014), so will provide only a brief description of the limitations here. In brief, the giving rules that one gives to oneself can be either proper or improper, and the difference involves the degree to which the giving is motivated by the great epistemic goods, such as love of truth. To the extent that one's motivations involve other factors, to that degree autonomy of the right sort is not present.

Though these brief remarks do not give anything like a full characterization of the role of autonomy in epistemic contexts, they are adequate for present purposes, since even the cursory treatment above shows that humility isn't the problem in epistemic contexts but rather pride and arrogance. The proud are so sure of themselves that it is often hard to see this feature as an honest appraisal arising out of love of truth, but rather an exaggerated sense of self arising from other motives. The self-sufficiency bluster of the arrogant is thus evidence of a trait that is contrary to the kind of autonomy central to the theory of rationality. But an honest humility, arising out of an awareness of and attention to one's limits in securing the great epistemic goods, is not evidence that autonomy has been violated. At worst, it is a character trait that is neutral on the question. Furthermore, to the extent that the great epistemic goods include understanding the world and our place in it, such an honest humility would seem to be indispensable to such an achievement and thus fully compatible with the expression of Kantian autonomy involved in that great good. We can thus conclude that autonomy of the right sort can be reconciled with the epistemic value of intellectual humility.

8.7 Conclusion

The explanation of the tension, then, involves a more circumspect account of the proper role for autonomy in the theory of rationality, one that doesn't exaggerate the independence of self to such an extent that autonomy in intellectual life would be a vice. We also have seen that we can achieve a better understanding of the relationships between humility and modesty, as well as pride and vanity, by granting that the pairs are generally associated, but that neither is a form of the other. Thus when investigating the nature of humility, we should be careful not to confuse it with closely related character traits, and when discussing the virtue and value of humility, we need not be encumbered by the worry that any goodness to be found in humility will conflict with autonomy in epistemic contexts.

What remains, then, is a more direct examination of the nature of this character trait within the logical and valuational space so delineated. We have the needed background for a more direct inquiry in the the nature, virtue, and value of humility, the topic of the next and final substantive chapter.

9

Humility: Nature, Value, and Virtue

9.1 Introduction

What remains of our project of explaining and defending the balancing roles of faith and humility is an account of the nature, value, and virtue of humility, one that leaves intact the explanations and arguments for the complementarity role between these two character traits. We can begin this task by considering a current controversy concerning the virtues.

The traditional account of the virtues is Aristotelian, where virtue requires (but is not to be identified with) knowledge, but this view has been opposed in recent literature, which has emphasized the importance of ignorance in a proper account of some virtues, including humility.[1] The dominant question in these discussions is whether these character traits require a false opinion about oneself. The ignorance view requires that humility involve an incorrect, and (in all likelihood) epistemically unwarranted, underestimating of oneself, since it requires denying (to ourselves) that our abilities and accomplishments are sometimes extraordinary, splendid, magnificent, or at least mildly admirable. Such misestimation is a defect in a person, and though defects can sometimes be part of a larger whole that is not defective, we are forced to climb a considerable incline from this starting point if we are going to be able to defend humility as a virtue. So let us take a closer look to see if this path is one that is required or whether there is perhaps a better path to follow.

9.2 Humility: Relational or Non-relational?

A full assessment of this ignorance view of humility requires distinguishing two issues. One issue is internal to the individual. In the intellectual context, for example, it is a matter of assessing one's attitude toward the possibility of having currently mistaken opinions. In the more general context, it involves an assessment of one's abilities and accomplishments, not in terms of comparison to other individuals, but in non-relational terms. It is an accomplishment to be a hunter-gatherer who is successful enough to feed a family, for example, and that assessment involves no comparison

---

[1] See, e.g., Slote (2004), Flanagan (1990), Driver (1989), Schueler (1997), Ridge (2000), Raterman (2004), Ben-Ze'ev (1993), Richards (1988), Driver (2001), Sinha (2012), Garcia (2006), and Allhoff (2010).

with others and how good they are at the task in question. The other issue is relational. If it is central to a proper attitudinal expression of humility to underestimate oneself, the crucial question is the standard against which one is comparing oneself. Here two possibilities stand out. The non-relational approach would counsel, in the intellectual context for example, having an opinion that one has lots and lots of false beliefs, lots more than one actually has. The relational approach would counsel having an opinion that one has lots of false beliefs, perhaps at least more than one's intellectual superiors.[2]

No matter which approach is taken, however, there are problems with this ignorance approach. When we think about the intellectual component of these character traits, both require, first, a reasonably accurate non-comparative, understanding of one's abilities and accomplishments. One can't be humble or modest about one's abilities when one is totally clueless what they are or when they have been misidentified. In addition, a full understanding of any ability or accomplishment involves a *normative* dimension—one concerning the *importance*, the *significance* of that ability or accomplishment. It is a tremendous accomplishment to have climbed Mount Everest, and it puts one in a truly elite group of people. But for those who have done so, a full understanding of their accomplishment must acknowledge that on the scale of significant human accomplishments, it pales in comparison to saving the life of a drowning infant, for example, even though the latter takes much less strength and endurance than the former. There may be more glory in climbing the mountain, but it is in large part vainglory too. It is easy to fail to notice this evaluative dimension, which leads even the most highly accomplished to understand (if they are suitably humble, that is) that attention and accolades are more worthily focused on other abilities and accomplishment than the ones toward which the fickle flash of fame focuses. Moreover, an accurate self-assessment also contains an awareness that any recognition, admiration, or celebration of one's successes is, by its very nature, one which ignores the failures, weaknesses, absences, and defects we all possess. So accolades are, by their very nature, imbalanced—they do not present an accurate picture, and to that extent, conflict with a full understanding of oneself and one's abilities and accomplishments. Finally, it is the very nature of celebratory attention to ignore the dimensions of success that are not fully attributable to the person in question. Not only does good luck play a significant role, but the basic capacities involved in success are products of nature, not effort. Hence, the agent-centered focus of celebration, admiration, and recognition will seem distorted to one with the accurate understanding of self that is central to modesty and humility.

So, from the completely internal components involved in an understanding of self, the proper conclusion to draw is that correctness of understanding and adequacy of

---

[2] I leave out in the text the probabilist's possibility of only having beliefs about the likelihood of having false beliefs, since such beliefs under-report. It is a rarer thing than they imagine to have beliefs whose content involves a probability judgment, even if it is common to have gradeable degrees of belief in a content without a probability operator.

self-assessment are central to both modesty and humility, rather than taking some secondary position to more important elements of ignorance and underestimation. Hence, if elements of ignorance or misestimation are central to these character traits, they will have to be found in some relational component instead.

This second, relational aspect of humility requires there to be some standard of comparison, relative to which one is underestimating one's worth or abilities or accomplishments (or attractiveness). There are reasons for concern here. First, note that if the standard of comparison is other people, and humility involves underestimating one's abilities and accomplishments relative to one's contemporaries, it makes humility (and modesty) more difficult to achieve, the greater one's disadvantages. If one is dumb as dirt, it is hard to underestimate one's intelligence relative to one's contemporaries. Such an underestimation view makes the possibility of humility arise as splendor in a person emerges, since only the gifted can underestimate their gifts relative to others. No such implication should be tolerated.

Second, if humility requires misestimation of some sort, we have strong grounds, not easily overridden, for concluding that it is a character trait best avoided. First, self-awareness and self-understanding is a good thing in itself, something that a suitably reflective approach to life is prized for fostering. Socrates claimed that an unreflective life is not worth living, a claim best taken hyperbolically I expect, but the reflection needed as corrective is surely the sober sort leading to a proper understanding of oneself and one's place in the world, not some close relative leading to accurate understanding of the world but mistakes about oneself. Moreover, if humility were a virtue involving misestimation, how exactly does one go about trying to acquire such a virtue? Are there 12-step programs that make such self-deception easy or at least more likely to occur? I think we should prefer the Aristotelian dictum that virtues are acquired by practicing acts of the correct type, but self-deception is something at which one cannot aim: nobody can engage in an activity that expresses a direct and immediate intention to self-deceive. We should find the idea implausible that there are developed, virtuous character traits for which there is no adoptable plan for acquiring. Finally, about the only value one can find for such a virtue of ignorance is a social value—it is much more fun to be around people who don't have high opinions of themselves than it is to be around those who do. But, as noted by Ridge (2000), obsequiousness will work just as well for such purposes, and no one should think of it as a virtue.

We can distance our understanding of humility from such misestimation views by noting also that the kind of ignorance posited in such accounts isn't sufficient for humility either. "Of sinners the worst, to grace the least responsive" can be both an expression of humility but also one of pride: "Oh no, good sir, you have nothing on me there: no one is worse than I!" Inverse competitiveness is not humility, but an important contrast to it.

In light of these problems, I suggest there is a good diagnosis available for how one comes to view underestimation as crucial for humility. The internal account above focuses on both a descriptive and an evaluative feature of one's view of oneself and one's abilities and accomplishments. If we ignore the evaluative dimension here, then the descriptive feature, combined with an accuracy requirement, forces us to think of humble but splendid people in terms of a correct recognition that, for example, they are spendid in certain ways. That description is jarring, however, and doesn't explain at all how humility is present in light of that conception of self. But adding the evaluative dimension can generate the right tone: they recognize their own true giftedness, but also recognize that (i) good fortune played a role, (ii) the accomplishments pale in significance when compared with others, and (iii) they have many other failures and weaknesses that are ignored by the accolades. Even those robed in splendor can be humble in a way explained by these evaluative recognitions.

Moreover, this picture also explains why humility arises in Christian and other religious contexts, for in such contexts people experience a deep sense of their own fallenness and inadequacy, and an awe and respect for something greater than themselves, yielding a context in which the evaluative dimensions that underlie humility are pronounced. An Aristotelian magnanimous soul may engage in a bit too much comparison with the general lot of humanity, whereas religious foci bring a different set of comparisons and evaluations to the fore.

9.3 Intellectualist Accounts

Resistance to the "virtues of ignorance" approach to humility and modesty leads to replacement views that attempt to explain these virtues in terms of accurate self-assessment (see, for example, Kupfer (2003), Grenberg (2007b,a), Schueler (1997), and Schueler (1999)). While it is important to recognize that ignorance is not essential to these virtues, it is important to consider the issue of whether accurate self-assessment is either necessary or sufficient for them as well. We will see that a full picture of the role of accurate self-estimation in understanding the nature of humility is more complicated than this turn in the literature suggests.

Let's consider the sufficiency claim first. The sufficiency claim suffers at the thought of the greats. Michael Jordan may be the greatest basketball player ever, and if he recognizes this fact, it doesn't follow that he is humble about it. He could be (though I doubt it), but more likely is that he is not. When Muhammad Ali declared "I am the greatest," it wasn't the remark of a humble man honoring the sincerity or knowledge norms of assertion, saying merely what he thought or knew to be true. The greatest among us might also be humble, but if so, their humility is not found in their recognition of their greatness.

What of necessity? Here things are more difficult, but we can begin with the general recognition that humility doesn't involve thinking less of yourself, but is more characteristically about focus: thinking of yourself less.[3] It is possible to generate

---

[3] Hear C. S. Lewis on this point from *The Problem of Pain*: "True humility is not thinking less of yourself; it is thinking of yourself less."

recognition of excellence in a person for the first time, and find out in doing so that the recognition is immediately accompanied by humility with respect to that excellence. "Oh, that? I've never thought of that as something I was good at, but it's not really that big a deal." Nicolas Bommarito (2013) calls this possibility "quality inattention," and also notes that there is value inattention, as in when a humble person remarks, "Yes, but it's not really important enough to make a big deal about."

Perhaps the defenders of the requirement of accuracy of self-assessment can take some comfort, though, in the requirement that you can't be humble about a quality that you do not in fact possess. Such a requirement has been emphasized in Michael Slote (1983) that reflective virtues are dependent virtues, requiring some other good quality which the virtue is about. But perhaps that is too strong, since it is easy to imagine resistance here. Couldn't one be modest about an honor, for example, even if one didn't in fact receive it? Imagine a war veteran, at the end of life, being mistakenly told he'd won the Congressional Medal of Honor. His response could be humble, for sure, and I think that is all we have to say about the case. Moreover, if that is all we need to say, we can still preserve the facticity claim, insisting that he is not humble about winning the medal (since he didn't win it), but is nonetheless humble in the way he responds to the news.

Others see a greater possibility for mistakes compatible with humility, however. Here is Nicolas Bommarito's explanation of why such mistakes are compatible with humility and modesty:

> What is relevant is why a person overestimates his or her good quality. The attention of those who . . . overestimate because of misleading evidence or unmotivated irrationality is different from that of those who overestimate out of vanity. Vain desires will likely result in attention to one's own role in success rather than attention to the role of external factors and will also tend to draw one's attention toward one's own good qualities and the importance of such qualities. The patterns of attention associated with vain overestimation put pressure on the habits of attention that . . . overestimation associated with misleading evidence and superstition does not, by drawing attention to one's good qualities and one's own role in bringing them about.
>
> (Bommarito 2013, p. 106)

Bommarito's perspective is that misestimation can be motivated in a purely cognitive way (involving misleading evidence or simple irrationality) or can involve cognitive penetration from non-cognitive sources, such as vain desires. From this perspective, the line between the kinds of overestimation compatible with humility and the kinds not compatible with it has to do with the source of the misestimation. When the source is purely cognitive, there is no conflict; when the source involves cognitive penetration, there can be. In particular, if the overestimation is caused by a desire to look good to others, the overestimation undermines the attribution of virtue.

Here is Bommarito's example of overestimation that leaves room for humility:

> Ben can overestimate his own skill and still seem modest. For example, suppose he receives a very prestigious and influential ranking of world-class architects and, because of a misprint, sees his own name listed among the very best of the best. As a result of this reliable but

misleading evidence, he revises his estimation of his own skill and takes himself to be a world-class architect. In this case, Ben overestimates his own skill not because he wants to puff up his own ego, but because he simply got misleading evidence and responded to it in a rational way.

(Bommarito 2013, p. 105)

Bommarito claims that Ben is humble (modest) in the example because his misestimation results from an accurate evaluation of the force of his evidence, which leads him to misestimate. One must be careful, however, about the ascription being made. Is the ascription that Ben is modest overall, or that he is modest about his architectural abilities, or that he is modest about being a world-class architect? The latter is jarring, in the same way as the war veteran example given earlier. There can be humility and modesty in such cases, but the description needs to move away from the error being made in order to be defensible. The war veteran is humble in the face of the news he has received, and Ben is modest when seeing the report that he's a great architect. In each case, the cognitive error of overestimation is distanced from the ascription of humility or modesty, in keeping with Slote's approach that such virtues are dependent virtues.

Bommarito also suggests that modesty is compatible with irrational overestimation:

One might also be modest while overestimating in an irrational way. Suppose Sean has the superstition that European cars are more difficult to drive. He never reflects on this belief, but ever since he was a child, he got the sense from his somewhat ill-informed father that one had to be more skilled to drive cars from Germany and Italy. Because he drives a German car, he takes himself to be a better driver than he really is, though his attention is as described—rarely, if ever, reflects on his driving skill at all. His superstition is not self-serving but a case of unmotivated irrationality—for example, he would have the same superstition even if he happened to drive an American car, and he also overestimates the abilities of others, even people he dislikes, who happen to drive European cars. In this case, Sean does overestimate his own driving ability, but he does so because he has an unmotivated superstition that makes him a poor evaluator of driving skill in general. He seems like a modest guy, a good driver who doesn't make a big deal of it, whose unfortunate superstitions make him a bad judge of driving skill.

(Bommarito 2013, p. 106)

Sean, according to Bommarito, is humble but the basis of his humility is an irrational superstition, gotten from his father, that European cars are more difficult to drive. He is mistaken, of course, but the mistake doesn't impugn the judgment about his humility.

A first concern about the example involves the attribution of irrationality. If his belief comes by testimony from his father, it begins to look like a rational belief, not an irrational superstition, whether or not the father was ill-informed. (One doesn't need one's testimonial sources to have rational beliefs in order for one to acquire rational beliefs based on their testimony; one doesn't even need one's sources to know what they tell you in order for one to acquire knowledge from what they say.[4]) But

---

[4] See, e.g., Warfield (2005) and Fitelson (2010).

even if we grant that the belief is simply an irrational superstition, we have the same issue as before, one concerning the object of the modesty. If we are attributing overall modesty to Sean, there is no problem since the particular irrational belief doesn't require that he has an overall irrational assessment of himself; if we are attributing modesty with respect to his driving abilities, we also encounter no difficulty since his generic assessment of his driving abilities is again accurate and rational. But if we attribute modesty concerning the error being made, we encounter the same jarring experience as before: Sean is not modest concerning his being a better driver than the rest of us, because he isn't!

The point here is that across-the-board accuracy of self-evaluation need not be present in order for these virtues to be present, but only that inaccuracy prevents a specific instance of the virtue from being present. A generic attribution of such a virtue to a person is compatible with lack of humility over a wide range of abilities and excellences: Willy can be humble and yet not humble about being from the South. In this respect, it isn't surprising to find Sean to be modest even though he isn't modest about being a great driver. There is some other characteristic in the neighborhood regarding which he is modest, and the overestimation is inessential to that modesty, and also to the overall character assessment we make when we say that he is a modest person.

There is thus no need that arises from these cases to investigate the issue of cognitive penetration to determine what kinds of overestimation are compatible with these virtues. Even so, the idea of an accuracy-based account of humility is only the beginning of an account of humility, since mere accuracy of self-assessment is compatible with both the presence and absence of humility. So even if accuracy is important, understanding the nature of humility requires determining what, beyond accuracy, is needed. On this score, Bommarito's positive account is especially helpful.

9.4 The Virtues of Attention

One item that keeps recurring when thinking about the virtue of humility is the issue of focus or attention, for the humble direct attention away from themselves and their good qualities. Moreover, the nature of attention is different from awareness itself, for one can be aware of exactly the same surroundings while attending to different features of it. Since attention goes beyond awareness, perhaps there is a way of using attention to characterize the nature of humility, thereby endorsing the Slote thesis about accuracy of awareness while also accommodating the insufficiency of it.

This promising approach to humility treats it in terms of what a person attends to when reflecting on one's accomplishments and achievements rather than simply in terms of the accuracy or inaccuracy of the assessment itself. As Bommarito notes, there are virtues of attention:

The virtues of attention are virtues that are rooted in how we direct our attention. These virtues are sometimes moral but not always. It is an academic virtue of attention to be able to focus one's attention on a long and technical lecture. It is an aesthetic virtue of attention for one to pay attention to the relationship between the narrative and shot composition in a film. Gratitude is a moral virtue of attention because it involves directing one's attention to the value of what someone else has done for us.   (Bommarito 2013, p. 100)

Bommarito's account of the nature of humility (modesty) is an attention-based account. It is summarized in the following passage:

[I]t is necessary to have a good quality to be modest about. Contrary to most contemporary views, it is not necessary to underestimate the good quality nor is it necessary to have an accurate assessment. Instead, what is necessary is to direct one's conscious attention in certain ways—away from the trait or its value or toward the outside causes and conditions that played a role in developing it.

Attending in these ways, however, is not sufficient for modesty; it must happen for the right reasons.   (Bommarito 2013, p. 103)

The idea, then, is to view humility as a special kind of disposition, one which, when displayed, has a characteristic profile reflected in that to which the person in question attends. To have this disposition, there must be an underlying good quality, and Bommarito's way of developing the view is neutral as to the kind of accuracy involved in cognitive estimates regarding the quality in question. Instead, what is central is how one "direct[s] one's conscious attention."

Compare this account in terms of virtues of attention with another account that also uses the language of attentiveness, developed in Whitcomb et al. (2015). This account is of intellectual humility only and not humility in general, and it understands the former in terms of "proper attentiveness to, and owning of, one's intellectual limitations" (Whitcomb et al. 2015, p. 12). In characterizing attentiveness, the authors write,

On our view, humility partly consists in a disposition to be aware (even if just implicitly) of one's limitations, for them to come to mind when the occasion calls for it. In this connection, notice that the paradigmatically arrogant person is often oblivious to his limitations; they don't show up on his radar. The paradigmatically servile person, however, hardly sees anything else; his radar is perpetually peppered with his limitations. On our view, humility lies in the mean between these extremes. When life calls for one to be mindful of a limitation, then, and only then, will it appear on the ideally humble person's radar. And what goes for humility in general goes for [intellectual humility] in particular.   (Whitcomb et al. 2015, pp. 8–9)

This view of humility makes it a mean between two extremes, both involving what a person attends to and when, concerning one's limitations. In this way, it shares a feature with Bommarito's account. But it encounters two difficulties that Bommarito's account does not face. The first is that awareness isn't attention, so to grant a role to attention (humility involves, we are told, a proper attentiveness to one's limitations) in the account but then to clarify it in terms of a disposition toward awareness is a mistake. Attention implies awareness, but not vice versa: one can be aware of one's surroundings while attending only to the book one is reading while ambling across campus. Moreover, attentiveness to one's limitations isn't generated merely by some disposition to be aware of one's limitations, any more than my general disposition to be aware of being in the same room as my wife generates attentiveness to her presence (since I have the former disposition even when she's not in the room). Second, this account has no hope of accounting for the humility of Christ, where this humility is displayed in taking on limitations that are not part of his intrinsic nature and held up as an example to motivate the attitude of humility in his followers,[5] and must be judged to be less adequate than any account that provides hope of accounting for ordinary, mundane humility while also explaining divine humility.

Bommarito's attention-based account offers more hope on both of these scores.[6] His account clearly distinguishes between attention and awareness, and there is no focus on limitations in his account that would make it incapable of explaining divine humility. So the patterns of attention that are in focus can be but need not be on one's limitations. Such a broadening allows an explanation of the humility of Christ in terms of an attentional focus away from his own excellences and onto other things, including the importance of and need for the Divine plan of redemption. Such a focal orientation away from the good characteristics in question and towards something of greater value and significance is one typical way in which humility is displayed, and thus this attention-based account provides a useful approach both to ordinary humility and the kind of humility attributed to Christ in the Christian tradition. It is thus a good start toward the kind of account needed, though as we shall see, some of the details will need development in order to show how it can accommodate the hope of providing an account that is adequate to both ordinary and divine humility. To see how to do so, we need some background on the notion of attention itself.

9.5 The Nature of Attention

One central feature that needs to be considered and addressed involves the distinction in the psychological literature between endogenous and exogenous attention.[7] The difference is whether control of the patterns of attention are internal or external. When they are under voluntary control, the the kind of attention is endogenous; when the response is reflexive and automatic, it is exogenous. So, for example, when one's attention is drawn to a sonic boom from an unnoticed plane, that attention is

---

[5] See Philippians 2:3–8: "Do nothing out of selfish ambition or vain conceit. Rather, in humility value others above yourselves, not looking to your own interests but each of you to the interests of the others. In your relationships with one another, have the same mindset as Christ Jesus: Who, being in very nature God, did not consider equality with God something to be used to his own advantage; rather, he made himself nothing by taking the very nature of a servant, being made in human likeness. And being found in appearance as a man, he humbled himself by becoming obedient to death—even death on a cross!" (NIV).

[6] It is worth noting here that Bommarito's work is not cited in the bibliography of Whitcomb et al. (2015).

[7] See Mulckhuyse and Theeuwes (2010). Useful literature on the topic can also be found in Koralus (2014) and Mole (2011).

exogenous attention, but the way in which a hunter scans a landscape looking for movement is endogenous attention.

A good example of endogenous attention can be given using the following array of shapes and colors, where the task is to find the gray triangle:

Figure 9.1 Find the Gray Triangle

With Koralus (2014), we can say that there is a task here that is attentively performed (searching for the gray triangle), and that the way in which it is done involves focus marking on successive objects in the array.

Even if there are paradigm examples of each type of attention, the distinction is not precise, since, for example, peripheral visual cues are external but attract attention in a way affected by the values, interests, and concerns of the individual in question. But they do not engage the will, or the executive function of mentation, and thus are categorized as examples of exogenous attention. Endogenous attention is "top-down," involving this executive function, whereas exogenous attention is "bottom-up," even if the elements needed for attention involve internal mental states rather than external cues alone.

We can use this distinction to get a better understanding of Bommarito's proposal, where endogenous attention is primary. According to his proposal, a proper expression of humility involves putting the focus of attention elsewhere than on one's successes or abilities, and a humble person adopts a stance, and reinforces it, involving such re-direction of focus. The primary language Bommarito focuses on is how one "direct[s] one's conscious attention."

We need to distinguish, though, between the character trait itself and any expression of it. If we do so, on Bommarito's approach, we say that there is an underlying character trait whose characteristic expression involves patterns of endogenous attention. Once described in this way, the natural question to ask is why the patterns of attention have to be endogenous. Wouldn't exogenous patterns work just as well?

Here is a story in favor of an attention-based account that refuses to rule out exogenous patterns. We might say that some people are more naturally humble, while others show a predilection for pride and arrogance. Among the less naturally humble, efforts of will are needed to focus attention patterns in the way required for humility, but among the naturals, attention patterns connected with humility will tend to be exogenous. Moreover, even among the less naturally humble, the activity of the will diminishes as strength of character trait increases, so that what started out as endogenous need not remain so.

Notice, moreover, that in the context of specifically Christian faith, this alternative approach to the attentional element involved in humility allows us to make sense not only of ordinary humility but also the humility of Christ. An account of humility that focuses on endogenous attention fits better with expressions of humility among fallen creatures, and no account of the humility of Christ will make sense when it tries to explain it in terms of his sense of fallenness, or in terms of the role good fortune played in his accomplishments or in the way in which those accomplishments pale in comparison with the accomplishments of others. In the central example of the humility of Christ, there is no awareness of and owning of limitations, but rather an attentional focus away from self and toward a great good that may be a function of the will but may also only be a function of the nature of the person in question rather than a function of the will.

This approach to the humility of Christ is thus one that is sensitive to the central features of the Incarnation itself. The humility of Christ is, first and foremost, a settled disposition arising from Divine love that involves an openness to taking on whatever role is needed in order to address the problems that plague the objects of his love. Such a settled disposition may involve an activity of the will, but need not: it might be the same kind of exogenous attentional patterns we display when our values, cares, and concerns attune us to certain features of our environment more than others.

For those attracted to the idea that humility must involve endogenous attention, there may be a line of defense to pursue. One might argue that love itself isn't possible without the engagement of the will, so if Christ's humility is prompted by Divine love, it will involve the will and thus the attentional feature will be endogenous. I am sympathetic to this view about the relationship between love and the will, but I don't think we need any extended discussion of this defense of the idea of endogenous attention in the Incarnation. For even if it is true, that will only be one example in which the values, cares, and concerns underlying patterns of attention end up counting as endogenous, and all that is needed in order to refuse to endorse the requirement that attention must involve the activity of the will is one case in which the patterns of attention arise out of values, cares, and concerns without engaging the will.

Perhaps, though, one will want to argue that the will is always involved in any case in which patterns of attention arise out of values, cares, and concerns. I am less sympathetic to this claim than to the claim that love itself always involves the will, for we should remember that the fuzzy distinction between endogenous and exogenous attention is supposed to be connected with the idea that the control in question can be either bottom-up or top-down. If there is some way in which the will is always involved in values, cares, and concerns, it remains the case that patterns of attention motivated by these items will still be bottom-up, whereas searching for the gray triangle in Figure 9.1 will be top-down. To the extent that we want to characterize the two sets of distinctions so that they line up with each other, to that extent we should be unmoved by this kind of argument for the requirement that the attention involved in humility must always be endogenous.

Given such a story about the function of humility in the life of an individual, it becomes fairly straightforward to explain why intellectual humility is a virtue, since a central part of an accurate self-assessment involves taking into account which standards are most important and which are less important. The conclusion to draw is not that humility is a virtue only given the cultural context of Christianity, or the cultural context of religions within the Abrahamic tradition, or even the cultural context of the great world religions. It is rather that the kind of self-awareness constitutive of such a character trait involves evaluative dimensions that can be too easily overlooked when the only comparison class that comes to mind is that of the general lot of humanity. Humility, so conceived, still has claim to being a universal virtue, one's whose value is explained by the characterization given of it, even though it is unsurprising that an appreciation of its value is made more likely by certain cultural contexts rather than others.[8]

What remains in a full characterization of humility is the final element in Bommarito's account, that element involving the directing of attention *for the right reasons*. A full account of what the right reasons involve goes beyond our present needs and would require a book of its own, one that we can bypass including here, since we have seen enough of what humility involves to explain how and in what way humility and faith are balancing virtues.

9.6 Conclusion

We thus see that, as a virtue of attention, humility is well-situated both to be in need of being balanced by faith worth having and to provide a balance to any such faith that is distorted, exaggerated, or excessive in some way. We have seen quite a bit of the former by noting the way in which arrogance provides an advantage to its possessors, so it is useful at this point to emphasize the latter. Faith worth having can focus on the wrong objects, and the zeal involved can be excessive or exaggerated, leading to behavior that interferes with achieving a good life. A pattern of attention that involves comparison with proper standards, with people of wisdom and temperance, provides a useful counterweight to these disturbing potentialities of faith.

---

[8] For a different, but related approach, see Grenberg (2005).

10

Conclusion

It will come as no surprise for those familiar with the language of faith and humility in Christian contexts to hear someone claim that they are intimately connected, but it is a more surprising claim within ordinary, mundane contexts. Even in those contexts in which the claim isn't very surprising, the precise way in which the two are related is the distinctive element articulated here. In the Christian context, the connection between the two has not been properly appreciated because of the cognitive hijacking of faith, making the balancing relationship between faith and humility disappear in a sea of obfuscation.

A better approach begins with questions of value, asking what kind of faith could possibly have the kind of value that might explain counting it as a virtue. One disastrous consequence of the cognitive hijacking of faith, claiming it to be, at bottom, some kind propositional belief or other cognitive state, is that such an explanation gets threatened. To get it back, the beliefs in question have to be combined with some other features that generate something of value. A better approach, and the one taken here, is to focus on the behavior sought and the dispositions that lead to it. It is here that we find a faith worth having, and the resulting functional account of faith allows it to be realized in substrates that involve cognitive as well as affective and conative states, but not in a way that comports well with any view of faith on which doctrinal elements lead the parade. Moreover, this account of the nature of faith meshes nicely with an account of the value of faith, thereby generating a unified explanation that makes clear why faith is a virtue.

In Christian contexts, the cognitive hijacking of faith has led to translational distortions of sacred texts that then get used for abusive purposes, such as we find in the damnatory clauses of the Athanasian Creed. We should not think of these clauses as rare and perplexing elements in the history of Christianity: they are the stuff and substance to be expected in a religion that depends so centrally on the virtue of faith and yet in which the understanding of faith has been so seriously distorted. There is plenty of blame to go around for the causes of such distortion, but the central and singular role of politics, under the initial efforts of Constantine to secure a uniformity of thought in the face of disagreements about the doctrines of the Trinity and Incarnation, take center stage in the story. It is, of course, a truism that real community depends on commonalities of one sort or another, but it is worth considering the possibility that there is another kind of commonality which could have been the focus, rather than a doctrinal one. On this point, it is worth remembering the distinctively Johannine perspective on Christian life and community, one that elevates love over other factors. It is easy to imagine this disciple counseling Christian churches to endorse a commonality that makes the affections of greater importance than cognitions for achieving the kind of unity required for community. We might even use a verse out of context to convey this perspective, reminding members that whatever their disagreements, they must always (metaphorically) "greet each other with a holy kiss." In short, it is an unnecessary hijacking of Christianity that makes doctrinal matters central, and results in the schisms and offshoots and denominational proliferation that is the direct result of such a central obsession with doctrinal conformity. While it might be true that a different focus would still have ended similarly, it is enough of an objection to a doctrinal focus to see its consequences. Moreover, the alternative picture of the nature and value of faith makes an affective source of unity much more natural and attractive, and it is a perspective on such unity that can be gleaned from the Johannine corpus. If there is a practical takeaway to this academic inquiry, it is this: when you are thinking about faith in Christian contexts, and you see the language of belief, substitute the language of having faith in its place. And then, when thinking about this language of having faith, think of it in terms of dispositions in service of the relevant ideal, not in terms of some substrate of belief that one might think has to be in place in order for one to have the faith in question.

The implications of such a notion of faith are wide-reaching. First, educational efforts need to be aimed at developing lives worth living, and there is a fairly good case to be made that faith of the sort described here is central to such a life. But educational systems aimed at preservation of doctrinal commitments do not fit with such an educational mission. A better understanding of faith would result in educational systems emphasizing *process* rather than *preservation* when it comes to the question of what is true and what is false. It has always struck me as genuinely inscrutable how to reconcile endorsing the obvious ways in which the great heroes of the faith all demonstrate theological understandings that evolve over time, even while faith remains the same, only changing by growing in strength, with creedal and confessional requirements for later adherents of the faith that are rigid and inflexible. In one sense, such incoherence doesn't surprise, since incoherence, both noticed and unnoticed (though in my judgment, much more commonly of the second variety), is such a basic aspect of human life. Yet, for this incoherence to go unrecognized and embraced so adamantly in religious circles borders on, to my mind, the unfathomable.

How could such a thing happen? The best analogy I can think of to help us see how such a thing is possible is the way in which our assessments of human intelligence and competence have been molded by political powers and organizations when it comes to public language. It is well-known that standardization of language was one of the central tools used in the creation of nation states, acting as a force for the kind of unity needed to keep the state from dissolution into warring tribes and factions. Spelling and punctuation and grammar get codified in service of patriotic goals and the greater good of political unity. And yet, we don't look on those that misspell and get their grammar wrong as political rebels or anarchists of some sort or people who don't sufficiently love their country. Instead, the more common reaction is to view such people as lacking in intelligence and competence. It is a sign of the extent of the power of an entity to be able not only to stimulate compliance in such matters but also to do so by getting subjects to internalize these linguistic conventions in such a way that the invented rules get used unreflectively in evaluations of intelligence. It is a remarkable feature of human beings that they can be manipulated in this way, and it is a fascinating fact about political power that it has such reach.

I suggest that we see something of the same in the history of Christianity, where those in power managed not only to secure allegiance to doctrinal positions but also managed to get the faithful to internalize a conception of their faith that makes about as much sense as holding that you can't be very smart if you misspell 'sycophant'. The two phenomena are twin offspring of the manipulability in human nature.

A further point about the Christian context is worth noting as well: in the Synoptics, the disciples of Jesus are called "followers," never "believers". It is not until after the rise of theology in the writings of St. Paul that we get a cognitive distortion of faith, but the distortion is not due to St. Paul himself, since his focus on justification by faith is best understood in terms of the functional account presented here and does not fit well at all with a cognitive picture of what faith involves. For those who see a cognitive picture of faith in St. Paul, perhaps I should say that the the present account is more Johannine that Pauline, but a remark such as that is unfair. There is no question that doctrinal questions occupy St. Paul more than St. John, but one shouldn't confuse questions of the alethic adequacy of doctrinal commitments with those of salvific adequacy, as one must do to see in St. Paul's writings any hint of a fundamentally doctrinal approach to faith.

One can thus characterize this account of faith as decidedly non-fundamentalist, where fundamentalism is understood as the position defining membership in various groups in terms of those who are true believers, in the sense of Hoffer (1951). Such an approach focuses on the cognitive element to such an extent that the difference between those on the inside and those on the outside is fundamentally doctrinal. The idea explained and defended in this work is that a true person of faith and a true believer are not variants of each other, for the former welcome many to the fold with whom they disagree on doctrinal issues. Such welcoming is not a sign of a lack of concern for truth, but rather a clear sense that solidarity in service of an ideal is primary, with agreement on alethic matters having subsidiary significance. This point holds, it should be emphasized, whether we are thinking in terms of religious contexts or more mundane ones.

For those who see in this account a downplaying of the importance of truth, I recommend further reflection on the significance of truth of the sort I undertake to provide in Kvanvig (2008). I argue that truth matters immensely, both from a purely intellectual point of view and in terms of quality of life more generally. We aim for comprehensive and accurate systems of understanding for precisely these reasons. But there are sophisticated attempts to tie intellectual accomplishments to quality of life and there are ham-fisted ones. Among the latter attempts are those that make the value of truth a matter of some direct and immediate effect on quality of life, so that failure to find the truth should result in death or disability of a very serious sort. Truth matters, but not in such a direct and immediate way, and it takes only a small understanding of the nature of science and its dramatic capacities for good to see that the connections between basic research and well-being are present but in a way that is much more subtle than ham-fisted approaches can tolerate. So instead of concluding that the account presented here downplays the importance of truth, the reality is that it is fully compatible with, and sustains, a high respect for it. Disrespect for it is rather to be laid at the feet of those who pursue an anti-intellectual, ham-fisted pragmatism that requires immediate payoffs before committing to finding the truth in a particular area. In religious contexts, we get precisely such a ham-fisted pragmatism when we confuse alethic and salvific adequacy. Such positions not only depend on a fundamental philosophical mistake but they also tend to encourage a life of the mind that is guided, not by a love of truth, but by mindless assents to creedal slogans, in service of avoiding a purported eternal catastrophe. Instead of showing a proper concern for truth, cognitive and doctrinal approaches to faith say such strong things about truth that they end up disrespecting it, in much the same that way hyperbolic praise leads us to suspect we are being made fun of rather than honored. It is a virtue of the functional account of faith presented here that it meshes well with an account of the legitimate value of truth, both from a purely intellectual point of view and more generally.

Such a picture of faith has significant advantages, not the least of which is the intimate relationship it paints with the virtue of humility. The central claim of this work is that faith, properly understood, is a virtue central to human flourishing and that so is humility; moreover, there is a *pro tanto* relationship between the two, in spite of the fact that human flourishing is ultimately a holistic matter of having all of one's character traits balanced by the executive function of *phronesis*. In spite of this overarching holism, some virtues are more intimately connected with other virtues, and in this case, the intimate connection between faith worth having and humility is the way in which each of them complements the other. Faith without humility can be extreme and distorted, failing to attend to the important ways in which our intellect and affections can attach to ideals that are intolerable. In addition, humility without faith can lead to diminished efforts, either through failure to embrace any ideals at all or through loss of heart and failure of will to devote one's life to ideals worth pursuing even if the chances of success are (nearly) hopeless.

What our study doesn't answer is the pressing question of whether the elements of faith and humility are ones that must be present for wisdom to carry out its balancing function regarding the virtues present in a given individual to the, or a, good life for that individual. I believe we do not know enough about the interactions of the variety of virtues there are to be able to give a definitive answer to this question: much more needs to be investigated concerning the downsides and upsides of various virtues and how they interact with each other. In the process, we may get ourselves in the position of identifying some virtues as *cardinal virtues*, the kind that must be present in order to achieve the good life. It is clear that wisdom itself in one such virtue, and I suspect, at a very minimum, that a good life will be deeply improbable without faith and humility, and perhaps that a case will arise for taking them to be cardinal virtues along with wisdom.

Moreover, even if we could achieve the goal of showing that faith and humility are cardinal virtues, it would be hopelessly unrealistic to expect such a defense to tell us what ideals must be present for the faith in question. No matter how important faith is to a well-lived life, the variety of good lives that are possible undermines any attempt to defend limitations on ideals that are worth serving. This point should be obvious, since what ideals are worth pursuing depends to a great extent on conclusions regarding metaphysical disputes that go beyond the normative theorizing that addresses which virtues, if any beyond wisdom itself, are cardinal virtues. To name just one such dispute, note that which ideals are worth pursuing depends centrally on the issue of whether there is an afterlife and what its aspects might be. Such issues are surely among the most important to resolve in search of the good life, but the issue of which virtues are cardinal ones is an issue that gets resolved prior to resolution of that issue rather than depending on it. So no defense of faith and humility as cardinal virtues can depend on any particular answer to such metaphysical issues. To some, this point will suggest that neither virtue is essential to the good life, and that may be true, but at this point the best conclusion to draw is that we don't know enough about the virtues and the way in which they interact with each other to draw any confident conclusions about which virtues, beyond wisdom itself, are cardinal ones.

Even in the absence of the stronger conclusion, however, what we have seen about the nature, value, and virtue of faith reveals how important it is, together with humility, to human flourishing (not to mention the flourishing of life more broadly). As I see it, then, a life of both faith and humility is a thing of beauty, grace, and goodness, at least when not distorted by failures along other dimensions of virtue and behavior. Models of such lives are found among the great heroes of every major world religion and also among our greatest voices for moral progress and social justice. They are also found in ordinary lives history will always overlook, lives that are not only good for the individuals in question but also for the contribution they make to the communities that thrive because of them.

It is in hope for more such lives that I write to articulate the connection between the two. The question to humbly ask is whether our hearts and minds have been placed on things that matter, or whether our cares and concerns are but a chasing after the wind. And, finally for the ideals that capture, conquer, compel, and vanquish, whether today is a good day to die.

Bibliography

Adams, Robert Merrihew. 2006. *A Theory of Virtue: Excellence in Being for the Good*. Oxford: Clarendon Press.

Alfano, Mark. 2013. *Character as Moral Fiction*. New York: Cambridge University Press.

Allhoff, Fritz. 2010. "What is Modesty?" *International Journal of Applied Philosophy* 23: 165–87.

Alonso, Facundo M. 2014. "What is Reliance?" *Canadian Journal of Philosophy* 44 (2): 163–83.

Alston, William P. 1996. "Belief, Acceptance, and Religious Faith." In *Faith, Freedom, and Rationality*, edited by Jeff Jordan and Daniel Howard-Snyder. 3–27. Lanham, MD: Rowman & Littlefield.

Annas, Julia and Jonathan Barnes. 1985. *The Modes of Scepticism: Ancient Texts and Modern Interpretations*. Cambridge: Cambridge University Press.

Arnold, Matthew. 1924 [originally published in 1873]. *Literature and Dogma: An Essay Toward a Better Apprehension of the Bible*. New York: The Macmillan Co.

Audi, Robert. 1982. "Believing and Affirming." *Mind* 91 (361): 115–20.

Audi, Robert. 1994. "Dispositional Beliefs and Dispositions to Believe." *Noûs* 28.4: 419–34.

Audi, Robert. 2011. "Faith, Faithfulness, and Virtue." *Faith and Philosophy* 28 (3): 294–309.

Bach, Kent and Robert M. Harnish. 1979. *Linguistic Communication and Speech Acts*. Cambridge, MA: MIT Press.

Baier, Annette C. 1986. "Trust and Antitrust." *Ethics* 96.2: 231–60.

Bellah, Robert N. 1991. "Religion and Belief: The Historical Background of 'Non-Belief.'" In *Beyond Belief: Essays on Religion in a Post-Traditionalist World*. Ch. 13, 216–30. Berkeley: The University of California Press.

Ben-Ze'ev, Aaron. 1993. "The Virtue of Modesty." *American Philosophical Quarterly* 30: 235–46.

Bommarito, Nicolas. 2013. "Modesty as a Virtue of Attention." *The Philosophical Review* 122.1: 93–117.

Bratman, Michael. 1999. *Faces of Intention*. Cambridge: Cambridge University Press.

Bratman, Michael E. 1992. "Practical Reasoning and Acceptance in a Context." *Mind* 101 (401): 1–16.

Brown, Dee. 1970. *Bury My Heart at Wounded Knee*. New York: Henry Holt and Co.

Buchak, Lara. 2012. "Can It Be Rational to Have Faith?" In *Probability in the Philosophy of Religion*, edited by Jake Chandler and Victoria S. Harrison. 225–46. Oxford: Oxford University Press.

Chisholm, Roderick. 1957. *Perceiving*. Ithaca: Cornell University Press.

Choi, Sungho and Michael Fara. 2014. "Dispositions." In *The Stanford Encyclopedia of Philosophy*, edited by Edward N. Zalta. Spring 2014 edn.

Christensen, David. 1992. "Confirmational Holism and Bayesian Epistemology." *Philosophy of Science* 59 (4): 540–57.

Christensen, David. 2001. "Preference-Based Arguments for Probabilism." *Philosophy of Science* 68 (3): 356–76.

Clegg, Jerry S. 1979. "Faith." *American Philosophical Quarterly* 16: 225–32.

Clifford, W. K. 1877 [1999]. "The Ethics of Belief." In *The Ethics of Belief and Other Essays*. 70–97. Amherst, NY: Prometheus Books.

Cohen, L. Jonathan. 1989. "Belief and Acceptance." *Mind* 89 (391): 367–89.

Cohen, L. Jonathan. 1992. *An Essay on Belief and Acceptance*. Oxford: Oxford University Press.

Cohen, Stewart. 1987. "Knowledge and Context." *Journal of Philosophy* 83: 574–83.

Cohen, Stewart. 1998. "Contextualist Solutions to Epistemological Problems: Scepticism, Gettier, and the Lottery." *Australasian Journal of Philosophy* 76.2: 289–306.

Cohen, Stewart. 1999. "Contextualism, Skepticism, and the Structure of Reasons." *Philosophical Perpectives* 13: 57–89.

Coleman, James. 1990. *Foundations of Social Theory*. New York: Cambridge University Press.

Craig, Edward. 1990. *Knowledge and the State of Nature*. Oxford: Oxford University Press.

Cunningham, William. 1862. *The Reformers; and the Theology of the Reformation*. Edinburgh: T. and T. Clark.

Currie, Greg and Anna Ichino. 2012. "Aliefs Don't Exist, Though Some of Their Relatives Do." *Analysis* 72 (4): 788–98.

Darley, John M. and C. Daniel Batson. 1973. "'From Jerusalem to Jericho': A Study of Situational and Dispositional Variables in Helping Behavior." *Journal of Personality and Social Psychology* 27: 100–8.

D'Arms, Justin and Daniel Jacobson. 2000. "The Moralistic Fallacy: On the 'Appropriateness' of Emotions." *Philosophy and Phenomenological Research* 61 (1): 65–90.

Darwall, Stephen. 2009. *The Second-Person Standpoint: Morality, Respect, and Accountability*. Cambridge, MA: Harvard University Press.

Dawkins, Richard. 2006. *The God Delusion*. London: Bantam Press.

de Finetti, Bruno. 1974. *Theory of Probability*. Vol. I. New York: Wiley.

De Graaf, David. 2005. "Some Doubts about Doubt: The New Testament Use of Diakrino." *Journal of the Evangelical Theological Society* 48.4: 733–55.

Dennett, Daniel. 2006. *Breaking the Spell: Religion as a Natural Phenomenon*. New York: Viking Penguin.

DeRose, Keith. 1991. "Epistemic Possibilities." *Philosophical Review* 100 (4): 581–605.

DeRose, Keith. 1992. "Contextualism and Knowledge Attributions." *Philosophy and Phenomenological Research* 52: 913–29.

DeRose, Keith. 1995. "Solving the Skeptical Problem." *The Philosophical Review* 104 (1): 1–52.

DeRose, Keith. 2002. "Assertion, Knowledge, and Context." *The Philosophical Review* 111 (2): 167–203.

DeRose, Keith. 2008. *The Case for Contextualism*. Oxford: Oxford University Press.

Dewey, John. 1934. *A Common Faith*. New Haven: Yale University Press.

Dewey, John. 2008. "A Common Faith." In *The Later Works of John Dewey, Volume 9, 1925–1953: 1933–1934, Essays, Reviews, Miscellany, and A Common Faith (Collected Works of John Dewey)*, edited by Jo Ann Boydston. 1–58. Carbondale, IL: SIU Press.

Doggett, Tyler. 2012. "Some Questions for Tamar Szabó Gendler." *Analysis* 72 (4): 764–74.

Doris, John. 2002. *Lack of Character: Personality and Moral Behavior*. Cambridge: Cambridge University Press.

Doris, John M. 1998. "Persons, Situations, and Virtue Ethics." *Noûs* 32 (4): 504–30.

Dougherty, Trent and Patrick Rysiew. 2009. "Fallibilism, Epistemic Possibility, and Concessive Knowledge Attributions." *Philosophy and Phenomenological Research* 78.1: 123–32.

Driver, Julia. 1989. "The Virtues of Ignorance." *The Journal of Philosophy* 86: 373–85.

Driver, Julia. 2001. *Uneasy Virtue*. New York: Cambridge University Press.

Erikkson, Lina and Alan Hájek. 2007. "What are Degrees of Belief?" *Studia Logica* 86 (2): 183–213.

Field, Hartry. 1978. "A Note on Jeffrey Conditionalization." *Philosophy of Science* 45 (3): 361–7.

Fitelson, Branden. 2010. "Strengthening the Case for Knowledge From Falsehood." *Analysis* 70 (4): 666–9.

Flanagan, Owen. 1990. "Virtue and Ignorance." *The Journal of Philosophy* 87: 420–8.

Fodor, Jerry. 1983. *The Modularity of Mind*. Cambridge, MA: MIT Press.

Fodor, Jerry. 1984. "Observation Reconsidered." *Philosophy of Science* 51: 22–43.

Foley, Richard. 1979. "Justified Inconsistent Beliefs." *American Philosophical Quarterly* 16.4: 247–57.

Foley, Richard. 1991. "Evidence and Reasons for Belief." *Analysis* 51.2: 98–102.

Foley, Richard. 1993. *Working Without a Net: Essays in Egocentric Epistemology*. New York: Oxford University Press.

Foley, Richard F. 1992. "The Epistemology of Belief and the Epistemology of Degrees of Belief." *American Philosophical Quarterly* 29.2: 111–21.

Foley, Richard F. 2007. *Intellectual Trust in Oneself and Others*. New York: Cambridge University Press.

Foot, Philippa. 1978. *Virtues and Vices and Other Essays in Moral Philosophy*. Oxford: Oxford University Press.

Foot, Philippa. 2001. *Natural Goodness*. New York: Oxford University Press.

Foot, Philippa. 2002. *Moral Dilemmas and Other Topics in Moral Philosophy*. Oxford: Oxford University Press.

Frankish, Keith. 2004. *Mind and Supermind*. Cambridge: Cambridge University Press.

Fricker, Elizabeth. 2006. "Testimony and Epistemic Autonomy." In *The Epistemology of Testimony*, edited by Jennifer Lackey and Ernest Sosa. 225–53. Oxford: Oxford University Press.

Garber, Daniel. 1980. "Field and Jeffrey Conditionalization." *Philosophy of Science* 47 (1): 142–5.

Garcia, J. L. A. 2006. "Being Unimpressed with Ourselves: Reconceiving Humility." *Philosophia* 34 (4): 417–35.

Gendler, Tamar Szabó. 2008a. "Alief and Belief." *The Journal of Philosophy* 105 (10): 634–63.

Gendler, Tamar Szabó. 2008b. "Alief in Action (and Reaction)." *Mind & Language* 23 (5): 552–85.

Gendler, Tamar Szabó. 2012a. "Between Reason and Reflex: Response to Commentators." *Analysis* 72 (4): 799–811.

Gendler, Tamar Szabó. 2012b. "Summary." *Analysis* 72 (4): 759–64.

Gertler, Brie. 2011. "Self-Knowledge and the Transparency of Belief." In *Self-Knowledge*, edited by Anthony Hatzimoysis. 125–45. Oxford: Oxford University Press.

Gibbs, Jr., Raymond W., ed. 2008. *The Cambridge Handbook of Metaphor and Thought*. Cambridge: Cambridge University Press.

Goodman, Nelson. 1955. *Fact, Fiction, and Forecast*. Cambridge, MA: Harvard University Press.

Grenberg, Jeanine. 2005. *Kant and the Ethics of Humility: A Story of Dependence, Corruption and Virtue*. Cambridge: Cambridge University Press.

Grenberg, Jeanine. 2007a. "Courageous Humility in Jane Austen's *Mansfield Park*." *Social Theory and Practice* 33 (4): 645–66.

Grenberg, Jeanine M. 2007b. "Précis of Kant and the Ethics of Humility: A Story of Dependence, Corruption and Virtue." *Philosophy and Phenomenological Research* 75 (3): 622–3.

Hájek, Alan. 2008. "Arguments for—or Against—Probabilism?" *British Journal for the Philosophy of Science* 59 (4): 793–819.

Hardin, Russell. 2002. *Trust and Trustworthiness*. New York: Russell Sage Foundation.

Harman, Gilbert. 1999. "Moral Philosophy Meets Social Psychology: Virtue Ethics and the Fundamental Attribution Error." *Proceedings of the Aristotelian Society* 99 (1999): 315–31.

Harman, Gilbert. 2003. "No Character or Personality." *Business Ethics Quarterly* 13 (1): 87–94.

Harman, Gilbert H. 1986. *Change in View*. Cambridge, MA: The MIT Press.

Harris, Sam. 2004. *The End of Faith: Religion, Terror, and the Future of Reason*. New York: W. W. Norton.

Hartshorne, Hugh and M. A. May. 1928. *Studies in the Nature of Character*. Vol. 1 of *The Nature of Deceit*. New York: McMillan.

Hawthorne, James. 2009. "The Lockean Thesis and the Logic of Belief." In *Degrees of Belief*, edited by Franz Huber and Christoph Schmidt-Petri. Vol. 342 of *Synthese Library*, 49–74. New York: Springer.

Hawthorne, James and Luc Bovens. 1999. "The Preface, the Lottery, and the Logic of Belief." *Mind* 108 (430): 241–68.

Hawthorne, John and Jason Stanley. 2008. "Knowledge and Action." *Journal of Philosophy* 105.10: 571–90.

Hazlett, Allan. 2012. "Higher-Order Epistemic Attitudes and Intellectual Humility." *Episteme* 9 (3): 205–23.

Henderson, David and Terence Horgan. 2014. "Replies to Our Critics." *Philosophical Studies* 169 (3): 549–64.

Henderson, David K. and Terence Horgan. 2011. *The Epistemological Spectrum: At the Interface of Cognitive Science and Conceptual Analysis*. Oxford: Oxford University Press.

Hintikka, Jaakko. 1962. *Knowledge and Belief*. Ithaca: Cornell University Press.

Hitchens, Christopher. 2007. *God is Not Great: How Religion Poisons Everything*. New York: Twelve.

Hoffer, Eric. 1951. *The True Believer: Thoughts on the Nature of Mass Movements*. New York: Harper & Brothers.

Holton, Richard. 1994. "Deciding to Trust, Coming to Believe." *Australasian Journal of Philosophy* 72: 63–76.

Horgan, Terry and Matjaž Potrč. 2010. "The Epistemic Relevance of Morphological Content." *Acta Analytica* 25 (2): 155–73.

Horgan, Terry and Matjaž Potrč. 2011. "Attention, Morphological Content and Epistemic Justification." *Croatian Journal of Philosophy* 11 (1): 73–86.

Howard-Snyder, Daniel. 2013. "Propositional Faith: What It Is and What It Is Not." *American Philosophical Quarterly* 50.4: 357–72.

Huemer, Michael. 2007. "Epistemic Possibility." *Synthese* 156 (1): 119–42.

Hume, David. 1777 [1748]. *An Enquiry Concerning Human Understanding*. London: A. Millar.

Hunter, David. 2011. "Alienated Belief." *Alienated Belief* 65.2: 221–40.

Isen, Alice M. and Paula F. Levin. 1972. "Effect of Feeling Good on Helping: Cookies and Kindness." *Journal of Personality and Social Psychology* 21: 384–8.

Jackson, Frank. 1998. *From Metaphysics to Ethics*. Oxford: Oxford University Press.

Jackson, Frank. 2005. "Ramsey Sentences and Avoiding the *Sui Generis.*" In *Ramsey's Legacy*, edited by H. Lillehammer and D. H. Mellor. 122–36. Oxford: Clarendon Press.

James, William. 1897. "The Will to Believe." In *The Will to Believe and Other Essays in Popular Philosophy.* 1–15. New York: Longmans, Green, and Co.

Jeffrey, Richard. 1992. *Probability and the Art of Judgment.* New York: Cambridge University Press.

Jones, Karen. 1996. "Trust as an Affective Attitude." *Ethics* 107.1: 4–25.

Kagan, Shelly. 1989. *The Limits of Morality.* Oxford: Clarendon Press.

Kamtekar, Rachana. 2004. "Situationism and Virtue Ethics on the Content of Our Character." *Ethics* 114 (3): 458–91.

Kaplan, Mark. 1998. *Decision Theory as Philosophy.* New York: Cambridge University Press.

Kaplan, Mark. 2010. "In Defense of Modest Probabilism." *Synthese* 176 (1): 41–55.

Kaplan, Mark. 2013. "Coming to Terms with Our Human Fallibility: Christensen on the Preface." *Philosophy and Phenomenological Research* 87 (1): 1–35.

Keller, Simon. 2004a. "Friendship and Belief." *Philosophical Papers* 33 (3): 329–51.

Keller, Simon. 2004b. "Presentism and Truthmaking." In *Oxford Studies in Metaphysics I*, edited by Dean Zimmerman. 83–106. Oxford: Oxford University Press.

Kittel, Gerhard, Gerhard Friedrich, and Geoffrey W. Bromiley. 1964. *Theological Dictionary of the New Testament.* Grand Rapids, MI: Eerdmans.

Koralus, Philipp. 2014. "The Erotetic Theory of Attention." *Mind & Language* 29.1: 26–50.

Kripke, Saul. 1980. *Naming and Necessity.* Cambridge, MA: Harvard University Press.

Kripke, Saul A. 1979. "A Puzzle About Belief." In *Meaning and Use*, edited by A. Margalit. 239–83. Dordrecht: Reidel.

Kupfer, Joseph. 2003. "The Moral Perspective of Humility." *Pacific Philosophical Quarterly* 84 (3): 249–69.

Kvanvig, Jonathan L. 1993. *The Problem of Hell.* New York: Oxford University Press.

Kvanvig, Jonathan L. 1995a. "Coherentism: Misconstrual and Misapprehension." *Southwest Philosophy Review* 11: 159–69.

Kvanvig, Jonathan L. 1995b. "Coherentists' Distractions." *Philosophical Topics* 23: 257–75.

Kvanvig, Jonathan L. 1997. "In Defense of Coherentism." *Journal of Philosophical Research* 22: 299–306.

Kvanvig, Jonathan L. 2003. *The Value of Knowledge and the Pursuit of Understanding.* Cambridge: Cambridge University Press.

Kvanvig, Jonathan L. 2008. "Pointless Truth." *Midwest Studies in Philosophy* 32: 199–212.

Kvanvig, Jonathan L. 2009a. "Knowledge, Assertion, and Lotteries." In *Williamson on Knowledge*, edited by Duncan Pritchard and Patrick Greenough. 140–60. Oxford: Oxford University Press.

Kvanvig, Jonathan L. 2009b. "Religious Pluralism and the Buridan's Ass Paradox." *European Journal for Philosophy of Religion* 1.1: 1–26.

Kvanvig, Jonathan L. 2011a. "Coherentism and Justified Inconsistent Beliefs: A Solution." *Southern Journal of Philosophy* 50.1 (March 2012): 21–41.

Kvanvig, Jonathan L. 2011b. "Norms of Assertion." In *Assertion*, edited by Jessica Brown and Herman Cappellan. 233–51. Oxford: Oxford University Press.

Kvanvig, Jonathan L. 2011c. "The Rational Significance of Reflective Ascent." In *Evidentialism and Its Critics*, edited by Trent Dougherty. 34–54. Oxford: Oxford University Press.

Kvanvig, Jonathan L. 2013a. "Affective Theism and People of Faith." *Midwest Studies in Philosophy* 37: 109–28.

Kvanvig, Jonathan L. 2013b. "Curiosity and a Response-Dependent Account of the Value of Understanding." In *Knowledge, Virtue, and Action*, edited by Timothy Henning and David Schweikard. 151–75. London: Routledge.

Kvanvig, Jonathan L. 2013c. "Epistemic Normativity." In *Epistemic Norms: New Essays on Action, Belief, and Assertion*, edited by John Turri and Clayton Littlejohn. 115–35. Oxford: Oxford University Press.

Kvanvig, Jonathan L. 2013d. "Perspectivalism and Reflective Ascent." In *The Epistemology of Disagreement*, edited by David Christensen and Jennifer Lackey. 223–43. Oxford: Oxford University Press.

Kvanvig, Jonathan L. 2014. *Rationality and Reflection*. Oxford: Oxford University Press.

Kyburg, Henry E., Jr. 1961. *Probability and the Logic of Rational Belief*. Middletown, CT: Wesleyan University Press.

Lackey, Jennifer. 2008. *Learning from Words: Testimony as a Source of Knowledge*. Oxford: Oxford University Press.

Lakoff, George. 1993. "The Contemporary Theory of Metaphor." In *Metaphor and Thought*, edited by Andrew Ortony. 202–51. Cambridge: Cambridge University Press.

Lange, Marc. 2000. "Is Jeffrey Conditionalization Defective by Virtue of Being Non-Commutative? Remarks on the Sameness of Sensory Experiences." *Synthese* 123 (3): 393–403.

Langford, Cooper Harold. 1942. "The Notion of Analysic in Moore's Philosophy." In *The Philosophy of G. E. Moore*, edited by Paul A. Schilpp. 321–42. LaSalle, IL: Open Court Press.

Lehrer, Keith. 1990. *Metamind*. Oxford: Oxford University Press.

Lehrer, Keith. 1997. *Self Trust: A Study of Reason, Knowledge and Autonomy*. Oxford: Oxford University Press.

Lehrer, Keith. 2000. *Theory of Knowledge*. 2nd edn. Boulder: Westview Press.

Leiter, Brian. 2012. *Why Tolerate Religion?* Princeton, NJ: Princeton University Press.

Lewis, Clive Staples. 1952. *Mere Christianity*. London: Macmillan.

Lewis, David. 1996. "Elusive Knowledge." *Australasian Journal of Philosophy* 74.4: 549–67.

Lewis, David. 1997. "Finkish Dispositions." *The Philosophical Quarterly* 47.187: 143–8.

Locke, John. 1698. *Essay Concerning Human Understanding*. London: William Tegg.

McKaughan, Daniel J. 2013. "Authentic Faith and Acknowledged Risk: Dissolving the Problem of Faith and Reason." *Religious Studies* 49: 101–24.

Mackie, J. L. 1974. *The Cement of the Universe: A Study of Causation*. Oxford: Oxford University Press.

McMyler, Benjamin. 2011. *Testimony, Trust, and Authority*. Oxford: Oxford University Press.

Maher, Patrick. 1993. *Betting on Theories*. Cambridge: Cambridge University Press.

Makinson, D. C. 1965. "The Paradox of the Preface." *Analysis* 25 (6): 205–7.

Martin, Charles Burton. 1994. "Dispositions and Conditionals." *The Philosophical Quarterly* 44: 1–8.

Merritt, Maria. 2000. "Virtue Ethics and Situationist Personality Psychology." *Ethical Theory and Moral Practice* 3 (4): 365–83.

Milgram, Stanley. 1963. "Behavioral Study of Obedience." *Journal of Abnormal and Social Psychology* 67: 371–8.

Milgram, Stanley. 1974. *Obedience to Authority*. New York: Harper and Row.

Moberly, R. W. L. 2000. *The Bible, Theology, and Faith: A Study of Abraham and Jesus.* Cambridge: Cambridge University Press.

Mole, Christopher. 2011. *Attention is Cognitive Unison: An Essay in Philosophical Psychology.* Oxford: Oxford University Press.

Mulckhuyse, Manon and Jan Theeuwes. 2010. "Unconscious Attentional Orienting to Exogenous Cues: A Review of the Literature." *Acta Psychologica* 134: 299–309.

Nagel, Jennifer. 2012. "Gendler on Alief." *Analysis* 72 (4): 774–88.

Nuyen, A. T. 1998. "Just Modesty." *American Philosophical Quarterly* 35 (1): 101–9.

Parfit, Derek. 2001. "Rationality and Reasons." In *Exploring Practical Philosophy*, edited by Jonas Josefsson, Dan Egonnson, Bjorn Petersson, and Toni Ronnow-Rasmussen. 17–39. Aldershot, UK: Ashgate Press.

Pascal, Blaise. 1966 [1669]. *Pensées.* Baltimore: Penguin Books.

Plantinga, Alvin. 1983. *Faith and Rationality: Reason and Belief in God.* Notre Dame: University of Notre Dame Press.

Plantinga, Alvin. 1993. *Warrant: The Current Debate.* Oxford: Oxford University Press.

Plantinga, Alvin. 2000. *Warranted Christian Belief.* Oxford: Oxford University Press.

Pojman, Louis. 1986. "Faith Without Belief?" *Faith and Philosophy* 3 (2): 157–76.

Pollock, John. 1986a. *Contemporary Theories of Knowledge.* Totowa, NJ: Rowman and Littlefield.

Pollock, John L. 1986b. "The Paradox of the Preface." *Philosophy of Science* 53 (2): 246–58.

Preston-Roedder, Ryan. 2013. "Faith in Humanity." *Philosophy and Phenomenological Research* 87 (3): 664–87.

Prinz, Jesse. 2009. "The Normativity Challenge: Cultural Psychology Provides the Real Threat to Virtue Ethics." *Journal of Ethics* 13 (2–3): 117–44.

Quine, Willard V. O. 1951. "Two Dogmas of Empiricism." *Philosophical Review* 60 (1): 20–43.

Rabinowicz, Wlodek and Toni Rønnow-Rasmussen. 2004. "The Strike of the Demon: On Fitting Pro-Attitudes and Value." *Ethics* 114 (3): 391–423.

Ramsey, F. P. 2010 [1926]. "Truth and Probability." In *Philosophy of Probability: Contemporary Readings*, edited by Antony Eagle. 52–94. London: Routledge.

Ramsey, F. P. 1990. *F. P. Ramsey: Philosophical Papers.* Cambridge: Cambridge University Press.

Raterman, Ty. 2004. "On Modesty: Being Good and Knowing It Without Flaunting It." *American Philosophical Quarterly* 43: 221–34.

Richards, Norvin. 1988. "Is Humility a Virtue?" *American Philosophical Quarterly* 25.3: 253–9.

Ridge, Michael. 2000. "Modesty as a Virtue." *American Philosophical Quarterly* 37: 269–83.

Ross, Lee and Richard E. Nisbett. 1991. *The Person and the Situation.* Philadelphia: Temple University Press.

Ross, W. D. 1930. *The Right and the Good.* Oxford: Oxford University Press.

Rowbottom, Darrell P. 2007. " "In-Between Believing" and Degrees of Belief." *Teorema* 26 (1): 131–7.

Sabini, John and Maury Silver. 2005. "Lack of Character? Situationism Critiqued." *Ethics* 115 (3): 535–62.

Salmon, Nathan. 1989. *Frege's Puzzle.* Oxford: Oxford University Press.

Schellenberg, John L. 2009. *The Will to Imagine: A Justification of Skeptical Religion.* Ithaca, NY: Cornell University Press.

Schueler, G. F. 1999. "Why IS Modesty a Virtue?" *Ethics* 109 (4): 835–41.

Schueler, George F. 1997. "Why Modesty Is a Virtue." *Ethics* 107: 467–85.

Schwitzgebel, Eric. 2010. "Acting Contrary to Our Professed Beliefs Or The Gulf Between Occurrent Judgment and Dispositional Belief." *Pacific Philosophical Quarterly* 91 (4): 531–53.

Sessions, William Lad. 1994. *The Concept of Faith: A Philosophical Investigation.* Ithaca, NY: Cornell University Press.

Sider, Theodore. 2011. *Writing the Book of the World.* Oxford: Oxford University Press.

Siegel, Susanna. 2005. "The Contents of Perception." Edward N. Zalta (ed.). http://plato. stanford.edu/archives/spr2005/entries/perception-contents/.

Siegel, Susanna. 2013. "The Epistemic Impact of the Etiology of Experience." *Philosophical Studies* 162 (3): 697–722.

Simpson, Thomas W. 2012. "What Is Trust?" *Pacific Philosophical Quarterly* 93 (4): 550–69.

Sinha, G. Alex. 2012. "Modernizing the Virtue of Humility." *Australasian Journal of Philosophy* 90 (2): 259–74.

Skyrms, Brian. 1975. *Choice and Chance: An Introduction to Inductive Logic.* Vol. 18. Encino, CA: Dickenson Pub. Co.

Slote, Michael. 1983. *Goods and Virtue.* Oxford: Clarendon Press.

Slote, Michael. 2004. "Driver's Virtues." *Utilitas* 16: 22–32.

Smith, Michael. 1994. *The Moral Problem.* Oxford: Blackwell.

Sommers, Fred. 2009. "Dissonant Beliefs." *Analysis* 69 (2): 267–74.

Sosa, Ernest. 2007. *A Virtue Epistemology.* Oxford: Oxford University Press.

Sreenivasan, Gopal. 2002. "Errors About Errors: Virtue Theory and Trait Attribution." *Mind* 111 (441): 47–68.

Stanley, Jason. 2005. *Knowledge and Practical Interests.* Oxford: Oxford University Press.

Statman, Daniel. 1992. "Modesty, Pride and Realistic Self-Assessment." *Philosophical Quarterly* 42 (169): 420–38.

Strong, James. 2007 [1890]. *Strong's Exhaustive Concordance of the Bible.* Peabody, MA: Hendrickson Publishers.

Stroud, Sarah. 2006. "Epistemic Partiality in Friendship." *Ethics* 116 (3): 498–524.

Stump, Eleonore. 2010. *Wandering in Darkness: Narrative and the Problem of Suffering.* Oxford: Oxford University Press.

Stump, Eleonore. 2012. "Divine Simplicity." In *Oxford Handbook to Thomas Aquinas.* Oxford: Oxford University Press.

Sturgeon, Scott. 2008. "Reason and the Grain of Belief." *Noûs* 42.1: 139–65.

Swinburne, Richard. 2005. *Faith and Reason.* 2nd edn. Oxford: Oxford University Press.

Tatz, Akiva. 1993. *Living Inspired.* Southfied, MI: Targum Press.

Tennant, Frederick R. 1943. *The Nature of Belief.* London: Centenary Press.

Thompson, Christopher. 2017. "Trust Without Reliance." *Ethical Theory and Moral Practice* 1–13.

Tucker, Christopher, ed. 2013. *Seemings and Justification: New Essays on Dogmatism and Phenomenal Conservatism.* Oxford: Oxford University Press.

van Fraassen, Bas. 1980. *The Scientific Image.* Oxford: Oxford University Press.

van Fraassen, Bas. 1989. *Laws and Symmetry.* Oxford: Oxford University Press.

Velleman, David. 2000. *The Possibility of Practical Reason.* Oxford: Oxford University Press.

Wagner, Carl G. 2002. "Probability Kinematics and Commutativity." *Philosophy of Science* 69 (2): 266–78.

Warfield, Ted A. 2005. "Knowledge from Falsehood." *Philosophical Perspectives* 19: 405–16.

Weiner, Matt. 2005. "Must We Know What We Say?" *The Philosophical Review* 114.2: 227–51.

Weirich, Paul. 2004. "Belief and Acceptance." In *Handbook of Epistemology*. 499–520. Dordrecht: Kluwer Academic Pub.

Weisberg, Jonathan. 2009. "Commutativity or Holism? A Dilemma for Conditionalizers." *British Journal for the Philosophy of Science* 60 (4): 793–812.

Whitcomb, Dennis, Heather Battaly, Jason Baehr, and Daniel Howard-Snyder. 2015. "Intellectual Humility: Owning Our Limitations." *Philosophy and Phenomenological Research* 91 (1): 1–31.

Williams, Bernard. 2002. *Truth and Truthfulness: An Essay in Genealogy*. Princeton, NJ: Princeton University Press.

Williamson, Timothy. 1996. *Vagueness*. Oxford: Oxford University Press.

Williamson, Timothy. 2000. *Knowledge and Its Limits*. Oxford: Oxford University Press.

Zagzebski, Linda. 1996. *Virtues of the Mind: An Inquiry into the Nature of Virtue and the Ethical Foundations of Knowledge*. Cambridge: Cambridge University Press.

Zagzebski, Linda T. 2012. *Epistemic Authority: A Theory of Trust, Authority, and Autonomy in Belief*. Oxford: Oxford University Press.

Zimmerman, Aaron. 2007. "The Nature of Belief." *Journal of Consciousness Studies* 14.11: 61–82.

Index